THE OFFICIAL HANDBOOK OF THE LEGION OF MARY

SECOND AMERICAN EDITION

By

CONCILIUM LEGIONIS MARIAE

PUBLISHED BY

CONCILIUM LEGIONIS MARIAE

Nihil obstat:

MICHAEL L. DEMPSEY, S.T.D.,
CENSOR THEOL. DEPUT.

Imprimi potest:

✠ EDUARDUS,
ARCHIEP. DUBLINEN,
HIBERNIAE PRIMAS.

DUBLINI, *die* 7 *Martii anno* 1937.

FOR AMERICAN EDITION

Imprimatur:

✠ JOANNES,
ARCHIEPISCOPUS LUDOVICOPOLITANUS

LUDOVICOPOLI, DIE 14 QUINTILIS, ANNO 1941.

Publishers Printing Co.
Incorporated
Louisville, Kentucky

Printed in U. S. A.

Pope Pius XII and the Legion of Mary

ACTIO CATHOLICA

Palazzo S. Callisto,
ROME.

12th. June, 1939.

Dear Sir,

In my audience with the Holy Father last Sunday, I spoke to His Holiness of the Legion of Mary and of the good which it has accomplished as a fervent auxiliary of Catholic Action.

The Holy Father recalled with pleasure the spirit of affectionate and humble devotion which inspired you and Mr. Duff to come to the feet of the Vicar of Christ, so soon after his elevation to the Chair of St. Peter, in order to assure him of the spirit of loyalty towards the Holy See which animates the Legion and of its solemn intention of remaining always faithful to the instructions and wishes of the Bishops. The Holy Father then asked me to convey to all the officers and members of the Legion of Mary his Apostolic Blessing, and to urge them on to even greater efforts for the glory of God and the extension of Christ's Kingdom on earth.

For my part I assure you of my great admiration for the work of the Legionaries, who serve under the noble banner of our Lady. Inspired by the love of their neighbour and by that zeal for souls which is the root of the apostolate, they go out two by two on their beautiful mission of spiritual charity. Most especially do I admire the work which the Legionaries are accomplishing in the Mission Lands, in Africa and India, where they have placed themselves at the disposal of several of the Bishops for the works of the apostolate. May Jesus Christ bless the labours of these zealous souls, and may His Blessed Mother keep them in her love!

With my very best wishes to you and to Mr. Duff, and with sentiments of deep esteem, I am

Yours faithfully in Christ,

I. Card. Pizzardo

Mr. John Nagle,
President of the Legion of Mary,
De Montfort House,
DUBLIN.

PIUS XI

TO THE

Legion of Mary

16th September, 1933.

"We give a very special blessing to this beautiful and holy work—the Legion of Mary. Its name speaks for itself. The image of Mary Immaculate on its Standard portrays high and holy things.

"The Blessed Virgin is mother of the Redeemer and of us all. She co-operates in our Redemption, for it was under the Cross that she became our mother. This year we are celebrating the centenary of that co-operation and of that universal maternity of Mary.

"I pray for you that you may exercise still more earnestly that apostolate of prayer and work to which you have set your hands. So doing, God will make you, too, co-operators in the Redemption. This is the best of all ways in which to show your gratitude to the Redeemer."

TABLE OF CONTENTS

If past experience is an indication, no branch of the Legion will fail which is worked faithfully according to rule.

If unprepared to work the system exactly as described in these pages, please do not start the Legion at all. In this connection, read carefully the Section "Legion System Invariable," page 63.

Without affiliation to the Legion (through one of its approved Councils), there is no Legionary Membership.

"Who is she that cometh forth as the morning rising, fair as the moon, bright as the sun, terrible as an army set in array?"—(Cantic. Cantic. VI. 9).

"The Virgin's name was Mary."—(St. Luke I. 27).

"The Legion of Mary! What a perfectly chosen name!"—(Pius XI).

NAME AND ORIGIN.

The Legion of Mary is an Association of Catholics, who, with the sanction of the Church and under the powerful leadership of Mary Immaculate, Mediatrix of all Graces (who is fair as the moon, bright as the sun and—to Satan and his legionaries—terrible as an army set in battle array), have formed themselves into a

Legion for service in the warfare which is perpetually waged by the Church against the world and its evil powers. The Legionaries hope to render themselves worthy of their great heavenly Queen by their loyalty, their virtues, and their courage. The Legion of Mary is therefore organised on the model of an army, principally on that of the army of ancient Rome, the nomenclature of which is adopted also—but the army and the arms of Legionaries of Mary are not of this world.

This army, now so considerable, had the most humble of beginnings. It was not a thought-out organisation. It sprang up spontaneously. There was no premeditation in regard to rules and practices. A suggestion was simply thrown out. An evening was fixed, and a little group came together, unaware that they were to be the instruments of most loving Providence. To look at that meeting, it was identical with what would be seen to-day were one to attend a Legion meeting anywhere in the world. The table around which they met bore a simple altar, of which the centre was a statue of the Immaculate Conception (of the Miraculous Medal model). It stood on a white cloth, and was flanked by two vases with flowers, and two candlesticks with lighted candles. This setting, so rich in atmosphere, was the inspired notion of one of the earliest comers. It crystallised everything for which the Legion of Mary stands. The Legion is an army. Well, their Queen was there before they assembled. She stood waiting to receive the enrolments of those who she knew were coming to her. They did not adopt her. She adopted them; and since then they have marched and fought with her, knowing that they would succeed and persevere just to the extent that they were united to her.

The first corporate act of those Legionaries was to go on their knees. The earnest young heads were bent down. The Invocation and Prayer of the Holy Ghost were said; and then through the fingers which had, during the day, been toilsomely employed, slipped the beads of the simplest of all devotions. When the final ejaculations died away, they sat up, and under the auspices of Mary (as represented by her statue), they set themselves to the consideration of how they could best please God and make Him loved in His world. From that discussion came forth the Legion of Mary, as it is to-day, in all its features.

What a wonder! Who, contemplating those inconspicuous persons—so simply engaged—could in his wildest moments imagine what a destiny waited just a little along the road! Who among them could think that they were inaugurating a system which was to be a new world-force: possessing—if faithfully and forcefully administered—the power, in Mary, of imparting life and sweetness and hope to the nations! Yet so it was to be.

That first enrolment of Legionaries of Mary took place at Myra House, Francis Street, Dublin, Ireland, at 8 p. m. on September 7th, 1921, the eve of the Feast of Our Lady's Nativity. From the title of the parent branch, viz., Our Lady of Mercy, the organisation was for a time known as "The Association of Our Lady of Mercy."

Circumstances which one would regard as accidental determined this date, which seemed at the time less appropriate than the following day would have been. In after years only—when countless proofs of a truly maternal love had made one reflect—was it realised that not the least exquisite touch of Mary's hand had been shown in the moment of the Legion's birth. Of the evening and the morning was the first day made (Genesis i, 5), and surely the first, and not the last fragrances of the Feast which honours her own Nativity were appropriate to the first moments of an organisation, whose first and constant aim has been to reproduce in itself the likeness of Mary, thus best to magnify the Lord and bring Him to men.

"Mary is the Mother of all the members of the Saviour, because by her charity she has co-operated in the birth of the faithful

in the Church. Mary is the living mould of God, that is to say, it is in her alone that the God Man was naturally formed without losing a feature, so to speak, of His Godhead; and it is in her alone that man can be properly and in a life-like way formed into God, so far as human nature is capable of this by the grace of Jesus Christ."—(St. Augustine).

OBJECT.

The object of the Legion of Mary is the sanctification of its members by prayer and active co-operation, under ecclesiastical guidance, in Mary's and the Church's work of crushing the head of the serpent and advancing the reign of Christ.

Subject to the approval of the Concilium, and to the restrictions specified in the official Handbook of the Legion, the Legion of Mary is at the disposal of the Bishop of the Diocese and the Parish Priest for any and every form of Social Service and Catholic Action which these authorities may deem suitable to the Legionaries and useful for the welfare of the Church. Legionaries will never engage in any of these services whatsoever in a Parish without the sanction of the Parish Priest or of the Ordinary.

By the Ordinary in these pages is meant the Ordinary of the Diocese.

"Tell your faithful children of the laity that when, united with their pastors and their bishops, they participate in the works of the Apostolate, both individual and social, the end purpose of which is to make Jesus Christ better known and better loved, then they are more than ever 'a chosen generation, a kingly priesthood, a holy nation, a purchased people,' of whom St. Peter spoke in such laudatory terms (I Peter II. 9). Then, too, they are more than ever united with Us and with Christ, and become great factors in bringing about world peace, because they work for the restoration and spread of the Kingdom of Christ."—(Pius XI. Encyclical of 23rd December, 1922, on Peace of Christ).

SPIRIT OF THE LEGION.

The spirit of the Legion of Mary is that of Mary herself. Especially does the Legion aspire after her profound humility, her perfect obedience, her angelical sweetness, her continual prayer, her universal mortification, her altogether spotless purity, her heroic patience, her heavenly wisdom, her self-sacrificing courageous love of God, and above all her faith, that virtue which has alone in her been found in its utmost extent and never equalled. Inspired by this love and faith of Mary, her Legion essays any and every work and "complains not of impossibility, because it conceives that it may and can do all things." (Imit. Christ, Bk. III, C.5.)

"To all these calls to the 'impossible,' the first answer that comes tremblingly to human lips is the 'How can this be done'? and the second, 'Behold the handmaid of the Lord.' When this has been uttered in its fullest sense, by what St. Francis of Sales calls 'an incomparable act of resignation,' the work is accomplished by the overshadowing of the Spirit of God."—(Monahan—Life of St. Madeleine Sophie Barat).

LEGIONARY SERVICE.

(1). Must be "a living sacrifice, holy, pleasing unto God, . . . and not conformed to this world."—(Romans, XII, 1 and 2)

The Roman Legion, from which the Legion takes its name, has come down through the centuries illustrious for loyalty, courage, discipline, endurance, and success, and this for ends that were often base and never more than worldly. Manifestly, Mary's Legion cannot offer to her the name (like a setting stripped of the jewels which adorned it) accompanied by qualities less notable, so that in these qualities is indicated the very minimum of Legionary Service. (See Appendix I.)

From this foundation will spring in the faithful Legionary, virtues as far greater as his cause is superior, and in particular a noble generosity which will echo that sentiment of St. Teresa: "To receive so much and to repay so little: O! that is a martyrdom to which I succumb." Contemplating his Crucified Lord, Who devoted to him His last sigh and the last drop of His blood, the Legionary's service must strive to reflect such utter giving of self.

"Tell me my people what have I not done for my vineyard that I ought to have done."—(Isaias Ch. 5. 4).

(2). Must not turn from "Labour and Painfulness."—(II Cor. xi. 27).

There will ever be places, as recent events have instanced, where Catholic zeal must be prepared to face the instruments of death or torture. Generally, however, Legionary devotedness will have a humbler stage, but still one giving ample opportunity for the practice of a quiet but true heroism. The Legion Apostolate will involve the approaching of many who would prefer to remain remote from good influences, and who will manifest their distaste for receiving a visit from those whose mission is good, not evil. These may all be won over, but not without the exercise of a patient and brave spirit.

Sour looks, the sting of insult and rebuff, ridicule and adverse criticism, weariness of body and spirit, pangs from failure and from base ingratitude, the bitter cold and the blinding rain, dirt and vermin and evil smells, dark passages and sordid surroundings, the laying aside of pleasures, the taking on of the anxieties which come in plenty with the work, the anguish which the contemplation of irreligion and depravity brings to the sensitive soul, sorrow from sorrows whole-heartedly shared—there is little glamour about these things, but if sweetly borne, counted even a joy, and persevered in unto the end, they will come, in the weighing-up, very near to that love, greater than which no man hath, that he lay down his life for his friend.

"What shall I render to the Lord for all the things that He hath rendered to me?"—(Psalm 115, 12).

(3). Must "walk in love as Christ also hath loved us and hath delivered Himself for us."—(Ephesians v. 2).

The secret of all success with others lies in the establishment of personal contact, the contact of love and sympathy. This love must be more than an appearance. It must be able to stand up to the tests that real friendships can bear. This will frequently involve little mortifications. To greet, in fashionable surroundings, one who a little while before was the subject of one's visitation in a jail, to be seen walking with bedraggled persons, to grasp warmly the hand which is coated with grime, to partake of a proffered meal in a very poor or dirty home, may to some be difficult, but if avoided, the attitude of friendship is shown to have been a pretence, the contact breaks, and the soul that was being lifted sinks back in disillusion.

At the bottom of all really fruitful work must be the readiness to give oneself entirely. Without this readiness, one's service has no substance. The Legionary who somewhere sets up the barrier: "thus far and no farther is self-sacrifice to go," will accomplish only the trivial, though great exertions may be made. On the other hand, if that readiness exist, even though it may never, or but in small measure, be called upon, it will be fruitful of immense things.

"Jesus answered him: wilt thou lay down thy life for Me?"—(St. John xiii. 38).

(4). Must Finish the Course.—(II.Tim. iv. 7).

Thus the call of the Legion is for a service without limit or reservations. This is not entirely a counsel of perfection, but of necessity as well, for if excellence is not aimed at, a persevering membership will not be achieved. A life-long perseverance in the work of the apostolate is in itself heroic, and will only be found as the culmination of a continuous series of heroic acts, as indeed it is their reward.

But not alone to the individual membership must the note of permanence attach. Each and every item of the Legion's round of duty must be stamped with this self-same seal of persevering effort. Change, of course, there must necessarily be. Different places and persons are visited: works are completed, and new works are taken on. But all this is the steady alteration of life, not the fitful operation of instability and novelty-seeking, which ends by breaking down the finest discipline. Apprehensive of this spirit of change, the Legion appeals unceasingly for a sterner temper, and from each succeeding meeting sends its members to their tasks with the unchanging watchword, as it were, ringing in their ears: "Hold firm."

Real achievement is dependent upon sustained effort, which in turn is the outcome of an unconquerable will to win. Essential to the perseverance of such a will is that it bend not often nor at all. Therefore, the Legion enjoins on its branches and its members a universal attitude of refusal to accept defeat, or to court it by a tendency to grade items of work in terms of the "promising," the "unpromising," the "hopeless," etc. A readiness to brand as "hopeless" proclaims that, so far as the Legion is concerned, a priceless soul is free to pursue unchecked its reckless course to hell. In addition, it indicates that an unthinking desire for variety and signs of progress tends to replace higher considerations as the motive of the work. Then, unless the harvest springs up at the heels of the sower, there is discouragement, and sooner or later the work is abandoned.

Again, it is declared and insisted that the act of labelling any one case as hopeless automatically weakens attitude towards every other case. Consciously or unconsciously, approach to all work will be in a spirit of doubt as to whether it is justifying effort, and even a grain of doubt paralyses action.

And worst of all, faith would have ceased to play its due part in Legion affairs, being allowed only a modest entrance when deemed approvable to reason. With its faith so harnessed and its determination sapped, at once rush in the natural timidities, the pettinesses, and the worldly prudence, which had been kept at bay, and the Legion is found presenting a casual or half-hearted service which forms a shameful offering to Heaven.

Hence it is that the Legion is concerned only in a secondary way about a programme of works, but much about intensity of purpose. It does not require from its members wealth or influence, but faith unwavering: not famous deeds but only unrelaxed effort: not genius but unquenchable love: not giant strength but steady discipline. A Legionary service must be one of holding on, of absolute and obstinate refusal to lose heart. A rock in the crisis: but constant at all times. Hoping for success: humble in success: but independent of it. Fighting failure: undismayed by it: fighting on, and wearing it down: thriving upon difficulties and monotony, because they give scope for the faith and effort of an enduring siege. Ready and resolute when summoned: on the alert though not called upon: and even when there is no conflict and no enemy in sight, maintaining a tireless precautionary patrol for God. With a heart for the impossible: yet content to play the part of stop-gap: nothing too big: no duty too mean: for each the same minute attention, the same inexhaustible patience, the same inflexible courage: every task marked with the same golden tenacity. Always on duty for souls: ever at hand to carry the weak through their many weak moments: vigilantly watching to surprise the hardened at their rare moments of softness: unremitting in search for those that have strayed. Unmindful of self: all the time standing by the Cross of others, and standing there till the work is consummated.

Unfailing must be the service of the organisation consecrated to the Virgo Fidelis, and bearing—either for honour or dishonour—her name!

"Everything belonging to the gentle Virgin, everything which is under her protection remains intact; the virtue and strength of those vowed to her worship, no less than the garment of flesh which she gave her Son, and of which it was said: 'Not a bone of Him shall be broken'; no less than the linen tunic which was not torn."—(Bolo: Tragedy of Calvary).

THE DEVOTIONAL OUTLOOK OF THE LEGION.

The devotional outlook of the Legion is reflected in its prayers. The Legion is built in the first place upon a profound faith in God and in the love He bears His children. He wills to draw great glory from our efforts, and He will purify them and render them fruitful and persevering. Our feverish anxiety, or alternately, our apathy, shows that we believe Him merely to be watching us at our work. Instead, let us realise that we only have the good purpose because He has implanted it, and that we shall only bring it to fruition if He sustains us all the time. The success of the enterprise in hand is more by far to Him than it is to us. Infinitely more than we, does He desire that conversion we are seeking. We wish to be saints: He yearns for it a million times more than we.

The Legionaries' essential mainstay must be this knowledge of the companionship of God, their good Father, in their two-fold work of sanctifying themselves and serving their neighbor. Nothing can stand in the way of success except want of trust. If there be but faith enough, God will utilise us to conquer the world for Him.

"For whatsoever is born of God, overcometh the world; and this is the victory which overcometh the world, our faith."—(I. Ep. St. John V. 4).

God and Mary.

Under God, the Legion is built upon devotion to Mary, "that ineffable miracle of the Most High."—(Pius IX). But what is the place of Mary herself in relation to God? It is that He brought her, as He did all the other children of earth, out of nothing; and though He has since then exalted her to "a point of grace immense and inconceivable," nevertheless, in comparison to her Maker, she still remains as nothing. Indeed, she is—far more than any other—His creature, because He has wrought more in her than in any other of His creatures. The greater the things He does to her, the more she becomes the work of His hands.

Very great things He hath done to her. From all eternity, the idea of her was present to His mind along with that of the Redeemer. He associated her to the intimacies of His plans of grace, making her the true mother of His Son and of those united to that Son. He did all these things because, in the first place, He would gain from Mary herself a return greater than He would from all other pure creatures together. In the second place, He thereby intended, in a way which our minds cannot adequately grasp, to enhance the glory which He would receive from ourselves also. Thus, the prayer and loving service, with which we recompense Mary, our Mother and the helper of our salvation, can represent no loss to Him who made her so. What is given to her goes none the less surely and fully to Him. But there is question of more than undiminished transmission; there is question of increase. And Mary is more than a faithful messenger. She has been set by God to be a vital element in His gracious scheme, in such sort that both His glory and our grace are the greater by reason of her presence there.

As it is the pleasure of the Eternal Father so to receive through Mary the homages intended for Him, so too He has been graciously pleased to appoint her to be the way by which shall pass to men the various outpourings of His munificent goodness and omnipotence, beginning with the cause of them all—the Second Divine Person made man, our true life, our only salvation.

"If I will to make myself dependent on the Mother, it is in order to become the slave of the Son. If I aspire to become her possession, it is in order to render more surely to God the homage of my subjection."—(St. Ildephonsus).

Mary, Mediatrix of All Graces.

The Legion's trust in Mary is limitless, knowing that, by the ordinance of God, her power is without limit. All that He could give to Mary, He has given to her. All that she was capable of receiving, she has received in plenitude. For us God has constituted her a special means of grace. Operating in union with her we approach Him more effectively, and hence win grace more freely. Indeed we place ourselves in the very flood-tide of grace, for she is the spouse of the Holy Ghost: she is the channel of every grace which Jesus Christ has won. We receive nothing which we do not owe to a positive intervention on her part. She does not content herself with transmitting all: she obtains all for us. Penetrated with belief in this office of Mary, the Legion enjoins it as a special devotion and sets in its Catena, for daily recitation by every member, the proper prayer of the Feast of Mary, Mediatrix of all Graces (May 31st).

"Judge as to the ardent love with which God would have us honour Mary, seeing that He has set in her the fullness of all good: in such manner that all we have of hope, all of grace, all of salvation, all—I say and let us doubt it not—flows to us from her."—(St. Bernard: Sermo de Aquaeductu).

Mary Immaculate.

A second aspect of Legion devotion is towards the Immaculate Conception. At the very first meeting, the members prayed and deliberated round a little altar of the Immaculate Conception, identical with that which now forms the centre of every Legion meeting. Moreover, the very first breath of the Legion may be said to have been drawn in an ejaculation in honour of this privilege of Our Lady, which formed the preparation for all the dignities and all the privileges afterwards accorded to her. The Immaculate Conception is referred to by God in the same sentence in which Mary herself is first promised to us. The privilege is part of Mary: Mary is the Immaculate Conception; and, together with the privilege, prophecy is made of its heavenly sequel: the Divine Maternity, the crushing of the Serpent's head in Redemption, and Mary's Motherhood of men.

"I will put enmities between thee and the woman, and thy seed and her seed: She shall crush thy head and thou shalt lie in wait for her heel."—(Gen. III. 15).

To these words, addressed to Satan by Almighty God, the Legion turns as the source of its confidence and strength in its warfare with sin. It aims with all its heart to become in fulness the seed, the children of Mary, for there is the pledge of victory. In the measure that it makes her more and more its Mother, is the Legion's enmity with the powers of evil intensified and victory made more complete.

"In the actual exercise of our apostolate, our great means of action consists in depending upon Mary, in keeping ourselves so closely united to Mary that in all things and everywhere we act as instruments of Mary and are, as it were, the 'heel' of that Immaculate Virgin. It is less our apostolate that we carry on than Mary's own apostolate. She herself acts with us, in us, by us, to the degree in which we make our life one of entire subjection to Her."—(Petit Traité de Marialogie: Marianiste.)

Mary Our Mother.

But if we claim the inheritance of children, there must be esteem for the motherhood through which it comes. A third aspect of Legion devotion to Mary is the special honouring of her as our real Mother, which in very fact she is.

Mary became the Mother of Christ when to the Angel's salutation she pronounced her meek assent, "Behold the handmaid of the Lord: be it done to me according to thy word." She became our Mother in the midst of the sorrows of Calvary when Jesus said to her from the cross, "Woman, behold thy son," and to St. John, "Behold thy Mother." Through St. John, these words were addressed to all the elect. Fully co-operating by her consent and sorrows in the Redemption, Mary became at that moment and in the fullest sense our Mother.

Truly her children, we must deport ourselves as such, and indeed as very little children, dependent utterly upon her. We must look to her to feed us, to guide us, to teach us, to cure our ailments, to console us in our griefs, to counsel us in our doubts, to recall us when we wander; so that wholly confided to her care, we may grow to the resemblance of our elder brother, Jesus, and share His mission of combating sin and conquering it.

Incessantly must the Legionary dwell upon the reality of Mary's motherhood of us, "so that the faith in her maternal role will expand and urge us on to practices which will translate into action the firmness of our conviction and the ardour of our love," and make us worthy children of so true a mother.

"We give a very special blessing to this beautiful and holy work—the Legion of Mary. Its name speaks for itself. The image of Mary Immaculate on its Standard portrays high and holy things.

"The Blessed Virgin is mother of the Redeemer and of us all. She co-operates in our Redemption, for it was under the Cross that she became our mother. This year we are celebrating the centenary of that co-operation and of that universal maternity of Mary.

"I pray for you that you may exercise still more earnestly that apostolate of prayer and work to which you have set your hands. So doing, God will make you, too, co-operators in the Redemption. This is the best of all ways in which to show your gratitude to the Redeemer,"—(Pius XI. to the Legion of Mary: September 16, 1933).

Legionary Devotion the Root of the Legionary Apostolate.

One of the dearest duties of the Legion shall be to show forth this whole-hearted devotion to the Mother of God. It can only do so through its members, so that each one of those is bidden to associate himself with it by serious meditation and zealous practice.

If the devotion is to be in real truth a Legionary tribute, it must be an essential part of the Legion—as much an obligation of membership as the weekly meeting or active work: all must participate therein in a perfect unity. This is a point of view with which members cannot be too deeply impressed.

But this unity is something most delicate, for each member in a measure controls it, and can mar it. So on each one devolves a solemn trusteeship in the matter. If there is default, if the Legionaries are not "as living stones built up, a spiritual house." (I Peter 11. 5), then is a vital part of the structure of the Legion defective. In measure as the living stones are found in this way wanting, will the Legion system tend more and more to become a ruin, which will not shelter, and hence with difficulty will retain its children. Still less will it be the home of high and holy qualities, or a starting-point for heroic endeavour.

But with all as one in adequate discharge of this item of Legionary service, not only will the Legion be distinguished amongst organisations for its exalted devotion to Mary, but will, moreover, be found possessed of a marvellous unity of mind and purpose and action. This unity is so precious in the sight of God that He has vested it with an irresistible power; so that, if for the individual a true devotion to Mary is a special channel of grace, what shall it bring to an organisation which is persevering with one mind in prayer with her (Acts I. 14) who has received **all** from God; participating in her spirit; and entering fully into the design of God with regard to the distribution of grace! Shall not such an organisation be filled with the Holy Ghost, (Acts II. 4) and shall there not be "many wonders also and signs done?" (Acts II. 43).

"The Virgin in the Cenacle, praying in the midst of the Apostles and pouring out her heart for them with intensity unspeakable, calls down upon the Church that treasure which will abound in it for ever: the fulness of the Paraclete, the supreme gift of Christ." —(Leo XIII. Encycl. Jucunda Semper, 1894).

If Mary were but known!

To the priest struggling almost despairingly in a sea of religious neglect, the following words of Father Faber—taken from his preface to B. Grignion de Montfort's "True Devotion to Mary" (an abounding source of inspiration to the Legion)—are commended as a preliminary to his consideration of the possible value to him of the Legion. The argument of Father Faber is that Mary is not half enough known or loved, with sad results for souls:—"Devotion to her is low and thin and poor. It has no faith in itself. Hence it is that Jesus is not loved, that heretics are not converted, that the Church is not exalted; that souls, which might be saints, wither and dwindle; that the Sacraments are not rightly frequented, or souls enthusiastically evangelised. Jesus is obscured because Mary is kept in the background. Thousands of souls perish because Mary is withheld from them. It is the miserable unworthy shadow which we call our devotion to the Blessed Virgin, that is the cause of all these wants and blights, these evils and omissions and declines. Yet, if we are to believe the revelations of the Saints, God is **pressing** for a greater, a wider, a stronger, quite another devotion to His Blessed Mother. . . . Let a man but try it for himself, and his surprise at the graces it brings with it, and the transformations it causes in his soul, will soon convince him of its otherwise almost incredible efficacy as a means for the salvation of men, and for the coming of the Kingdom of Christ."

"God is willing to give us all; all now depends on us, and on thee by whom all is received and treasured up, by whom all is transmitted, O Mother of God! All depends on the union of men with her who receives all from God."—(Gratry).

Bringing Mary to the World.

If devotion to Mary will work such wonders, then the great purpose must be to bring that instrument to bear, to bring Mary to the world. And how more effectively can this be done than through an apostolic organisation; lay—hence illimitable as to numbers; active—hence penetrating everywhere; loving Mary with all its might, and binding itself to involve the hearts of all others in that love; utilising all its avenues of action to fulfill this purpose.

And so, bearing her name with an inexpressible pride; built as an organisation upon an unbounded and child-like trust in her, to which it gives solidity by planting it in the heart of each individual one of its members: possessing then the latter as working parts acting in a perfect harmony of loyalty and discipline—the Legion of Mary does not think it presumption, but rather a right degree of confidence to believe that its system forms, as it were, a mechanism which only requires operating by the hand of Authority to compass the world, and which Mary will deign to use as an agency to accomplish her maternal work for souls, and to carry on her perpetual mission of crushing the head of the serpent.

"'Whosoever shall do the will of God, he is my brother and sister and mother' (St. Mark iii. 35). What a marvel! What an honour! To what a height of glory Jesus elevates us! The women proclaim as most happy Her who brought Him into the world; but what prevents them from participating in that same maternity? For here the Gospel speaks of a new mode of generation, a new parenthood."—(St. John Chrysostom).

THE LEGION APOSTOLATE.

Its Dignity.

To portray the dignity of the Apostolate to which the Legion summons its members, and its importance to the Church, one can find no more emphatic words than those on the subject of Catholic Action, which are set out below. They are the words of Pius XI, and authoritative:—

"Would that (they) may be convinced that they are called and chosen for this office, which is not too far removed from the Priestly office, by an altogether special grace of God; for Catholic Action is nothing else but the Apostleship of the Faithful who, under the leadership of the Bishops, lend a helping hand to the Church and in a measure complete its Pastoral ministry.

"But as those who participate in and promote Catholic Action do so only by prayer, work, and self-sacrifice, it is abundantly clear that they are animated and carried along by one and one only desire—the noblest that can be found—that of preparing for the Lord an entrance into the hearts of men, and of daily extending the confines of the Lord's Kingdom, that is, in a word, of restoring all things in Christ.

"They must remember, however, that their work will be not only feeble and halting, but indeed utterly fruitless unless, as is fitting to citizens who are also apostles, they are inflamed and burn with charity for their brethren and their neighbour without distinction.

This fire of charity—since it alone can remove the difficulties and soften down and moderate the asperities which result between men from differences in temperament, occupation, race, and customs—will it not also pave the way slowly, little by little, for the solution on Catholic principles of even the gravest questions of equity and justice affecting the welfare of the State and human Society?" (Pius XI, Acta Apostolicae Sedis, Vol. xx, p. 296).

"Mary exercises over the human race a moral influence which we cannot better determine than by comparing it to those physical forces of attraction, affinity and cohesion, which in the order of nature unite together bodies and the parts of which they are composed. . . . We believe we have shown that Mary took part in all the great movements which constitute the life of societies and their real civilisation."—(Petitalot).

An Apostolic Laity Essential.

The proposition is ventured upon that the health of a Catholic community depends upon the presence of a large apostolic class—belonging to the laity, yet sharing the outlook of the priest, and providing points of contact with the people, and intimacy of control. Security depends on this complete union of priest and people. Either without the other is helpless.

But the essential idea of apostleship is an intense interest in the welfare and the work of the Church, and such interest there can hardly be without some feeling of participation. Thus the apostolic organisation is a mould which produces apostles. This mould can be handled with full effectiveness by the Priest alone, and in the handling of it is the true pastor made manifest.

Wherever these qualities of apostleship are not sedulously cultivated, it is certain that the next generation will have a serious problem to face in the lack of all real interest in the Church, and of all sense of responsibility. Out of this infantile Catholicism what good can come? And where is its safety but in a complete calm? History teaches that such a nerveless flock is readily stampeded even unto the destruction of its own pastors, or else that it is devoured by the first fierce pack of wolves which comes upon the scene.

"In all times the laity have been the measure of the Catholic spirit."—(Newman: Present Position of Catholics, ix.).

The Legion and Catholic Action.

Like many another great principle, Catholic Action is in itself something cold and abstract. Hence there is a very real danger that it may not exercise an appeal, so that the laity do not respond to the high destiny which has been held out to it, and, worse still, may even be deemed to be incapable of responding. The disastrous sequel would be that the effort to make the laity play its proper and indispensable part in the battle of the Church would be abandoned.

"But," says one qualified to judge (H. E. Mgr. Riberi, the Apostolic Delegate to Missionary Africa): **"the Legion of Mary is Catholic Action decked out in attractive and alluring form; throbbing with life so that it wins all to it; undertaken in the manner stipulated by Pius XI, that is, in dependence on the Virgin Mother of God; insistent on quality as the foundation of membership and even as the key to numerical strength; safeguarded by plenteous prayer and self-sacrifice, by exact system, and by complete co-operation with the Priest."**

To the Priest the Legion gives the respect and obedience which are owing to lawful superiors, yet more than this. Its apostolate is built upon the fact that the main channels of Grace are the Mass and the Sacramental System, of which the Priest is the essential minister. All the strivings and expedients of that apostolate must have in view this great end: the bringing of the divinely-appointed nourishment to the multitude, sick and hungering. It follows that a first principle of Legionary action must be the bringing of the Priest to the People, not always in person—for that may be impossible—but everywhere in influence and in understanding.

This is the essential idea of the Legion apostolate. Lay it will be in bulk of membership, but working in inseparable union with its Priests, and under their captaincy, and with absolute identity of interest. It will ardently seek to supplement their efforts, and to widen their place in the lives of men, so that men, receiving them, shall receive Him who sent them.

"Amen, amen, I say to you, he that receiveth whomsoever I send, receiveth Me; and he that receiveth Me, receiveth Him that sent Me."—(Our Lord's Discourse to the Apostles; St. John xiii. 20).

The Priest and the Legion.

The idea of the Priest, with a devoted band pressing round him to share his labours, has the holiest of all sanctions: the example of Our Lord Himself, whose preparation for the conversion of the world was to surround Himself with a band of chosen ones, whom He tutored Himself and filled with His own spirit.

That divine lesson was learned and applied by the Apostles, who called on all to help them in the winning of souls. As has been beautifully said (Card. Pizzardo), it may well be that the strangers from Rome (Acts II. 10), who heard the preaching of the Apostles on the day of Pentecost, were the first to announce Jesus Christ in Rome, thus sowing the seeds of the Mother Church which Saint Peter and Saint Paul soon after established officially.

Certainly, "the first diffusion of Christianity made at Rome itself was made by Catholic Action. Could it have been otherwise? What would the Twelve have done, lost in the immensity of the world, if they had not gathered around them men and women, the old and the young, saying: 'We carry with us the treasure of heaven. Help us to scatter it abroad.' "—(Allocutio of Pius XI.).

The words of one Pontiff have been quoted. Let those of another be added to demonstrate finally that the example of Our Lord and His Apostles in relation to the conversion of the world is divinely meant to form pattern for **every Priest** (the alter Christus) in relation to his own little world, be it parish, or district, or special work:—

"Happening to be one day amidst a group of Cardinals, the Holy Father (Pius X.) said to them:—'What is the thing most necessary at the present time to save society?' 'Build Catholic schools,' said one. 'No.' 'Multiply churches,' replied another. 'No again.' 'Increase the recruiting of the clergy,' said a third. 'No, no,' replied the Pope. 'What is most necessary at the present time is to have in each parish a group of laymen at the same time virtuous, enlightened, determined, and really apostolic.' This holy Pope, at the end of his life, counted for the salvation of the world on the training, by the zeal of the clergy, of Catholics devoting themselves to the apostolate by word and action, but above all, by example. In the dioceses in which, before being Pope, he had exercised the ministry, he attached less importance to the census of parishioners than to the list of Catholics capable of radiating an apostolate. He considered that in any class whatever chosen ones could be formed. And so he classified his priests according to the results which their zeal and their abilities had obtained on this point." (Chautard: The Soul of the Apostolate, Pt. III. 1. f.).

"The priest must be that husbandman who, at every hour of the day, from dawn to dusk, goes out into the public places to call for labourers in the Lord's vineyard. Without that call of his, there is a great risk that the majority will remain standing there 'all the day idle.' (Matt. xx. 6)."—(Civardi: Manual of Catholic Action).

The Legion as an Asset in the Parish.

In the first place, it is declared and emphasised that this Handbook represents, not the sketching of an ideal, but the effort to depict with photographic fidelity the organisation as it actually is at work.

It will be found that the interests of general parochial organisation will be served by the establishment of a branch of the Legion, on to which would be grafted all the miscellaneous activities which form part of the parish system. Ordinarily, each of these activities has its own periodic meeting, which involves a multiplication of meetings for the priest and for the zealous worker who may be engaged on several works. Moreover, these meetings are usually formless, with little or no prayer. Though necessary for the regulation of the work, they serve little higher purpose. Sometimes, even, the effort is made to conduct a work without any meeting, i. e., by a system of informal or personal guidance of the workers by the person chiefly responsible. This method, which can hardly be termed organisation at all, represents the least efficient application of zeal, and will secure neither efficiency, nor numbers, nor perseverance.

On the other hand, at least the advantages, which invariably arise from the setting up of central machinery, will attend the establishment of a branch or branches of the Legion. In such a branch will be united some or all of the parish works and workers. There will be one weekly meeting instead of many, one worker encouraged by another, the experience of each teaching all, reports of interesting work helping out reports of works which are more useful than they are lively. In addition, the Legion will supply a tradition, a methodical system, and a spiritual mould for the members themselves.

In many places, the fact that the most notable contributions to work of an apostolic or social character are being made by non-Catholics constitutes a humiliating and serious situation. For the Church, in any place, to occupy a position of apparent inferiority in works of zeal has a bad mental effect upon the Catholics there, producing innumerable unfortunate reactions. More than that! it is intolerable that Catholic neglect should thus deck out the Church of Christ in the habiliments of a fool—to be mocked at by those who are still living by the Catholic inspiration which they verbally repudiate. For those other Churches, called Christian, bear but the same relation to the Catholic Church that the moon bears to the sun; they got and get their light from it. With its destruction, their borrowed light would go out.

The Legion will speedily remove such a reproach. Its spiritual and methodical system cannot fail to win the day against the best efforts and results of the separated brethren who, no matter what their qualities may be, lack the spirit of the Church and are unprovided with its weapons.

"Catholic Action must be considered by priests as a definite part of their ministry, and by the faithful as a duty of the Christian life."—(Pius XI.).

Its Fruits are intense Idealism and Action.

Again, the Church by exhibiting only a cautious routine would place the Truth, of which it is the custodian, in a very disadvantageous setting. If the young once form the habit of looking to purely worldly or even irreligious systems for the active idealism for which generous natures crave, a terrible harm has been done, for which future generations will pay.

Here the Legion can aid by making its programme one of enterprise and effort and sacrifice, such as will help to capture for the Church those two words "idealism" and "action," making them handmaids of the Church's doctrine.

According to the saying of the historian, Lecky, the world is ruled by its ideals. If this is so, those who create a higher ideal thereby lift all mankind; it being understood, of course, that the ideal is a practical one, and that it is sufficiently in evidence to constitute it a headline. Possibly it may be conceded that the ideals held up by the Legion conform to both of these requirements.

An important feature of the Legion is that its work will be graced by many religious vocations among its members.

But the objection will be made that, in the midst of a universal selfishness, there are none who will assume the heavy burden of Legion membership. This reasoning is wrong. The many who answer the call to trivial action will quickly fade away and leave not a trace. The few who respond to the call to high endeavour will persevere, and little by little their spirit will communicate itself to the many. In time, the strange anomaly is manifest that multitudes have become holy who had refused to be good.

What a piece of powerful machinery is to the hand that operates it, such will a Praesidium of the Legion be to the Priest (or the Religious) who avails of it. A few controls and levers are touched and a multiplication of power is effected, accomplishing the normally impossible. Just so, the hour and a half spent once a week at the meeting, guiding, encouraging, spiritualising the members, will enable him to be everywhere, to hear everything, to influence everybody, to overcome all his physical limitations. Indeed, it seems as if zeal could not be employed to better purpose than in the directing of more than one Praesidium.

Thus armed with his Legionaries (in themselves such another humble equipment as staff, scrip, sling, and pebbles, yet because of Mary made the instruments of Heaven), he can, like another David, go forth with certainty of victory against the grisliest Goliath of unbelief and sin.

"It is a moral force, not a material, which will vindicate your profession and secure your triumph. It is not giants who do most. How small the Holy Land! Yet it subdued the world. How poor a spot was Attica! Yet it has formed the intellect. Moses was one, Elias was one, David was one, Paul was one, Athanasius was one, Leo was one. Grace ever works by few; it is the keen vision, the intense conviction, the indomitable resolve of the few; it is the blood of the martyr, it is the prayer of the saint, it is the heroic deed, it is the momentary crisis, it is the concentrated energy of a word or a look, which is the instrument of heaven. Fear not, little flock, for He is mighty who is in the midst of you, and will do for you great things."—(Newman: Present Position of Catholics).

OBJECTIONS WHICH MAY BE ANTICIPATED.

1. "No need for the Legion here."

Zealous persons desirous of starting the Legion in a new area may expect the objection that the Legion is not required in that particular place. As the Legion is not an organisation for the doing of any one special type of work, but is primarily one for the development of Catholic zeal and spirit (which can then be applied to the doing of any work desired), such an objection usually amounts to a statement that there is no local need for Catholic zeal—an assertion which sufficiently confutes itself.

In every place, without exception, there is vital need for such an intense apostolate, and this for many reasons:—Firstly, because those members of the flock, who are capable of it, should be given an effective opportunity of living the apostolic life. Secondly, because the stirrings of such an apostolate in the general populace are necessary in these days, if religion is to be prevented from settling down into routine or materialism. Thirdly, the patient and intensive labours of such workers are required for the shepherding of those whose lives are bound in shallows and in misery, or of those whose tendency is to stray.

2. "Persons suitable for membership are not available."

As this objection usually proceeds from a misconception as to the type of worker required, it may in general be stated that every office, shop, and place of work holds potential Legionaries. Every Sodality and every Confraternity have, at least in their best members, excellent material for the Legion. In sending them into the Legion ranks, these associations effectively fulfil their own obligations to those members to develop them to the fullest extent possible.

Those potential Legionaries may be learned or unlettered, labourers or leisured, or in the ranks of the unemployed. They are not the monopoly of any particular colour, race, or class, but can be found in all. The Legion has the special gift of being able to enlist in the service of the Church this hidden force, this undeveloped loveliness of character. Professor Alfred O'Rahilly, as the result of a study of Legion activity, was moved to write as follows: "I made a great discovery, or rather I found that the discovery had been made, that there is a latent heroism in seemingly ordinary men and women; unknown sources of energy had been tapped."

Standards for membership should not go beyond those which the Popes have had in mind when they declare that in any class whatever an élite could be formed and trained to the apostolate.

In this connection, paragraph 3 (b) of the Section on Extension and Recruiting should be read most carefully; also the Section entitled "The Legion as the Handmaid of the Foreign Missionary," which urges the wide extension of Legionary membership among the native peoples.

A genuine difficulty in finding members would betoken an extraordinarily low spiritual standard in that locality, and so far from proving the need for inaction, would demonstrate conclusively the paramount need for a branch of the Legion to play the part of a good leaven. Be it remembered that a Praesidium can be formed with as few as four or five or six members. When these apply themselves to the work and understand its requirements, they will quickly find and introduce other suitable members.

3. "The Legion visitation would be resented."

Were such indeed to be the case, the conclusion indicated is that other work should be selected, not that the idea of the Legion (with all its possibilities of good to members and community) should be abandoned. Be it stated, however, that nowhere so far has the Legion experienced a permanent or general difficulty in this matter of its visitation. Assuming that the visitation is being undertaken in the true spirit of the Legion Apostolate (see Article thereon), it may ordinarily be taken that a coldness towards the Legionaries testifies to the existence of religious indifference or worse, so that, just where the Legionaries are least desired, exists the greatest need for their labours. Initial difficulties of this description do not justify the discontinuance of the visitation. Almost invariably have the Legionaries, who braved these icy barriers, been able to thaw them, and to remove as well the graver underlying causes.

4. "My child has to work hard during the day and requires his or her free time for rest."

These words delayed for years the start of the Legion in a large city. Constantly, they cost it excellent members. How reasonable they sound, yet if acted upon, they would leave the world a religious wilderness, for it is not by the leisured that the Church's work is done. Moreover, is it not to a more or less disordered amusement, rather than to a genuine rest, that those free hours are given by the high-spirited young? In such an alternation between a day of toil and an evening of pleasure, it is very easy to drift into a practical materialism, which, after a few years, leaves hearts without an ideal, eating themselves out for the youth which has prematurely fled, taking with it the only things they had been taught to prize. And things may end even more unhappily. Does not St. John Chrysostom say that he had never succeeded in persuading himself that any one could achieve salvation who had never done anything for the salvation of his brethren?

Infinitely wiser would it be to urge that child to give to the Lord, in a Legionary membership, the first fruits of that free time. Those first fruits will inspire the whole life and keep the heart, and face too, serene and young. And there is still left an abundance of time for recreation, doubly enjoyed because doubly earned.

5. "The Legion is only one among many organisations with the same ideals and programme."

It is true that idealism abounds and, likewise, that a programme of desirable works can be drawn up in a few minutes by anyone possessing paper and a writing implement. It is, therefore, true that the Legion is only one among ten thousand organisations which propose a noble warfare for souls and a programme of important works. But it is also true that it is one of the few which make their apostolate definite. A vague idealism, with general appeals to members to do good in their surroundings, will always be attended by the vaguest performance, and indeed belongs rather to the sphere of ordinary Catholicity than to Catholic Action. The Legion reduces its warfare to a definite spirituality, a definite programme of prayer, a definite weekly task, a definite weekly report and, it will be found, to definite accomplishment. Last, but not least, it bases this methodical system on the dynamic principle of union with Mary.

6. "Does not the Children of Mary Sodality, with its work-obligation, obviate the need for the Legion?"

On the contrary, it is asserted that the Legion forms a desirable and even an essential supplement to that Sodality. The obligation to do active work inevitably entails a special meeting to regulate that work and to receive reports. Without such a meeting, even the most elementary work cannot long be carried on. The contrary view marks an insufficient appreciation of the requirements of efficiency, discretion, and safety, as a little reflection will show.

If then a work-meeting is to be introduced, why not let it be the Legion, with its developed scheme and its proved capacity to handle work and members?

7. "The Legion works are already being done by other agencies. The Legion might clash with them."

How strange to hear these words spoken of places where three-fourths or even higher proportions of the population are non-practising or non-Catholic, and where progress is negligible!

How sad if anyone should reconcile himself to such a *status quo*, which means that in that place Herod is to occupy the throne of men's hearts, while the Lord and His dear Mother are to remain permanently relegated to the miserable stable!

Often, too, those words, which deny admittance to the Legion, are used in the interest of organisations which represent a name without performance; armies which may exist, but never conquer any enemy territory.

Moreover, work is not being done except it is being adequately done. Therefore, work is not being done which is engaging dozens of apostolic workers where, properly, there should be hundreds or even thousands; and unhappily this is ordinarily the case. Frequently, too, the lack of organisation, which the small numbers bespeak, means corresponding lack of spirit and method.

Be certain of it, there is room for the Legion. Surely, it is wise to put such a claim to the test by assigning to the Legion even a tiny sphere of action. The sequel may be convincing, and the members of a single little branch may, like the five barley loaves, be multiplied so that they fill all the needs, and over and above. (St. Matt. xiv, 16-21).

The Legion has no particular programme of works. It does not presuppose new works, but rather a new "cadre" for existing works not already sufficiently systematised, with effects analogous to those which would follow upon the application of electric power to a work previously done by hand.

8. "There are already too many organisations. The proper course is to revive the existing societies or to extend their functions so as to cover the works proposed to be done by the Legion."

This may be a reactionary argument. The words "too many" can be applied with truth to every department of life around. Yet the new is not denied because it is new, and from time to time a great advance is made. So, too, the Legion claims the opportunity to prove itself. If it is not "just another," but from God, what loss to turn it from one's door!

Moreover, the above objection supposes that the work in question is not at present being done. In such circumstances, it is neither sensible nor the common practice of mankind to reject new machinery which has elsewhere demonstrated its capacity to do that work.

How quaint would sound the same objection, put as follows: "There is no need to import that aeroplane. There is already too much mechanism in this place. Let us, instead, develop the motor-car so that it will fly!"

9: "This is a small place. There is no room for the Legion here."

It is no uncommon experience to find these words spoken of places which, though not large, yet have an unenviable notoriety.

Again, a village may possess a routine goodness and yet be stagnant: stagnant in moral qualities, and stagnant in human interests, so that the young fly from the want of the latter to the populous centres, and there come to disaster from want of the former.

The trouble arises from the absence of religious idealism, following upon the spectacle of none doing more than their essential duties. With religious idealism gone, a religious desert remains (and villages are not the only such deserts). To make that desert bloom again, reverse the process: create a little apostolic band which will cast abroad its own spirit and set up new headlines of conduct. Works suitable to the place will be undertaken, life brightened, the exodus stemmed.

Many highly successful Praesidia of the Legion have now for years existed in villages with populations of less than 500. And surely the following instance will give encouragement to all who think their own conditions unfavourable. A Parish Priest has Praesidia in each of the three separated and widely scattered rural areas which compose his Parish. One of those areas is fairly populous, but the second contains only 70 Catholics, and the third only 40. The work of the Praesida is described as exercising a dynamic effect upon the Catholicism of those places.

10. "Certain of the works of the Legion consist in spiritual activities which, from their very nature, belong to the Priest, and which should only be allotted to the laity when the clergy cannot undertake them. As

it is, I am able to visit my flock several times in the year with satisfactory results."

This objection is answered generally by the Section on the "Legion Apostolate": also more particularly in what follows, but in advance it is pointed out that no work deemed undesirable need be undertaken.

The intimate knowledge of what is unquestionably one of the holiest cities in the world, reveals there vast multitudes sick with sin and worldliness, and seething with the terrible problems of modern-day civilisation. For it or any other city-community the feeling that all is safeguarded by a visitation—however fruitful—once, twice, four times in the year is not justified. If all is well, for instance, many will be approaching the altar daily, more weekly, and all at least once monthly. Why then do four or five hours a week in the Confessional so often suffice? Whence the dreadful disproportion?

Again, what degree of intimacy, or at least of personal touch, is required to satisfy the pastoral obligation towards each soul under its care: that soul which, as St. Charles Borromeo used to say, was diocese enough for a bishop? A simple calculation will show what even half-an-hour a year for each would mean in all. And would that half-an-hour be sufficient contribution? St. Madeleine Sophie Barat, in addition to interviews innumerable, wrote 200 letters to one difficult soul. How many Legionary pursuits have lasted ten years and more, and are still in progress! Yet, if the harassed priest cannot spare even that half-hour; and if (as is claimed) the Legion will supply him with zealous representatives: many where he is one: obedient to his every word: of solid discretion: as capable (with his help) as he of gaining access to individuals and families: of irresistible gifts to entice souls to higher things: affording him—in a word—the opportunity of giving souls more than a routine service; is it fair to his work and to himself to refuse that help?

11. "The people are all good. We have flourishing Societies. We have no problems. The Priests and the Nuns are able to cope with the work."

Even if the truth of this statement were to be granted, there is another consideration as important as that of coping with the work. On all superiors rests responsibility for developing to the full the spiritual capacity of those in their charge. For the majority, this will be met by urging the performance of the essential duties and the frequent reception of the Sacraments. But in every flock a proportion will have the capacity to lead the apostolic life; and, surely, to leave that capacity undeveloped—hidden in the earth, as it were, like the talent of the Gospel—is most serious default. (St. Matt. xxv. 24-30). Therefore, the call to the apostolate must be made. But to call, without providing the means for responding, is little better than silence, for few of those who hear will have the ability to work out the means for themselves. Thus, machinery, in the shape of an apostolic organisation, must be set up.

At a recent inaugural meeting of the Legion in a country town, the Spiritual Director asked those who were present (23 in number, representing the cream of the Catholic womanhood of the place) how many had done any apostolic work. The response showed that not one ever had. His comment was "how amazing!" But what other response can the talents hidden in the earth ever make?

12. "I fear possible indiscretions on the part of members."

There is lack here of a sense of the realities of the position. As well refuse to reap a harvest because some ears may be spoiled by clumsy handling! The harvest at stake is souls: souls, poor and feeble and blind and lame: in such need, in such numbers that there is a danger that one may accept the situation as irremediable. Yet it is for such that the Lord bids search to be made in the streets and lanes and the highways and hedges, so that His house may be filled with them (St. Luke xiv. 21-23). In no other way can a harvesting so vast be wrought than by the marshalling of the lay battalions. It may be that some indiscretions will ensue. In some measure, they are inseparable from zeal and life. There are two ways of insuring against indiscretions: a shameful inaction, and a careful discipline. The heart which echoes that yearning of Our Lord for the sick multitude will turn with horror from the former alternative, and throw itself with all its might into that harvesting of stricken souls.

The history of the Legion to date does not suggest that indiscretions, either serious or numerous, need be anticipated; and at the least there is exhibited a careful discipline.

13. Obstacles in the way of starting, there will always be. In this the Legion will not be alone amongst good works. A little resolution will show these difficulties, which seem so formidable in advance, to resemble a forest, which at a distance appears solid and impenetrable, but when once approached is found easy of entry.

Remember, too, that "they who are ever taking aim, make no hits; that they who never venture, never gain; that to be ever safe, is to be ever feeble; and that to do some substantial good, is the compensation for much incidental imperfection." (Newman).

14. In talking of a work of Grace, let no one be so worldly prudent as to ignore the existence of Grace. Objections and possibilities of harm should not be quoted without a thought as to the helps. The Legion is built upon prayer, works for souls, and belongs to Mary altogether. When considering it, therefore, speak not of human rules, tell of the rules of God.

"Mary is a Virgin Unique and unlike any other: Virgo Singularis. When considering her, speak not to me of human rules, tell me of the rules of God."—(Bossuet).

SCHEME OF THE LEGION.

Personal Sanctification its Object and Means.

The general and essential means by which the Legion of Mary is to effect its object is Personal Service acting under the influence of the Holy Ghost, i.e., having Divine Grace as its moving principle and support, and the Glory of God and the salvation of souls as its final end and purpose.

Personal sanctification is thus not only the object of the Legion of Mary, but it is also its primary means of action: "I am the vine; you the branches . . . he that abideth in me, and I in him, the same beareth much fruit: for without me you can do nothing." (John xv. 5).

"The Apostolate is one of the duties inherent in the Christian life. If we ponder upon it we shall see that the Sacraments of Baptism and Confirmation impose—among other duties—this Apostolate of Catholic Action which is a spiritual service of our neighbour. Through Confirmation we become soldiers of Christ. A soldier must labour and fight, not so much for himself as for others. . . . Baptism also, in a way less obvious, imposes the duty of the Apostolate, since through it we become members of the Church, the Mystical Body of Christ."—(Pius XI).

An Intensely Ordered System.

Aware that zeal unsystematised, enthusiasm undirected (like the great natural sources of power which, unharnessed, run to waste), never bring great results, interior or exterior, and seldom are durable, the Legion places before its members a mode of life rather than the doing of a work. It provides an intensely ordered system, in which much is given the force of rule that in other systems is merely exhorted or left to be understood, and in regard to every detail of which it enjoins a spirit of scrupulous observance. It promises, in return, perseverance and conspicuous growth in those qualities upon which that system is built (which are indeed nothing but an epitome of Christian perfection), namely, faith, love of Mary, fearlessness, self-sacrifice, fraternity, prayerfulness, prudence, patience obedience, humility, gladness, and the apostolic spirit.

"The growth of what is usually designated the Lay Apostolate is a special manifestation of our modern days, possessing—were it for no other reason than the numbers concerned—infinite potentialities. Yet, insufficient seems the provision for this giant movement. When one looks upon the multitude of beautifully conceived Orders which cater for those who are able to abandon the world, the contrast with the form of organisation, thought good enough for those who are not so circumstanced, is very striking. On the one hand, what intensity and exact science making the most of its material! On the other, how elementary and superficial is the provision made! The system calls indeed for some service from its members, but it forms for the generality of them little more than an incident in the week's round, and it hardly even endeavours to play a more considerable part. There must be a higher conception of it. Should it not be the staff of their earthly pilgrimage—the very backbone of their whole spiritual life?

"Undoubtedly the Religious Order must form the pattern foı workers in common and, other things being equal, it may be taken that the quality of the work done will improve in the measure that there is approximation to the Order idea. Still this brings with it the difficulty of determining the exact degree of rule which is to be imposed. Desirable though discipline is in the interests of efficiency, there is always the danger of overdoing it, and narrowing the appeal of the organisation. The fact must be borne in mind that the object in view is permanent lay organisation (and these last three words are underlined)—not something equivalent to a new Religious Order, or which would eventually drift into becoming one, and of which history is full of instances.

"The aim is this, and no other: the drawing into efficient organisation of persons living their ordinary life as we know it, and in whom the presence of various tastes and pursuits other than purely religious ones has to be allowed for. The amount of regulation attempted should be no more than will be accepted by the average of the class for whom the organisation is intended, but it should certainly be nothing less."—(Legionary Foundations).

Perfection of Membership.

The Legion wishes perfection of membership to be estimated according to exact adherence to its system, and not according to any satisfaction or apparent degree of success which may attend the efforts of the Legionary. It deems a member to be a member to the degree to which he submits himself to the Legion system, and no more. Spiritual Directors and Presidents of Praesidia are exhorted to keep this conception of membership ever before the minds of their members. It forms an ideal attainable by all (success and consolation do not), and in its realisation will alone be found the corrective to monotony, to distasteful work, to real or imagined failure, which otherwise bring to an inevitable end the most promising beginnings of apostolic work.

"It is to be noted that our services to the Society of Mary are to be measured not according to the importance of the post we fill, but according to the degree of the supernatural spirit and of the zeal for Mary with which we devote ourselves to the duty

assigned by obedience, however humble, however hidden it may be." —(Petit Traité de Marialogie: Marianiste).

The Primary Obligation.

Foremost in its system, the primary obligation of each member, the Legion sets the duty of attendance at its meetings. As the burning lens is to the rays of the sun, so is the meeting to the members. The focus collects them, begets the fire, and kindles everything that comes near it. It is the meeting which makes the Legion. This bond sundered or dis-esteemed, the members drop away and the work falls to the ground. Conversely, in measure as the meeting is exalted and systematised, so is the power of the organisation intensified.

The following, written in the first years of its life, represents now as it did then the outlook of the Legion on the subject of organisation, and thus upon the importance of the meeting, which is the focus-point of such organisation:—"In the organisation the individuals, however notable, are content to play the part of cogs. They yield up much of their independence to the machine, that is to their associates as a body, but thereby the work gains a hundredfold in the fact that a number of individuals, who would otherwise have been either ineffective or else standing idle, are brought into action—each one, not with his or her own individual weakness, but with the fervour and power of all the greatest qualities amongst them. Consider pieces of coal lying unused, and the same in the heart of the furnace. Such is the parallel which suggests itself.

"Then the organised body has a well-marked life of its own, apart from the individuals who compose it, and this characteristic, rather than the beauty or urgency of the work done, seems in practice to be the magnet which attracts new members. The association establishes a tradition, begets a loyalty, enjoys respect and obedience, and powerfully inspires its members. Talk to the latter, and you will see that they lean upon it as upon a wise old mother. And well it may be so. Does it not save them from every pitfall: the imprudences of zeal: the discouragement of failure: the elevation of success: the hesitancy of the unsupported opinion: the timidity of loneliness: and, in general, from the whole quicksand of inexperience? It takes the raw material of mere good intention and educates it; sets about its work with regular plan; secures expansion and continuity."—("Legionary Foundations.")

"Considered in relation to us, its members, the Society of Mary is the extension, the visible manifestation of Mary our Heavenly Mother. Mary has received us into the Society as into her loving and maternal bosom, so as to mould us to the likeness of Jesus, and thus make us her privileged sons; so as to assign to us our apostolic task, and thus give us share in her mission as Co-redemptrix of souls. For us, the cause, the interests of the Society are identified with the cause, the interests of Mary."—(Petit Traité de Marialogie: Marianiste).

The Weekly Meeting of the Praesidium.

In an atmosphere made supernatural by its wealth of prayer, by its devotional usages, and by its sweet spirit of fraternity, the Praesidium holds a weekly meeting, at which work is assigned to each Legionary, and a report received from each Legionary of work done. This weekly meeting is the heart of the Legion from which the life-blood flows into all its veins and arteries. It is the power-house from which its light and energy are derived. It is the treasury out of which its own special needs are provided for. It is the great Community exercise, where Someone sits unseen in the midst of them, according to promise; where the peculiar grace of the work is bestowed; whither members are bidden and come even when they have no reports to make; and where they are imbued with the spirit of religious discipline, which looks first to the pleasing of God and personal sanctification; thence to the organisation which is best calculated to achieve these ends, and then proceeds to do the work assigned, subordinating private likings.

The Legionaries shall therefore regard attendance at their weekly Praesidium meeting as their first and most sacred duty to the Legion, Nothing else can supply for this; without it their work will be like a body without a soul. Reason tells us, and experience proves, that neglect in regard to this primary duty will be attended by ineffective work, and will too soon be followed by defection from the Legion's ranks.

"To those who do not march with her, we apply the words of St. Augustine: 'Bene curris sed extra viam': 'you run well, but you are out of the path.' Where will you arrive in the end?"—(Petitalot).

THE EXTERNAL AIMS OF THE LEGION.

1.—The Actual Work in Hands.

The Legion aims not at the doing of any particular work, but has as its primary object the making of its members holy. For the attainment of this it relies, in the first place, upon its members' attendance at its various meetings, into which prayer and devotion are so wound and woven as to give their complexion to all the proceedings. But then the Legion seeks to develop that holiness in a specific way, to give it the character of apostleship, to heat it white hot so that it must diffuse itself. This diffusion is not simply a utilisation of developed force, but (by a sort of reaction) is a necessary part of the development of that force. for the apostolic spirit is best developed by the apostolate. Hence the Legion also imposes on each member, as an essential and paramount obligation, the weekly performance of some active work prescribed by the Praesidium. The work proceeds from the meeting as an act of obedience to it, and, subject to the exceptions later indicated, the Praesidium can approve of any active work as satisfying the member's weekly obligation. In practice, however, the Legion outlook would require the direction of the work-obligation towards actual needs, and amongst the latter, towards the gravest, for that intensity of zeal which the Legion strives to generate in its members requires a worthy objective.

Trivial work will react unfavourably upon it, so that hearts that were ready to spend themselves for souls, and to return love for the Christ-Love, and effort and sacrifice for His labours and Death, end by settling down to pettiness and lukewarmness.

"Not so easily was I remade as made; He spoke and all things were made. But while He made me simply and at once by a word, He has, in the remaking of me, said many words, and worked wonders, and suffered much."—(St. Bernard).

2.—The Remoter and Greater Aim—The Leaven in the Community.

Important, however, as may be the work in hand, the Legion does not regard it as the ultimate or even as the chief object of its members' apostolate. Such work may employ one, two, or several hours of the Legionary's week, whereas the Legion looks beyond this to every hour of that week as radiant from the apostolic fire which has been kindled at its hearth. The system that imparts this quality of fire to souls has put abroad a mighty force. The apostolic spirit enters in only as master, dominates every thought, word, and action; and in its external manifestations is not confined to set times and places. The most retiring and otherwise least equipped person becomes invested with a peculiar capacity to influence others, so that whatever the surroundings, and even without the pursuing of a conscious apostolate, sin and indifference will end by bowing to a power greater than themselves. Universal experience teaches this. Therefore, with the satisfaction with which a general contemplates important posts adequately held, does the Legion think of each home, shop, factory, school, office, and every other place devoted to purposes of work or recreation, in which a true Legionary may be set by circumstances. Even where scandal and irreligion are at their worst, entrenched so to speak, the presence of this other Tower of David will bar the way to further advance and menace the evil. The corruption will never be acquiesced in; efforts at remedy will be essayed; it will be a subject of sorrow, of prayer; will be contended against determinedly, unremittingly, and probably successfully in the end.

Thus the Legion, beginning by bringing its members together to persevere with one mind in prayer with their Queen: then sending them into the sinful and sorrowful places, there to do a good work, and by catching fire in the doing to do a greater: finally looks out over the highways and byways of the everyday life as the object of a still more glorious mission. Knowing what has been done by limited numbers, reflecting that the potential material for its ranks is almost beyond number, believing that its system, ecclesiastically administered, affords a strangely efficacious way of purifying a sinful world, the Legion yearns exceedingly for the multiplication of its members, that it may be legion in number as in name.

Between those working actively, and those giving Auxiliary service, and those being worked for, the whole population can be taken in, and raised from the level of neglect or routine to that of enthusiastic membership of the Church. Consider what this can mean to village or town; no longer merely in the Church, but a driving force in it, sending directly or through the Communion of Saints its impulses to the ends of the earth, and into the dark places thereof. What an ideal—a whole population organised for God! And yet this is no mere ideal. It is the most practical and possible thing in the world to-day—if eyes are but uplifted and arms unfolded.

"Behold, I say to you, lift up your eyes, and see the countries, for they are white already to harvest."—(St. John iv. 35).

3.—To Weld All Men Together.

This "seeking first of the Kingdom of God and His justice" (St. Matt. vi. 33), that is, its direct labours for souls, absorbs the Legion altogether. Nevertheless, it must not be overlooked that other things, which it did not seek, have been added unto it. For instance, the Legion has a social value. This becomes a national asset to the individual country, and represents spiritual gain to the souls comprised.

The successful working of the social machine demands, like any other machine, the harmonious co-operation of its component parts. Each part, that is the individual citizen, must do exactly what it is intended to do, and with the least possible amount of friction. If each does not render complete service, then waste enters in with a whole train of calamitous consequences. Repair is impossible, as it is infinitely difficult to detect the degree or the origin of the trouble; hence the remedy, which must be adopted, is to employ more force or lubricate with more money. This remedy still further impairs the idea of service or spontaneous co-operation, so that there is progressive failure. Communities have such vitality that they continue to function even though half their parts are misfits. But they work at a terrible price of poverty, friction, and unhappiness. Money and effort are poured out to drive parts which should be moving effortlessly, or which, indeed, should be sources of power. Result: problems, turmoil, crises.

Who can deny that this is what obtains even in the best regulated States to-day? Selfishness is the rule of the individual life. Hate turns the lives of many into purely destructive forces, and each new day brings new and universal demonstration of a vital truth which may effectively be stated thus: "Men who deny God, who are traitors to God, will be false to every person and to everything less than God, to all things on earth and in Heaven."—(Brian O'Higgins). The State is only the sum of the individual lives, so what heights can it be expected to reach? A danger and a pain to themselves, what are the nations offering to the world at large but a bit of their own turmoil.

But suppose that into the community there enters a force, which spreads like a contagion from one to another, and which makes the ideas of self-sacrifice, mutual love, and idealism pleasing to the individual, what a change is effected! The grievous sores heal up, and life is lived on a different level. Suppose a nation were to arise, which built its life on lofty standards, and held up to the world the example of a whole people putting its faith into practice, and hence, as a matter of course, solving its problems. Who can doubt that such a nation would be a shining light to the world, so that the world would come to sit at its feet for the purpose of learning.

Now, it is unquestionable that the Legion possesses the power of making the laity vitally interested in their religion, and of communicating an ardent idealism to those who come under its influence, so that they tend to forget their worldly divisions, distinctions and antagonisms, and are animated with the desire to labour for and love all mankind. This idealism, being rooted in religion, is not a mere sentiment. It makes the individual think in terms of service, it elicits great sacrifices, it reaches heights of heroism, and it does not evaporate.

Look, peoples of the world! If such be the Legion, would it not seem as if it offers, ready for use, a chivalry with magic in it to weld all men together in high enterprise for God: in service far transcending that legendary warfare of King Arthur, who—in Tennyson's beautiful verse—"drew the knight-errant-hood of his realm and all the realms, together in that Order of his Table Round: a glorious company: the flower of men: to serve as model for the mighty world: and be the fair beginning of a time."

"It is clear that Catholic Action merits every favour and support not only from bishops and priests, who know well that it is to us as the apple of our eye, but also from the heads and magistratures of any and every State. And if it indeed shall rejoice in this common support, it will certainly issue into a magnificent abundance of fruit for Catholic peoples, and by reawakening the religious sentiment in souls, will notably promote civil prosperity as well."—(Pius XI).

4.—In High Enterprise for God.

This new Chivalry has arisen at a time of particular peril for religion. The old armies of paganism and irreligion have been supplemented by that of militant atheism, which now dominates the landscape. Able organisation spreads its corrupting influences in constantly widening circles, and it seems capable of engulfing the world.

Compared with this terrible array, what a modest little flock the Legion is! Yet that very contrast emboldens one. The Legion is composed of souls who are united to the Virgin most Powerful. Moreover, it contains within itself great principles, and it knows how to apply them in effective ways. It may be that He who is mighty will do great things to it, and through it.

The aims of the Legion of Mary, and of that phalanx of Satan are diametrically opposed, but their methods are somewhat similar. Each concentrates on the individual. Each has its own vivid idealism, which it seeks to impress upon all men with enthusiasm; not that empty enthusiasm which talks much, but an enthusiasm which talks but little, and makes its members, under the influence of a firm discipline, pursue unwaveringly a thought-out plan of campaign. But there is a likeness more important than that of method. Each declares that it sets out to love and serve mankind. Each makes its campaign an instrument to a supreme purpose. That of the Legion is to bring God and religion to every soul; the avowed object of the other forces is to accomplish the very opposite. In fact, the antagonism of the aims is only equalled by the similarity of the methods. But it is not to be thought that the Legionary scheme was conceived in deliberate opposition to that Goliath who now stalks the earth hurling defiances at God. Things worked out otherwise. A little band gathered round Our Lady and said to her, "Lead us." She brought them into an immense infirmary, filled with the sick and sorrowful and broken ones of a great city; and she said: "Behold in each of these my Beloved Son. So also, He is in each member of humanity. Join me in my mother-work for Him in each one." So hand in hand with her, they set about their simple work of service, and lo! they have grown into a legion; and over the world that Legion is doing those simple acts of the love of God in man, and of the love of men for the sake of God; and in every place that love shows its power to stir and win hearts.

Likewise, the materialistic systems profess the love and service of man. They have preached a hollow gospel of fraternity. Millions have believed that gospel. In its name, they deserted a religion which they thought to be inert, and they submitted enthusiastically to despotisms. They were convinced that their new leaders loved them best; so they followed them, and now they are trying ardently to induce all mankind to join them. They seem to be in the ascendant. And yet the position is not a hopeless one. There is a way of bringing back to faith those determined millions, and of saving countless other millions. That hope lies in the application of a great principle which rules the world, and which the Saint of Ars has stated thus: "The world belongs to him who loves it most, and who proves that love." Those millions will never listen to the enunciation of the truths of faith. But they cannot help seeing, and being moved by, a real faith which operates through a real heroic love for all men. Convince them that the Church loves them most, and they will turn their back on those who rule them now. They will return to Faith in spite of everything. They will even lay down their lives for that Faith.

No common love can conquer men thus. Neither will it be accomplished by a mediocre Catholicism which can hardly preserve itself. It can be done by a Catholicism which loves Christ its Lord with all its heart, and then sees Him and loves Him in all men of whatsoever description. But this supreme charity of Christ must be practised on such a scale that they who look on are driven to admit that it is indeed a characteristic of the Church, and not merely the acts of sublime members of the Church. Therefore, it must be exhibited in the lives of the general body of the laity.

But it seems a hopeless thing to fire the entire household of the Church with this exalted spirit? Yes, the task is herculean! So unending, indeed, are the perspectives of the problem, so infinite the hosts which possess the land, that even the courage of the strongest heart might well fail. But Mary is the heart of the Legion, and that heart is faith and love unutterable. So thinking, the Legion looks out over the world, and all at once excited hope is born: "The world belongs to him who loves it most." Then it turns to its great Queen, as it did at the beginning: "Lead us!"

"To the powerful Virgin it is given to crush the Serpent's head; to souls who are united to her, it is given to overcome sin. In this we must believe with an unshaken faith, with a firm hope."—(Gratry).

MEMBERSHIP.

1. The Legion of Mary is open to all Catholics who:
   - (a) Lead edifying lives.
   - (b) Are animated by the spirit of the Legion, or at least desire to foster that spirit in themselves.
   - (c) Are prepared to fulfil each and every duty which membership of the Legion involves.

2. Persons who wish to join the Legion must apply for membership in a Praesidium.

3. The admission of new members is the exclusive privilege and function of the Praesidium.

4. Candidates under 18 years of age can only be received in Junior Praesidia. See relative Section.

5. No one shall be admitted as a Candidate for membership of the Legion of Mary until the President of the Praesidium, to which admission is sought, is, after careful enquiry, satisfied that the person seeking admission fulfils the conditions required.

6. A satisfactory probation of at least three months is required before the Candidate can be enrolled in the ranks of the Legionaries, but from the first the Candidate can participate fully in the works of the Legion.

7. No Candidate can be accepted without the consent of the Parish Priest, or, in the case of an Institution not engaged in parochial work, of the Ordinary. The Ordinary and the Parish Priest shall determine the precise manner in which their consent shall be signified. It is open to the Ordinary and the Parish Priest to signify a general acceptance of all those approved by the Spiritual Director.

8. A copy of the Tessera shall be given to every Candidate.

9. Formal admission consists essentially in the Legionary Promise, and the entry of the name of the Candidate on the membership roll of the Praesidium. The wording of the Legionary Promise is given in the next Section. It is set out in a form which will facilitate reading.

(a) When the period of Probation is judged to have been satisfactorily completed, the Candidate is given at least one week's notice of reception. During that week the Candidate should seek to become familiar with the words and the ideas of the Promise, so that, at the actual reception, it will be read with facility, understanding, and earnestness.

(b) Then at an ordinary meeting of the Praesidium, immediately after the recitation of the Catena, all the members still remaining standing, the Vexillum is moved near to the Candidate, who then takes in the left hand a copy of the Promise and reads it aloud, supplying his or her own name in the proper place. When beginning the reading of the third paragraph of the Promise, the Candidate places the right hand upon the staff of the Vexillum, and keeps it there till the reading of the Promise is completed.

After which, the Blessing of the Priest (if he is present) is given to the new Legionary. The latter's name is then entered on the Membership Roll.

(c) After this, the members resume their seats, the Allocutio is given, and the meeting follows its ordinary course.

(d) If the Vexillum is not yet in the possession of the Praesidium, the Candidate should instead hold a pictorial representation of it. That on the notepaper will serve.

10. Once the Candidate is deemed qualified, there should be no delay in taking the Promise. Two or more Candidates may be received simultaneously. But this is not desirable. For, it is pointed out that the greater the number of those received at the one time, the less solemn the ceremony becomes for each of them.

11. The ceremony of reception may constitute an ordeal for specially sensitive persons. But such are really favoured, inasmuch as the ceremony possesses for them a particular solemnity and seriousness which will have its effect upon their subsequent membership.

12. The duty of welcoming Candidates, instructing them in their duties, and fostering them through their Probation period and afterwards, is allocated in a special manner to the Vice-President; but this is a duty in which all should take a part.

13. A membership, discontinued for any reason, requires for renewal a further probation and the repetition of the Promise.

14. For the purposes of the work of the Legion, members are addressed by the title of "Brother" or "Sister" as the case may be.

15. Members may be grouped in Men's, Women's, Boys', Girls', or Mixed Praesidia, as the needs suggest, and as approved by the Curia.

The Legion came into existence as an organisation of women, and eight years passed before the first men's

Praesidium was established. Yet it forms an equally suitable basis for the organisation of men, and now there are in operation men's Praesidia and mixed Praesidia in great numbers. The first Praesidium in the New World was of men.

Though women have thus the place of honour in the organisation, the masculine pronoun is used throughout these pages to designate the Legionary of either sex. This is the legal custom. It avoids, moreover, a tiresome repetition of the phrase "he or she."

"A united, disciplined and co-ordinated body of all the Catholic forces, acting in dependence on the Bishops. . . . It should be a great family of men and women, and boys and girls, moved by the one desire of sharing in the ministry of the Church and co-operating in the spreading of the Kingdom of Christ in individuals, in families, in society, a peaceful army of apostles eager to win souls to Christ and the Catholic Church, . . . a single, compact, disciplined army."—(Letter of His Holiness Pius XI. Acta Apostolicae Sedis, Vol. 21, p. 664).

THE LEGIONARY PROMISE.

Most Holy Spirit, I, (*Name of the Candidate*),
Desiring to be enrolled this day as a Legionary of Mary,
Yet knowing that of myself I cannot render worthy service,
Do ask of Thee to come upon me and fill me with Thyself,
So that my poor acts may be sustained by Thy power, and become an instrument of Thy mighty purposes.
But I know that Thou, who hast come to regenerate the world in Jesus Christ,
Hast not willed to do so except through Mary;
That without her we cannot know or love Thee;
That it is by her, and to whom she pleases, when she pleases, and in the quantity and manner she pleases,
That all Thy gifts and virtues and graces are administered;
And I realise that the secret of a perfect Legionary service
Consists in a complete union with her who is so completely united to Thee.

So, taking in my hand the Legionary Standard, which
seeks to set before our eyes these things,
I stand before Thee as her soldier and her child,
And I so declare my entire dependence on her.
She is the mother of my soul.
Her heart and mine are one;
And from that single heart she speaks again those
words of old:
"Behold the handmaid of the Lord";
And once again Thou comest by her to do great things.
Let Thy power overshadow me, and come into my soul
with fire and love,
And make it one with Mary's love and Mary's will to
save the world;
So that I may be pure in her who was made Immaculate by Thee;
So that Christ my Lord may likewise grow in me
through Thee;
So that I with her, His Mother, may bring Him to the
world and to the souls who need Him;
So that they and I, the battle won, may reign with her
for ever in the glory of the Blessed Trinity.

Confident that Thou wilt so receive me—and use me—
and turn my weakness into strength this day,
I take my place in the ranks of the Legion, and I
venture to promise a faithful service.
I will submit fully to its discipline,
Which binds me to my comrades,
And shapes us to an army,
And keeps our line as on we march with Mary,
To work Thy will, to operate Thy miracles of grace,
Which will renew the face of the earth,
And establish Thy reign, Most Holy Spirit, over all.

In the name of the Father and of the Son and of the
Holy Ghost. Amen.

"It was pointed out that the Legionary Promise was addressed to the Holy Ghost, who received far too little devotion from the general body of Catholics, and for whom Legionaries must needs have special love. Their work, which is the sanctification of themselves and of the other members of the Mystical Body of Christ, is dependent on the power and operation of the Holy Ghost, and hence calls for a very close union with Him. Two things are essential to this: deliberate attention to Him, and devotion to the Blessed Virgin, with whom He works in inseparable union. Probably it was the lack of the latter, rather than lack of the former which has led to the general absence of a true devotion to the Holy Spirit, in spite of the many books which have been written and the many sermons which are preached on the subject. Legionaries are already full of the love of their Queen and Mother. If they join it to a definite devotion to the Holy Ghost, they will enter most fully into the Divine plan which has required the union of the Holy Ghost and Mary in the work of regenerating the world. As a consequence, their Legionary efforts cannot fail to be attended by a great addition of force and success.

"The first prayers ever said by Legionaries were the Invocation and Prayer of the Holy Ghost, followed by the Rosary. The same prayers have opened each Legion meeting ever since, so that it is most appropriate to place under the same holy auspices the ceremony which opens the Legionary membership itself. It returns to the idea of Pentecost, when the apostolic grace was conferred by the Holy Ghost through Mary. The Legionary, seeking the Holy Ghost through Mary, will receive abundantly of His gifts, and amongst those gifts will be a truly enlightened love of Mary herself.

"Moreover, the proposed form of promise would be in conformity with Legionary devotion as pictured by the Standard, which shows the Dove presiding over the Legion and its work, through Mary, for souls."—(Extract from the Minutes of the 88th Meeting of the Concilium Legionis).

[This quotation does not form part of the Legionary Promise].

THE PATRONS OF THE LEGION.

St. Joseph.

In the Legion's prayers, St. Joseph's name follows the invocations to the Hearts of Jesus and Mary, as he ranks next to them in the Court of Heaven. Belonging, according to Suarez, to the order of the Hypostatic Union, he surpasses all the saints and angels.

The part which he has played in regard to Jesus, he must likewise play in regard to the Mystical Body of Jesus. Guardian and protector of the one, he must likewise be guardian and protector of the other.

His Feast occurs on March 19th.

Solemnity of St. Joseph, Wednesday after the 2nd Sunday after Easter.

"The ministry of St. Joseph, both as spouse of the Blessed Virgin and as adopted father of Jesus, was closely conjoined with the very Person of Jesus Christ, in such wise that its dignity appears, more than any other whatsoever, to approach the most sublime dignity of the Mother of God."—(Carthagena).

St. John.

Designated in the Gospel as "the disciple whom Jesus loved," St. John appears therein as the model of devotion to the Sacred Heart. He clung to that Heart till, faithful to the end, he saw it stilled and pierced in death. Afterwards he is manifested as the model of devotion to the Immaculate Heart of Mary. Pure as an angel himself, he took the place which Jesus Himself had filled, and he continued to render her the love of a son till she too died.

But Our Lord's Third Word from the Cross contained more than a filial provision for His Blessed Mother. In St. John, Our Lord pointed out the human race, but above all, those who would by faith attach themselves to Him. Thus was proclaimed Mary's Motherhood of Men—the many brethren of whom Christ Himself was the first-born. St. John was the representative of all these new children, the first to enter upon the inheritance, a model to all who were to come after him, and a saint to whom the Legion owes tenderest devotion.

He loved the Church and every soul in it, and spent every faculty in its service. He was Apostle, Evangelist, and had the merit of Martyr.

He was Mary's Priest: therefore a special patron to the Legionary Priest in his service of the organisation which aims to be a living copy of Mary.

His Feast occurs on December 27th.

"When Jesus therefore had seen his Mother and the disciple standing whom He loved, He saith to His Mother: Woman, behold thy son! After that he saith to the disciple: Behold thy Mother. And from that hour the disciple took her to his own."—(From Gospel of Mass of Mary, Mediatrix of all Graces: St. John xix. 26, 27).

Blessed Grignion de Montfort.

"In view of other decisions as to the inadmissibility of particular and local patrons, the inclusion of the name of Blessed Grignion de Montfort would at first sight appear to be debatable ground. It can, however, be safely asserted that no Saint has played a greater part in the development of the Legion than he. The Handbook is full of his spirit. The prayers re-echo his very words. He is really the tutor of the Legion: thus invocation is due to him by the Legion almost as a matter of moral obligation."

(Decision of the Legion placing the name of Blessed Grignion de Montfort in the list of Invocations).

His Feast occurs on April 28th.

"Let no one be timid in asking from this powerful Beatus the most extraordinary favours, for the Most Holy Virgin will not fail to reward the confidence which any one reposes in the power with her of her most faithful slave of love."—(Cardinal Mercier).

St. Michael Archangel.

"Although the prince of all the heavenly court, St. Michael is the most zealous in honouring Mary and causing her to be honoured, while he waits always in expectation that he may have the honour to go at her bidding to render service to some one of her servants." (St. Augustine).

His Feast occurs on September 29th.

"There are cold shallow controversies on earth about Our Lady's greatness, while at this hour the great St. Michael is gazing on her throne with a rapture of astonishment, a delighted rapture which will grow to all eternity."—(Faber).

The Holy Guardian Angels.

"Mary is the general of the armies of God. The angels form the most glorious troops of her who is terrible as an army set in battle array!"—(Boudon: The Angels).

The Feast of this Heavenly Legion occurs on October 2nd.

"For He hath given His Angels charge over thee; to keep thee in all thy ways. In their hands they shall bear thee up; lest thou dash thy foot against a stone. Thou shalt walk upon the asp and the basilisk; and thou shalt trample under foot the lion and the dragon."—(Psalm 90).

St. Peter.

"St. Peter, as Prince of the Apostles, is pre-eminently the patron for an apostolic organisation. He was the first Pope, but stands for all the illustrious line of

Pontiffs, and for the present Holy Father. In invoking St. Peter, we express once again a Legion's loyalty to Rome, the centre of our faith, the source of authority, discipline, unity."—(Decision of the Legion placing St. Peter's name in the list of Invocations).

The Feast of Saints Peter and Paul occurs on June 29th.

"And I say to thee: That thou art Peter; and upon this rock I will build my church, and the gates of hell shall not prevail against it. And I will give to thee the keys of the kingdom of heaven. And whatsoever thou shalt bind upon earth, it shall be bound also in heaven; and whatsoever thou shalt loose on earth, it shall be loosed also in heaven."—(St. Matthew xvi. 18, 19).

St. Paul.

"A soul that is to win others must be great and wide as the ocean: to convert the world, one's soul must be greater than the world." Such was St. Paul from the day when a sudden light from Heaven shined round about him, and threw its radiance into his soul, and enkindled therein the burning desire to fill the world with the Name and Faith of Christ. The Apostle of the Gentiles—his work is his name. Untiringly he laboured till the sword of the executioner sent his indomitable spirit to God, and then his writings lived on, and ever will live, to continue his mission.

It is the way of the Church ever to join him with St. Peter in its prayer, which is praise indeed. It is fitting, too, for together these two great ones consecrated Rome by their martyrdom.

The Church celebrates their Feast on the same day.

"In many more labours, in prisons more frequently, in stripes above measure, in deaths often. Of the Jews five times did I receive forty stripes, save one. Thrice was I beaten with rods, once I was stoned, thrice I suffered shipwreck, a night and a day was I in the depth of the sea. In journeying often, in perils of waters, in perils of robbers, in perils from my own nation, in perils from the gentiles, in perils in the city, in perils in the wilderness, in perils in the sea, in perils from false brethren. In labour and painfulness, in much watchings, in hunger and thirst, in fastings often, in cold and nakedness."—(2 Corinthians, xi. 23-27).

THE PRAYERS OF THE LEGION.

The following are the prayers of the Legion of Mary, divided in the manner in which they are to be said at meetings. Privately recited, this order need not be followed.

1.—Prayers to be said at the Opening of the Meeting.

In the name of the Father, etc.

℣. Come, O Holy Ghost, fill the hearts of Thy faithful, and enkindle in them the fire of Thy love.

℣. Send forth Thy Spirit, and they shall be created.

℟. And Thou shalt renew the face of the earth.

Let us pray

O God, Who, by the light of the Holy Ghost, didst instruct the hearts of the faithful, grant that in the same spirit we may be truly wise, and ever rejoice in His consolation. Through Christ Our Lord. Amen.

℣. Thou, O Lord, wilt open my lips.

℟. And my tongue shall announce Thy praise.

℣. Incline unto my aid, O God.

℟. O Lord, make haste to help me.

℣. Glory be to the Father, etc.

℟. As it was in the beginning, etc.

Then follow Five Decades of the Rosary with the Hail! Holy Queen!

℣. Pray for us, O holy Mother of God.

℟. That we may be made worthy of the promises of Christ.

Let Us Pray

O God, Whose only-begotten Son, by His life, death, and resurrection, has purchased for us the rewards of eternal salvation; grant, we beseech Thee, that meditating upon these mysteries in the most holy Rosary of the Blessed Virgin Mary, we may imitate what they contain, and obtain what they promise. Through the same Christ our Lord. Amen.

℣. Most Sacred Heart of Jesus ℟. Have mercy on us.
℣. Immaculate Heart of Mary ℟. Pray for us.
℣. St. Joseph ℟. Pray for us.
℣. St. John ℟. Pray for us.
℣. Blessed Grignion de Montfort ℟. Pray for us.
In the name of the Father, etc.

2. The Catena Legionis: to be said mid-way through the Meeting; and daily by every Legionary, Active and Auxiliary.

Antiphon. Who is she that cometh forth as the morning rising, fair as the moon, bright as the sun, terrible as an army set in battle array?

My soul ✠ doth magnify the Lord.
And my spirit hath rejoiced in God my Saviour.
Because He hath regarded the humility of His handmaid: for behold from henceforth all generations shall call me blessed.
For He that is mighty hath done great things to me, and holy is His name.
And His mercy is from generation unto generations to them that fear Him.
He hath showed might in His arm: He hath scattered the proud in the conceit of their heart.
He hath put down the mighty from their seat: and hath exalted the humble.
He hath filled the hungry with good things: and the rich He hath sent empty away.
He hath received Israel His servant: being mindful of His mercy.
As He spoke to our fathers: to Abraham and to his seed for ever.
Glory be to the Father, and to the Son, and to the Holy Ghost.
As it was in the beginning, is now, and ever shall be, world without end. Amen.

Antiphon. Who is she that cometh forth as the morning rising, fair as the moon, bright as the sun, terrible as an army set in battle array?

℣. O Mary, conceived without sin,
℟. Pray for us who have recourse to thee.

Let Us Pray

O Lord Jesus Christ, our Mediator with the Father, who hast been pleased to appoint the Most Blessed Virgin, Thy Mother, to be our Mother also, and our Mediatrix with Thee, mercifully grant that whosoever comes to Thee seeking Thy favours, may rejoice to receive all of them through her. Amen.

3.—The Legion Prayer: to be said at the conclusion of the Meeting, and daily by all Auxiliary Members. It is set out in a form which will facilitate reading.

In the name of the Father, etc.

We fly to thy patronage, O Holy Mother of God; despise not our prayers in our necessities, but ever deliver us from all dangers, O glorious and blessed Virgin.

℣. (Invocation appropriate to Praesidium). ℟. Pray for us.

[On all occasions other than Praesidium meetings, the Invocation to be used by all members will be:—
℣. Mary Immaculate, Mediatrix of all Graces.
℟ Pray for us.]

℣. St. Michael Archangel ℟. Pray for us.
℣. Our holy Guardian Angels ℟. Pray for us.
℣. Saints Peter and Paul ℟. Pray for us.

Let us pray.

Confer, O Lord, on us,
Who serve beneath the standard of Mary,
That fulness of faith in Thee and trust in her,
To which it is given to conquer the world.
Grant us a lively faith, animated by charity,
Which will enable us to perform all our actions
From the motive of pure love of Thee,
And ever to see Thee and serve Thee in our neighbour;
A faith, firm and immovable as a rock,
Through which we shall rest tranquil and steadfast
Amid the crosses, toils and disappointments of life;

A courageous faith which will inspire us
To undertake and carry out without hesitation
Great things for God and for the salvation of souls;
A faith which will be our Legion's Pillar of Fire—
To lead us forth united—
To kindle everywhere the fires of Divine Love—
To enlighten those who are in darkness and in the shadow of death—
To inflame those who are lukewarm—
To bring back life to those who are dead in sin;
And which will guide our own feet in the Way of Peace;
So that—the battle of life over—
Our Legion may reassemble,
Without the loss of anyone,
In the Kingdom of Thy Love and Glory. Amen.
May the souls of our departed Legionaries
And the souls of all the faithful departed
Through the mercy of God rest in peace. Amen.

[*Then follows immediately the blessing of the Priest; or if no Priest be present*:—In the name of the Father, etc.]

"Mary's faith surpassed that of all men and all angels. She saw her Son in the stable at Bethlehem and she believed that He was the Creator of the world. She saw Him before Herod, and she never wavered in her faith that He was the King of kings. She saw Him being born, and she believed that He was from everlasting. She saw Him poor and without even the elemental necessities, and nevertheless she believed Him to be the Master of the universe. She saw Him lying on straw, and her faith told her that He was the All-powerful One. She saw that He spoke not a word, yet she believed that He was the eternal Wisdom itself. She heard Him cry, and she believed that He was the Joy of Paradise. And in the end she saw Him dying, exposed to all manner of insult, affixed to a Cross, and though the faith of all others was shaken, yet Mary persevered in her unhesitating belief that He was God."—(St. Alphonsus Liguori).

[This quotation does not form part of the Legion prayers.]

THE LEGION PICTURE.

1. This Handbook bears a reproduction of the Legion Picture. The original was painted by a brilliant young Dublin artist as an offering to the Legion. As to be expected from work animated by this spirit, the picture

is one of extreme beauty and inspiration, which is caught even by the small reproduction.*

2. The Picture is a most complete, in fact an astonishing showing forth of the devotional outlook of the Legion.

3. The general design reproduces the outline of the Vexillum.

4. The Legionary prayers are made visible. The Invocation and Prayer of the Holy Ghost and the Rosary, which comprise the Opening Prayers are pictured by the Dove overshadowing Mary, filling her with light and the fire of His love. In these prayers the Legion honours the moment which is the centre-point of all time. Mary's consent to the Incarnation made her alike Mother of God and Mother of Divine Grace; so her Legionary children bind themselves to her with her Rosary, taking to heart the words of Pius IX: "I could conquer the world if I had an army to say the Rosary."

Again, there is allusion to Pentecost, where Mary was the channel of that other outpouring of the Holy Spirit which formed the Church, the Mystical Body of Christ. Through Mary was received the apostolic fire which was to renew the face of the earth. Without her, it will not be kindled in the hearts of men.

5. The Catena is represented, as to its name, by the chain-border. Truly befitting the Antiphon is the portrayal of Mary, coming forth as the morning rising, fair as the moon, bright as the sun, terrible as an army set in battle array. On her brow she bears a brilliant star, to mark her who is the true Morning Star, bathed from the first in the beams of redeeming grace and heralding the dawn of salvation.

The Magnificat is represented by its opening verse, the ever-present thought of Mary's mind, appropriately set in letters of fire above her head. The Magnificat sings of the triumph of her humility. It is no less now than then the will of God to depend upon the humble Virgin of Nazareth for His conquests. By the agency

*A full-size reproduction is obtainable through the Curia.

of those united with her, He continues to accomplish great things for His Name.

The Versicle and Response are those of the Immaculate Conception, the primary devotion of the Legion, which is expressed in the crushing of the Serpent. The words set in the border: "I will put enmities between thee and the woman, and thy seed and her seed: She shall crush thy head"* have the same reference. The picture shows this undying warfare: Mary and the Serpent; her children and the Serpent's seed: the Legion and the powers of evil, which fall back scattered in defeat.

The Catena prayer is that of Mary, Mediatrix of all Graces, Mother of God and our Mother. At the top of the picture, the Holy Ghost the Giver of all good gifts: below, the globe surrounded by the good and the bad, typifying the world of souls: between the two, Mary full of grace, all aflame with charity, the universal channel of intercession and distribution. But first will she enrich those truest children who, like St. John, have rested on the Heart of Jesus and have lovingly accepted her as Mother. The words in the border: "Woman, behold thy Son: Behold thy Mother,"† point to the manifestation, amid the inconceivable sorrows of Calvary, of that Motherhood.

6. The Concluding Prayers are mirrored in every line of the Picture. The Legion is depicted as a host innumerable, advancing in battle-array under the leadership of its Queen and bearing her Standards, "the crucifix in their right hands, the Rosary in their left, the sacred names of Jesus and Mary in their hearts, and the modesty and mortification of Jesus Christ in their behaviour." Their prayer is for a faith which will supernaturalise every instinct and action of their lives, and enable them to dare and do all things for Christ the King. That faith is represented by the Pillar of Fire, which melts all Legionary hearts into

* "Inimicitias ponam inter te et mulierem; et semen tuum et semen illius; ipsa conteret caput tuum."—(Gen. iii. 15).

† "Mulier, ecce filius tuus: Ecce mater tua."—(St. John xix. 26, 27).

one, and guides them on to victory and to the Land of Eternal Promise, casting abroad as it proceeds the life-giving flames of Divine Love. The Pillar is Mary who saved the world by her faith ("Blessed art thou that hast believed."‡ in the border), and who now, through encircling gloom, leads on unerringly those who call her blessed, until the everlasting splendour of the Lord God come upon them.

7. The Prayers end with a pointing from the Legionary labours to that Roll-call of Eternity, when the faithful Legionaries will muster shoulder to shoulder, not a single one missing, to receive the incorruptible crown of their membership.

In the meantime: a prayer for those for whom the conflict has ceased and who await the glorious Resurrection, and who may need their comrades' supplication.

"In the Old Testament we read that the Lord conducted his people from Egypt to the land of promise, 'by day in a pillar of cloud and by night in a pillar of fire.'—(Exod. xiii. 21). This stupendous pillar, at one time of cloud and at another of fire, was a figure of Mary and of the various offices which she performs in our behalf."—(St. Alphonsus Liguori).

THE TESSERA.

A leaflet styled the "Tessera," containing the Prayers of the Legion and bearing a reproduction of the Legion Picture, shall be issued to every member, active and auxiliary.

In Latin, "tessera" had the particular meaning of a tally or token which was divided amongst friends, in order that they or their descendants might always recognise each other. As a military expression, it signified the square tablet upon which the watch-word was written and circulated through the Roman Legion.

The Legion of Mary applies the word "Tessera" to the leaflet containing its Prayers and Picture. Here, too, are contained the ideas of (a) universal circulation in the Legion; (b) the setting out of the true watch-word of the Legion—its prayers; and (c) a token of

‡ **"Beata quae credidisti."—(St. Luke i. 45).**

VEXILLUM LEGIONIS.

The Standard of the Legion

unity and fraternity between all Legionaries, wherever found.

"Travellers together in this miserable world, we are all so weak that we each mutually require the supporting arm of our brother to prevent our fainting by the way. But in the order of salvation and grace, God especially requires that we be united together. Prayer is the bond which thus unites all hearts and voices, making them as one. Our strength lies in united prayer; this alone will render us invincible. Let us then hasten to unite our prayers, our efforts, our desires together, all of which being powerful of themselves, will, by union, prove irresistible."—(Ramiére).

The Vexillum Legionis is an adaptation of the Standard of the Roman Legion. The eagle which surmounted the Standard is replaced by the Dove, the emblem of the Holy Ghost. Beneath the Dove a crossbar bears the inscription "Legio Mariae" (Legion of Mary). Intermediate between cross-bar and staff (and joined to the former by a rose and a lily) is an oval frame bearing a representation of the Immaculate Conception (the Miraculous Medal). The staff is set in a globe which, for use on a table, stands on a square base. The whole ensemble conveys the idea that the world is to be conquered by the Holy Ghost acting through Mary and her children.

(a) A representation of the Vexillum should appear on the official notepaper of the Legion.

(b) A model of the Vexillum should stand on the table at meetings, about six inches in advance of, and about six inches to the right of the Statue. The table model customarily used is, inclusive of the base, 12¾ inches in height. A photograph appears next page. If it cannot be obtained locally, a replica in metal may be ordered from the Concilium. The design is copyright.

(c) A large model will be required for processional purposes and for use at the Acies. It should be about 6½ feet high, of which about 2 feet would represent the length of staff below the sphere. This can readily be made in wood by a capable fretworker, and then painted. Branches desiring to possess more elaborate equipment will, no doubt, have recourse to other materials than wood. The design affords much scope for artistic treatment.

A photograph of a large Vexillum is likewise given. It will serve as a guide to manufacture.

(d) A miniature representation of the Vexillum may be used as a badge, and may be worn by Active Legionaries on ceremonial occasions, on Pilgrimages, at gatherings under Catholic auspices, and (if permitted by the Curia) during one's Legionary work. It may not be worn during Probation, nor during one's everyday life, nor by Junior or Auxiliary members.
Such badge is to be called the Vexillina.

"That beautiful and suggestive Standard of the Legion of Mary."—(Pope Pius XI).

THE PRAYERS INVARIABLE.

The prayers of the Legion are to be regarded as invariable. Even in the invocations, no alteration or addition is to be made, either in respect of national, local, or particular saints, or where such alteration or addition would be a debatable matter.

This is a demand for sacrifice, but the demand only follows on a sacrifice which is one of the greatest of its kind, as will readily be conceded by those who know the land from which these Articles have come, and who understand the unique place in its affections held by its National Apostle.

It is true that the toleration of special invocations would not in itself be a large departure from common usage. Yet therein is contained the germ of a divergence in system, and the Legion dreads even that germ.

Again, the soul of the Legion is shown forth in its prayers, and it is fitting that the latter, by a uniformity most exact, shall typify—in whatever language they may in time be said—the complete unity of mind, heart, rule, practice, to which the Legion exhorts all who may anywhere serve beneath its standard.

"As ye are the children of Christ, so be ye children of Rome."—(St. Patrick).

THE LEGION SYSTEM INVARIABLE.

1. What has just been said of the prayers applies no less to the other things which are prescribed in these pages. The Legion notifies its members that they are not at liberty to vary rules and practices as they choose. The system described is the Legion system. Each variation, however slight, makes others inevitable, till presently a body is in existence which indeed bears the name, but possesses little else of the Legion, and which the Legion, if made aware of the facts, would not hesitate to disown, even though work in itself valuable were being done.

2. Experience has shown that the name of an organisation has little definite meaning for some persons. For they regard it as a virtual tyranny if they are not permitted to cover with the name of a standard organisation some composition of their own minds.

3. And places—like persons—are apt to conceive that they are out of the common and that their case has to be specially legislated for. Hence, the proposals which are from time to time made that the Legion system should be flexed to meet alleged special circumstances. Such modifications, if made, will have an unhappy sequel. For almost invariably they spring, not from necessity (for the Legion has already demonstrated its universal adaptability), but from the operation of a false spirit of independence. Such will never attract the special blessings of Heaven, and the fruit of that independence will always be a falling away. However, as it will not always be possible to convince people of this, it is at least pointed out to those who are set upon exercising a right of private judgment in relation to the rules of the Legion, that their only course in honour

VEXILLUM LEGIONIS

MODEL FOR TABLE USE.

MODEL FOR ACIES OR PROCESSIONAL USE.

A TYPICAL BOOK BARROW AT WORK NEAR A BUSY STREET.

is to refrain from covering their transactions with the name of the Legion.

4. An imitation of the Legion system may exclude the Legion itself from a city or even a country, or else cripple its operations there. Possibly the new organisation may be better contrived than the Legion, but even so, it is to be doubted if equal good will come of it. Guerillas are set to work where, perhaps, Mary wanted a section of her Legionary army. Forces are divided where they should be one.

Moreover, this ingenious picking of parts, which too-clever men often indulge in, never succeeds in capturing a quality of sweetness and inspiration which was the real power of the original, so that the usual result of this species of surgery is a corpse. But at the very best, what is created is a beautiful machine and nothing more. When poor results or failure follow, there is a heavy responsibility to be faced.

5. The various councils of the Legion exist chiefly for the purpose of preserving intact the Legion system. **At all costs** they must be true to the trusteeship committed to them.

"You must accept the whole, or reject the whole; reduction does but enfeeble, and amputation mutilate. It is foolish to receive all but something which is as integral as any other portion."—(Newman: Essay on Development).

THE PRAESIDIUM.

1. The unit of the Legion of Mary is styled a "Praesidium."

This Latin word was used to designate a detachment of the Roman Legion performing special duty, i.e., a section of a military line, a fortified post, a garrison. The term "Praesidium" is, therefore, appropriately applied to the branch of the Legion of Mary.

2. Each Praesidium is named after a title of our Blessed Lady, e.g., "Our Lady of Mercy," or from one of her privileges, e.g., "The Immaculate Conception," or from an event in her life, e.g., "The Visitation."

"Thy Name is as oil poured out."—(Cantic. Cantic. I. 2.)

Happy the Bishop who in each town of his diocese sees Praesidia sufficient in number to form, as it were, a living Litany of Mary!

3. The Praesidium has authority over all its members and power to control their activities. The members on their part shall loyally obey all the legitimate orders of the Praesidium.

4. Each Praesidium must, either directly or through an approved council, as hereinafter defined, be affiliated to the Concilium Legionis. Otherwise there is no Legion membership. It follows that no new Praesidium shall be instituted without the formal permission of its Curia, or (failing a convenient Curia) of the appropriate Senatus, or in the ultimate resort, of the Concilium. The Praesidium shall depend directly upon such governing body, and shall be entitled to full representation thereon.

5. No Praesidium shall be established in any Parish without the consent of the Parish Priest or of the Ordinary. The Parish Priest or the Ordinary shall be invited to carry out the inaugural ceremony.

6. The Praesidium shall hold a regular weekly meeting, which shall be conducted after the manner described in the Section entitled "Order of the Praesidium Meeting."

This rule is absolutely invariable. Again and again it will be suggested that, for various excellent reasons, it is difficult to hold a weekly meeting, and that a monthly or fortnightly meeting would serve all purposes.

To this it is replied that in no circumstances can the Legion consent to other than a weekly meeting, nor does it give to any of its councils the power to vary this rule. Were the regulation of the active work on hand the only consideration, possibly a monthly meeting might serve, although this is to be doubted if the work is being done weekly according to rule. But a vital purpose of the meeting is weekly prayer in common, and it is superfluous to point out that this end will not be attained by a meeting held otherwise than weekly.

A weekly meeting may entail self-sacrifice. If the Legion cannot with confidence call for such, where is the whole groundwork on which to build its system?

7. Each Praesidium shall have a Priest as Spiritual Director. It shall also have a President, Vice-President, Secretary, and Treasurer.

A women's Praesidium may also have, with the approval of the Spiritual Director and the sanction of the Curia, an approved man, styled the Tribune, to be present at its meetings and assist it in its work.

The foregoing shall be the Officers of the Praesidium and its representatives on the Curia. Their duties are described in a later Section.

8. The Officers should give a report to their Praesidia on each meeting of the Curia, and thus keep their members in touch with the proceedings of the Curia.

9. The Spiritual Director is appointed to the office by the Parish Priest or by the Ordinary, and he holds his office at their pleasure.

A Spiritual Director may undertake the direction of more than one Praesidium.

If the Spiritual Director cannot attend the meetings of the Praesidium, he may appoint another Priest or a Religious to act in his place.

Although the Spiritual Director should be apprised of the meetings, it is not essential for the validity of the meetings that he should actually attend the meetings.

The Spiritual Director shall rank as an Officer of the Praesidium, and he shall uphold all due Legionary authority.

10. The Spiritual Director shall have decisive authority in all religious or moral questions raised at the meetings of the Praesidium, and he shall have a suspensive veto on all the proceedings of the Praesidium, with a view to obtaining the decision of the Parish Priest or of the Ordinary.

"This right is a necessary weapon; but, like any such weapon, must be used with great discretion and cautiously, lest it become an engine of destruction, not of protection. In an association well constructed and well guided, it will never be necessary to use it."—(Civardi: A Manual of Catholic Action.)

11. The Officers of the Praesidium, other than the Spiritual Director, shall be appointed by the Curia. Should there be no existing Curia, the Officers shall be appointed by the next-highest governing body.

It is desirable to avoid cross-table discussion as to the merits of possible Officers, some of whom may actually be present. Therefore, it is the practice, on the occasion of a vacant Officership, for the President of the Curia, after careful inquiry (above all from the Spiritual Director of the Praesidium in question) with a view to ascertaining the most suitable person, to submit a name to the Curia, which the Curia, if it thinks fit, may then ratify.

12. Every appointment of an Officer (other than the Spiritual Director) shall be for a term of three years, renewable for one further term of the same length, i.e., six years in all. The Tribune may, however, be appointed for more than two consecutive terms.

The transfer of an Officer to another office, or to the same office elsewhere, shall rank as a new appointment.

An Officer may, after an interval of three years, hold anew the same office in the same Praesidium.

"The question of tenure of office must be decided on grounds of general principle. The danger to be kept in view from first to last in any organisation—above all in a voluntary religious organisation—is that it, or any particular unit of it, would become fossilised. The danger of this is really great. It is the human tendency for enthusiasms to die down, for a spirit of routine to creep in, for methods to become stereotyped, whereas the evils to be met change constantly.

"This process of deterioration ends in ineffective work and indifference, so that the organisation fails to attract or retain the most desirable type of member. A state of half-death supervenes. At all cost, this must be guarded against in the Legion. The springing up of perpetual enthusiasm must be ensured in each and every one of its councils and Praesidia. Obviously, one's first care must be for the natural sources of zeal, the Officers. These must be kept always in the grip of first fervour; and this is best effected by change. If the Officers fail, everything withers. If they lose fire and enthusiasm, the body they control will reproduce the same process. And, worst of all, the members are satisfied with the state of affairs, to which they have become accustomed, so that except from outside there is no hope of remedy. In theory, such a remedy would exist in a rule providing for periodic renewal of the period of office. But, in reality, this would not be efficacious, as even the governing bodies would fail to realise that a settling down process was at work, and would in practice automatically grant extension after extension.

"It would seem, accordingly, that the only certain course lies in a system of changing the Officers irrespective of merit or other circumstances. The practice of Religious Orders suggests a model upon which to shape Legion practice, that is a restriction of the period of office to six years, modified by coupling with it a requirement that, after the first three years, a renewal would be necessary."—(Decision of the Legion limiting the period of office of Officers.)

13. The members will never rise above the standards of spirit and work created by the Officers. Therefore, the latter must be the best obtainable. Otherwise the action of the Praesidium will be fettered; and it would be a senseless thing to clip the wings of a bird when lofty flight is desired.

The appointment of a succession of good Officers should mean that the quality of the Praesidium will constantly improve. For each new Officer, while jealously guarding against the lowering of existing standards, will add something of value.

14. Especially should the appointment of the President be the subject of anxious thought. A mistake in

this direction may ruin the Praesidium. Choice should only be made after viewing each possible person in the light of the requirements which are set out later in the Article on the President, and in particular under heads 8 and 10. Persons likely to fail in these directions should on no account be selected, even though their merits in other directions may be great.

15. During probation a Legionary can only hold an acting or temporary officership. If that officership is made definite by the Curia at the end of the probation period, the time already served in it counts as part of the three years' term referred to above.

16. No member of a Praesidium shall leave it to join another without the consent of the President of the former, and the admission of such person into the latter shall be done in accordance with the Constitution and the rules for the admission of new members, except that the probation may be dispensed with. The said permission, when asked, should not be unreasonably withheld. An appeal in this matter lies to the Curia.

17. The President of the Praesidium, after consultation with the other Officers, shall have authority to suspend any member of the Praesidium for any reasons that they in their discretion deem sufficient, and they shall not be accountable to the Praesidium for such action.

18. The Curia has authority to expel or to suspend any member of a Praesidium subject only to a right of appeal to the next-highest governing body. The decision of the next-highest governing body shall be final.

19. Any dispute as to the allocation of work as between Praesidia shall be decided by the Curia.

20. It is an essential duty of the Praesidium to raise up and preserve around itself a strong body of Auxiliaries.

View a regiment of soldiers, well-officered, courageous, perfectly disciplined and armed, suggesting an irresistible strength! Yet, in itself that regiment represents only a short-lived efficiency. It depends from day to day on a great supporting host of workers who furnish it with munitions, food, clothing and medical help. Cut away from these services, what will a few days of conflict do with that fine body of men!

What that supporting host is to the regiment, the Auxiliaries are to the Praesidium. The Auxiliaries are part of the system. The Praesidium is incomplete without them.

The proper method of keeping in touch with the Auxiliaries is by personal contact. The issue of circulars is not by itself a sufficient way of attending to this important duty.

21. An army always provides for its future by the establishment of military training schools. Similarly, it should be regarded as a necessary part of the system of each Praesidium to conduct a Junior Praesidium. Two of the Senior Legionaries should be assigned to the Junior Praesidium as Officers. Their work in that capacity may be held to satisfy their work-obligation for their Senior Praesidium. They may represent the Junior Praesidium on the Curia, or on a Junior Curia if such exists, or on both, as decided by the (Senior) Curia.

The other two Officerships should be filled by Junior members, to whom they will afford admirable training in responsibility, and who will represent the Praesidium on a Junior Curia.

"The rays of the sun are numerous, but the light is one; the branches of a tree are many, but the trunk is one, strongly fixed on immovable roots."—(St. Cyprian: De Unitate Ecclesiae.)

GOVERNMENT OF THE LEGION.

OF APPLICATION TO ALL GOVERNING BODIES

1. The government, local and central, of the Legion shall be carried on by its councils, whose duty in their respective spheres shall be to ensure unity, to preserve the original ideals of the Legion of Mary, to guard the integrity of the Legion spirit and rules and practice, as set forth in the official Handbook of the Legion, and to spread the organisation.

The Legion in any area will be as good as these councils wish to make it.

2. All councils shall hold regular frequent meetings, i.e. as a general rule not less frequently than once a month.

3. The prayers, setting and order of the meetings of any council of the Legion shall be identical with that prescribed in the case of the Praesidium, save that (a) the time-limit on length shall not apply, (b) the choice of Spiritual Reading shall be free, (c) the Standing Instructions need not be read, (d) the Secret Bag Collection shall be optional.

4. A primary duty of any council is that of allegiance to its next-highest council.

5. No Praesidium or council shall be instituted without the formal permission of its next-highest council, or of the Concilium Legionis, and the approval of the appropriate Ecclesiastical Authority.

6. To the Bishop of the Diocese and to the Concilium Legionis severally is reserved by the Constitution of the Legion the right to dissolve an existing Praesidium or Curia. On dissolution, a Praesidium or Curia ceases at once to be a part of the Legion of Mary.

7. Each council shall have a Priest as Spiritual Director, who shall be appointed by the appropriate Ecclesiastical Authority, and shall hold office at the pleasure of the latter. He shall have decisive authority in all moral and religious matters raised at the meetings of the council, and he shall have a suspensive veto on all the proceedings, with a view to obtaining the decision of the Authority by whom he was appointed.

The Spiritual Director ranks as an Officer of such council, and he shall uphold all due Legionary authority.

8. Each council shall also have a President, Vice-President, Secretary, and Treasurer, and such other officers as may be sanctioned as necessary by the next-highest council. Their tenure and conditions of office shall be precisely as in the case of the Officer of a Praesidium. See Section on the Praesidium.

9. The raising of the status of a council (i. e. Curia to Comitium or Senatus, or Comitium to Senatus) shall not affect the terms of office of the existing officers.

10. The Officers of a council shall be elected by the members of the said council, and if not already members of the council shall become members *ex officio.* All appointments of Officers shall be subject to ratification by the next-highest council.

11. The election shall be made by secret ballot. The manner of such election shall be as follows:

The election for each officership is to be taken separately, and in descending order. Each name put forward must be formally proposed and seconded. If only one name be put forward, it is of course unnecessary to proceed to a ballot. If two or more names are duly proposed and seconded, a ballot shall be taken. A voting paper is to be given to each member of the council (including the Spiritual Directors) who is present and entitled to a vote. When filled up, the papers are to be folded carefully and then collected by the scrutineers. The name of the voter is not to appear on the voting paper.

If the count shows that one candidate has obtained a clear majority of the votes, that is a number greater than those of all the other candidates added together, then that candidate is to be declared elected. But if no one has secured a clear majority, the results of the voting are to be read out; then the same candidates are to be re-voted for. Should this second ballot fail to yield a clear majority to one candidate, then the candidate who has secured the lowest number of votes is to be eliminated and a re-vote taken on the remaining candidates. If this third ballot is also ineffectual, procedure is to be by way of successive eliminations and re-votes until one candidate has secured the necessary clear majority of the votes.

The fact that the election is in respect of officers of a spiritual organisation is not to be held to justify casual methods. The election must be carried out in strict and proper form, and with due regard to the secrecy of the individual voting paper.

12. The representatives of a Praesidium or of a Council to its next-highest council shall be its officers. A council shall elect, from amongst its Tribunes, the Tribune who will represent it on a higher council.

13. With the permission of a council, other persons, whether members of the Legion or not, may attend the meetings of that council in the capacity of visitors, but shall not be entitled to vote there.

14. The councils of the Legion shall be the Curia, the Comitium, the Senatus, and the Concilium Legionis, and any other councils which may be set up under the Constitution.

15. The Latin names of the various councils accord fairly well with the functions which those councils fulfil.

In the Legion, Mary is Queen. She it is who summons her Legionary hosts to their glorious warfare and commands them in the field, inspires them, and personally leads them on to victory. It is a natural step from the Queen to her special council, or "Concilium," which would represent her visibly and share her superintendence of all the other Legionary governing bodies.

The district councils will be essentially representative bodies, the higher councils less so, by reason of the practical impossibility of securing a full attendance at the regular meetings of central councils representative of extensive areas. Thus the titles of "Curia," "Comitium," and "Senatus," set forth the character and status of the respective bodies and are appropriate to the areas served.

16. Where the words Curia and Senatus are used in these Articles, and there is in fact no appropriate Curia or Senatus, the relevant word shall be read as referring to the next-highest governing body or, in the ultimate resort, to the Concilium. Any doubts arising in this connection shall be settled by the Concilium.

17. A higher council may combine with its own

proper functions the functions of a lower council. A Senatus, for instance, may also act as a Curia.

If the amount of business permits, this combination of functions will frequently be found of advantage:—

(a) Usually, it will be the same persons who will be concerned in the management both of the higher council in question and of the district council. It would spare those Legionaries if one meeting could be made to serve the purpose of two;

(b) But there is a more important consideration. The representation of the higher council is drawn from a large area, so that it may be found impossible to secure a full attendance at the regular frequent meetings which it is supposed to hold. As a result, a small group of earnest Legionaries will be found burdened with a heavy responsibility and a great volume of work. Inevitably, much of the work is performed indifferently or left undone, with serious hurt to the Legion.

The combination of the functions of such higher body with those of the lower will ensure a large and constant attendance of members. These will not only perform the duties proper to the lower council, but will be interested and educated in the work of the higher body. It then becomes possible to enlist them in the all-important supervisory, extension, and clerical work of the higher body.

It may be objected that such an expedient amounts to giving the government of a large area to a body which is virtually a district council. It may be urged as preferable that the higher council should function separately, contenting itself with, say, four meetings in the year. By this means it would be enabled to secure a large representative attendance. But indeed such a proposal, alleged to be in the interests of representative government, is far from being so in reality. For during the long intervals between its meetings, that council must necessarily leave its functions to be discharged by its Officers. Thus only in name is the council exercising the functions of government. As a consequence, its members soon lose the sense of responsibility and all real interest in its work.

18. The duty of contributing to its next-highest council is imposed on each Legionary body. In this connection see the Section on Funds.

19. The fullest liberty of discussion should be afforded. To win over, not to vote down, should be the key-note of any Legion meeting. A hasty forcing of a decision may leave two parties, a minority and a victorious majority, with irritated feelings and hardened differences. On the other hand, decisions which have been come to after patient examination and ample ventilation of views, will be received by all, and in such a spirit that the loser gains merit by his defeat, and the winner does not lose it by victory.

So, when differences of opinion are found to exist, those who are obviously in the majority must exhibit a complete patience. They may be wrong, and it would be a grievous thing to win an incorrect position. Decision should, if possible, be postponed to another meeting, and perhaps again and again, so as to allow minute consideration. Members should be made acquainted with every angle of the question, and taught to pray for light. All must be made to realise that it is not the victory of an opinion which is at stake, but a humble quest of God's wishes in the matter. Then, it will commonly be found that unanimity has come about.

20. If the interests of harmony are to be vigilantly guarded in the Praesidium, where occasions for differences of opinion occur but seldom, what caution must be exercised in the councils; because:—

(a) There, members are less accustomed to work together;

(b) Differences of opinion are many, one of the chief functions of the councils being to adjust such differences. The consideration of new works, efforts after higher standards, disciplinary interests in general, defects, all necessarily tend to create differences of opinion, which may develop unpleasantly;

(c) Where the members are numerous, it is only too easy to find among them a few persons who, though excellent workers, are of the type commonly termed "cranks." These exercise on an assembly a most unhappy influence. Their working abilities win for them a following. They bring about an atmosphere of disputation with its sequel of ill-feeling. In the end the body which should be the model to those below it, an object-lesson in fraternity and in the method of conducting business, is found setting a bad example to all Legionaries. The heart is pumping acid through the Legion circulation;

(d) False loyalties so often operate, i.e., a tendency to tilt against some neighbouring or higher council, which is alleged (O how easily a plausible case is made and wins acceptance!) to be exceeding its powers or acting unworthily;

(e) "Never do men come together in considerable numbers, but the passion, self-will, pride, and unbelief, which may be more or less dormant in them one by one, bursts into a flame and becomes a constituent of their union. Even when faith exists in the whole people, even when religious men combine for religious purposes, still when they form into a body, they evidence in no long time the innate debility of human nature; and in their spirit and conduct, in their avowals and proceedings, they are in grave contrast to Christian simplicity and straightforwardness. This is what sacred writers mean by the 'world,' and why they warn us against it; and their description of it applies in its degree to all collections and parties of men, high and low, national and professional, lay and ecclesiastical." —(Newman: In the World.)

These are startling words, but they come from a very profound thinker. St. Gregory Nazianzen says the same thing in different terms. When analysed, what seems so strange a statement resolves itself into this: that the "world" is lack of charity: that charity is weak in us: that this weakness is covered to some extent by ties of relationship, intimacy, friendship, (things proper to small numbers); but that when the numbers grow large, and criticism and disagreements operate, the weaknesses in that charity tend to declare themselves, with most unhappy results. "God Himself and Charity are one and the same thing," says St. Bernard. "Where Charity does not reign, the passions and lusts of the flesh rule. The torch of faith, if it be not lighted by the fire of charity, will never last long enough to guide us to eternal happiness. . . . There is no true virtue without charity."

It is of little use for Legionaries to read the above pronouncements of danger, and then to vow that amongst them "such shall never be." It can be, and will be, if there are defects of charity at their meetings, if the supernatural spirit is allowed to weaken there. Vigilance must never relax. We read in history that the Roman Legion never passed a night, even in the longest marches, without pitching a camp, entrenching it, and fortifying it most elaborately; and this even though only a single night would be spent in it, even though the enemy was afar, even in time of peace. With some approach to this exact discipline, let the Legion of Mary apply itself to the protection of its camps (which are its assemblies) against the possibility of invasion by this fatal spirit of "the world." This protection will lie in the exclusion of all words and attitudes which are hostile to charity, and, generally, in the saturation of the meetings with the spirit of prayer and full Legion devotion.

"Grace, no less than nature, has its feelings and its affections. It has its love, its zeal, its hopes, its joys, its sorrows. Now, those 'feelings' of grace have always been in their fulness in Our Blessed Lady, who lived much more by the life of grace than by the life of nature. The vast majority of the faithful are rather in the *state* of grace than in the *life* of grace. Quite different to them, the Holy Virgin has been always in grace and—more than that—in the life of grace, and in the very perfection of that life of grace, during the whole of her time on earth".—(Gibieuf: De la Vierge souffrante au pied de la Croix.)

THE CONCILIUM LEGIONIS.

1. There shall be a central council in which shall be vested the supreme governing authority of the Legion. To it alone (subject always to the rights of the Ecclesiastical Authority as provided for in these pages) shall belong the right to make, alter, or interpret rules; to set up or repudiate Praesidia and subordinate councils, wherever situated; to determine the policy of the Legion on all points, to decide all disputes and appeals, all membership questions, and all points as to the suitability of works or the manner of carrying them out.

2. The central council shall be styled the Concilium Legionis.

3. The Concilium may delegate portion of its functions to its subordinate councils or to individual Praesidia, and may at any time alter the amount of such delegation.

4. The Concilium may combine with its own proper functions the functions of a subordinate council or councils.

5. The Concilium Legionis shall consist of:—

(a) the representatives of every Legionary body (council or Praesidium) which is directly related to the Concilium;

(b) the members of the Dublin City Curia (or Curiae), subject to the right of the Concilium itself to reduce this representation.

6. The Spiritual Director of the Concilium shall be appointed by the Hierarchy of Ireland.

7. The duly authorised representatives of the Concilium may enter into any Legionary area, visit the Legionary bodies there, carry on work of a propagandist character, and generally exercise functions which it is allowable for the Concilium to exercise.

8. To the Concilium Legionis alone shall belong, subject to the constitution and rules of the Legion, the right to amend the Handbook.

9. Changes of Rule cannot be effected save with the agreement of the great bulk of the Legionary bodies.

These, through their appropriate councils, shall be notified of any proposed change of rule, and given sufficient time to signify their views on the subject. The views may be signified through their representatives actually present at the Concilium, or by writing.

"All the works of God are founded on unity, for they are founded on Himself, who is the most awfully simple and transcendent of possible unities. He is emphatically One; and whereas He is also multiform in His attributes and His acts, as they present themselves to our minds, it follows that order and harmony must be of His very essence. To be many and distinct in His attributes, yet, after all, to be but one—to be sanctity, justice, truth, love, power, wisdom, to be at once each of these as fully as if He were nothing but it, as if the rest were not,—this implies in the Divine Nature an infinitely sovereign and utterly incomprehensible order, which is an attribute as wonderful as any, and the result of all the others."—(Newman: Order, the Witness and Instrument of Unity. This and the next two quotations form, in the original, one passage).

THE SENATUS.

1. A council appointed to exercise authority over a region shall be styled a Senatus.

2. A Senatus shall exercise with regard to its subordinate councils or directly-related Praesidia all the functions delegated to it by the Concilium. In countries where, by reason of size or for other reasons, a single Senatus could not be expected to function well, two or more Senatus may be established, each of which shall depend directly on the Concilium, and shall exercise in its own area all the authority delivered to it.

3. A Senatus shall consist of the representatives of every Legionary body (council or Praesidium) which is directly related to that Senatus.

4. It is of paramount importance that there should be a good attendance at the meetings of the Senatus. If, by reason of distances, etc., such cannot be secured, a Senatus may, with the explicit permission of the Concilium, co-opt members for periods not longer than

those applicable generally to the tenure of officers.

5. The Spiritual Director of a Senatus shall be appointed by the Bishops of the Dioceses in which that Senatus has jurisdiction.

"God is an infinite law, as well as an infinite power, wisdom, and love. Moreover, the very idea of order implies the idea of the subordinate. If order exists in the Divine Attributes, they must have relations one to another, and though each is perfect in itself, it must act so as not to impair the perfection of the rest, and must seem to yield to the rest on particular occasions."—(Newman: Order, the Witness and Instrument of Unity).

THE CURIA.

1. When two or more Praesidia have been established in any city, town, or district, a governing body termed the Curia shall be set up. The Curia shall be composed of all the Officers (Spiritual Directors included) of the Praesidia in its area.

2. Where it is found necessary to confer on a Curia, in addition to its own proper functions, certain powers of superintendence over one or several Curiae, such higher Curia shall be styled more particularly a Comitium.

Each Curia, or Praesidium directly related to a Comitium, shall be entitled to representation on the latter.

In order to relieve the representatives of a Curia from attendance at all the meetings of the Comitium, (which, added to the meetings of their own Curia might form an undue burden) it would be permissible to deal with the business of that Curia and to require the attendance of its representatives only at every second or third meeting of the Comitium.

A Comitium shall not ordinarily cover an area larger than a Diocese.

3. The Spiritual Director shall be appointed by the Ordinary of the Diocese in which the Curia (or Comitium) functions.

4. The Curia shall exercise authority over its Praesidia, subject to the Constitution of the Legion. It shall appoint their officers (other than the Spiritual Director), and keep count of their terms of office.

As to the manner of appointment, see paragraph 11 of the Section on the Praesidium.

5. The Curia will ensure the scrupulous carrying out of the rules by the Praesidia and their members.

The following shall form important parts of the work of a Curia:

(a) the education and supervision of the Officers in their duties and in the general management of their Praesidia;
(b) the receiving of reports from Praesidia;
(c) the exchange of experiences;
(d) the consideration of new works;
(e) the creation of high standards;
(f) the ensuring that every Legionary satisfactorily performs the work-obligation;
(g) the extension of the Legion and the stimulation of Praesidia to recruit Auxiliaries (including the after-care and organisation of the latter.)

It is manifest, therefore, that a high degree of moral courage will be required from the Curia, and especially from its officers, for the proper discharge of its functions.

6. The fate of the Legion lies in the hands of its Curiae, and its future depends on their development. The state of the Legion in any district must be counted precarious until a Curia has been established there.

7. Substitutes for Officers unable to attend can only be sent to the Curia with the express permission of the latter. This permission must not be given without special reason, for the principle of substitution is opposed to that of official responsibility.

8. Legionaries under 18 years of age cannot sit on a Senior Curia. But if deemed advisable by the Curia, a Junior Curia, subject to the Curia, may be set up.

9. It is absolutely essential that the Officers of the Curia, and particularly the President, should be easily

accessible to the Legionaries who are subject to that Curia, so that difficulties, or proposals, or other matters which are not ripe for more public discussion, may be talked over.

10. It is most desirable that the Officers, and particularly the President, should be able to devote considerable time to the duties of their positions, on which so much depends.

11. When there are a large number of Praesidia attached to a Curia, the resulting number of representatives at the latter will be considerable. This fact may possibly involve disadvantages from the aspects of accommodation and of administrative perfection, but the Legion believes that these will be amply compensated for in other respects. The Legion looks to its Curiae to supply another function than that of administrative machinery. Each Curia is the heart and brain of the group of Praesidia which are attached to it. Being the centre of unity, it follows that the more numerous the bonds (i.e. the representatives) which link it to the individual Praesidia, the stronger will be that unity, the more certain will the Praesidia be to reproduce the spirit and methods of the Legion. It will be at the Curia meetings alone that the things which relate to the essence of the Legion can be adequately discussed and learned. Thence they will be transmitted to the Praesidia, and there diffused amongst the members.

12. The Curia shall cause each Praesidium to be visited frequently with a view to encouraging it and seeing that all things are being carried out as they should be. It is important that this duty be not fulfilled in a carping or fault-finding fashion, which would end by causing the advent of visitors to be dreaded and their recommendations to be resented, but in a spirit of affection and humility which will presume that there is as much to be learned from, as taught to, the Praesidium visited.

On the occasion of this visitation, the various membership rolls, the Secretary's and Treasurer's books, the

Work Sheet, and the other items of the Praesidium system must be examined with a view to judging if they are properly kept, and to ascertaining if the Legionary Promise has been made in the case of each qualified person.

At least a full week's notice of such intended visitation should be given to a Praesidium.

Once in a way one hears of this visitation being resented, on the score that it amounts to "outside interference." Such an attitude is not respectful to the Legion, of which those Praesidia are but parts, and of which they should be loyal parts: shall the hand say to the head "I need not thy help"? Furthermore, it is unthankful, for do not those units owe their very existence to that "outside interference." It is inconsistent, for how willingly they accept from their central authority things which they are pleased to regard as benefits. It is foolish, too, for thereby they set themselves against universal experience. It is the lesson of all organised life (whether religious, civil, or military) that an ungrudging, comprehensive and practical recognition of the "central principle" is essential to the preservation of spirit and efficiency. A regular visitation of the units of organisation is an all-important part of the application of that principle, and no competent form of authority neglects its duty in this respect.

Apart, however, from the fact that visitation from the Curia is necessary to health, each Praesidium should remember that it is part of the Rule, and hence should insist that this duty is not overlooked by the Curia. It goes without saying that a cordial welcome should be given to the visitors.

Defects, which are found, should not, in the first instance, be made the subject of open comment either at the Praesidium itself or at the Curia. They should be discussed with the Spiritual Director and the President of the Praesidium. If this does not secure rectification, the matter should be brought before the Curia.

13. Except very special reasons to the contrary exist,

the Curia must make the changing of the President an accompaniment of the reorganisation of a defective Praesidium. In almost every case the falling-away lies in the neglect or the inability of the President to govern.

14. The Curia stands in much the same relation to its members as a Praesidium does to its members. Thus, all that is said in these pages regarding the attendance and conduct of Legionaries at their Praesidium meetings is to be taken as applying equally to the attitude of Praesidium representatives towards their Curia meetings. Zeal in other respects will not compensate for failure on the part of Officers to give a faithful attendance at meetings of their Curia.

15. The Curia shall meet at times and places to be fixed by the Curia itself, with the approval of its next-highest council. Such meetings should, if possible, be held not less frequently than once a month.

16. An agenda for the meeting shall be prepared beforehand by the Secretary in consultation with the President, and circulated to each Spiritual Director and each President previous to the Praesidium meeting immediately before the Curia meeting. It shall be the duty of the President to notify the other representatives of the Praesidium.

Such agenda should be provisional, and as much liberty as possible should be extended to members to raise additional points.

17. Vigilant watch must be kept by the Curia to ensure that Praesidia do not drift into the giving of material relief, which marks the end of all really useful Legionary work. The periodic inspection of Treasurers' statements will help the Curia to discern the beginnings of any incorrect tendency.

18. The President (and of course the same applies to all those others in authority), should beware of falling into what is an exceedingly common fault, that of keeping even the most minute items of responsibility in his own hands. One result of such a tendency will be the slowing down of work. It may even paralyse

the whole system in large centres where the work is considerable in quantity. The narrower the neck of the bottle, the more slowly will the contents be given forth, until sometimes people break off that neck in their impatience.

But another serious feature is that the denial of some responsibility to those who are fit to assume it, does injustice both to those individuals and to the whole Legion. The exercising of some degree of responsibility is a necessary part of the development of great qualities in the individual. Responsibility, indeed, can transmute mere sand into gold!

The Secretary should not be held restricted to secretarial work, nor the Treasurer to the keeping of the accounts. All officers, and even senior and promising members, should be entrusted with spheres of initiative and control, for which—subject of course to the higher authority—they will be held responsible. The ultimate aim must be the filling of every Legionary with a sense of responsibility for the well-being and extension of the Legion as a potent means of helping souls.

"Thus God's power, indeed, is infinite, but it is still subordinate to His wisdom and His justice; His justice, again, is infinite, but it, too, is subordinate to His love; and His love, in turn, is infinite, but it is subordinate to His incommunicable sanctity. There is an understanding between attribute and attribute, so that one does not interfere with the other, for each is supreme in its own sphere; and thus an infinitude of infinities, acting each in its own order, are combined together in the infinitely simple unity of God."—(Newman: Order, the Witness and Instrument of Unity).

LEGIONARY LOYALTY.

The whole idea of organisation is the unification of the many. From the member up through the ascending grades of authority in the Legion must the principle of connection exist, and in the measure that it is wanting will there be a departure from the principle of life.

In a voluntary organisation, the cement of this connection is loyalty: the loyalty of the member to the Praesidium, of the Praesidium to its Curia, of Curia to Senatus, and of Senatus to the Concilium Legionis; and to the ecclesiastical authorities everywhere. True loyalty will inspire Legionary and Praesidium and council with a dread of independent action. On all doubtful points, in all difficult situations, and with regard to every new work or novel departure, recourse must be had to appropriate authority for guidance and sanction.

The fruit of loyalty is obedience, and the test of the latter is the readiness to accept situations and decisions which are unpalatable, and let it be remarked—to accept them cheerfully. This prompt and cordial obedience is always difficult. Sometimes, to give it violates one's natural inclinations to such an extent as to amount to heroism, to be in fact a sort of martyrdom. And in such terms does St. Ignatius of Loyola speak of it. "Those," he says, "who by a generous effort resolve to obey, acquire great merits; obedience in its sacrifice resembles martyrdom." The Legion expects from its children everywhere that spirit of heroic and sweet docility to proper authority of every sort.

The Legion is an army—the army of the Virgin Most Humble. It must exhibit in its everyday working, what is forthcoming in profusion from any earthly army—heroism and sacrifice, even supreme sacrifice. Who can doubt that demands of a supremely exacting character will be made on Legionaries, too. Not often, indeed, will they be called on to offer their bodies to laceration and death, like the soldiers of the world. But let them rise gloriously higher in the things of the spirit. Let them be ready to offer their feelings, their judgment, their independence, their pride, their will, to the wounds of contradiction and the death of a wholehearted submission, when authority requires.

"Deep harm to disobey, seeing obedience is the bond of rule," says Tennyson, but the Legion's life-line can be sundered by more than wilful disobedience. The same result is achieved by the officers, whose neglect of the duties of attendance or correspondence, cuts off their Praesidia or councils from the main tide of Legionary life. The same deep harm is done by those, whether officers or members, who attend their meetings, but whose attitude there—from whatever cause—is calculated to promote disunion.

"Jesus *obeyed* His Mother. You have read how all that the Evangelists tell us of Christ's hidden life at Nazareth with Mary and Joseph, is that 'He was subject to them' and 'advanced in wisdom and age' (St. Luke ii, 51-52). Is there anything incompatible with His divinity in this? Certainly not. The Word is made Flesh; He has stooped so far as to take a nature like to ours, sin excepted; He came, said He, 'not to be ministered unto, but to minister' (St. Matt. xx. 28); to be 'obedient unto death' (Philip ii. 8); that is why He willed to obey His Mother. At Nazareth He obeyed Mary and Joseph, the two privileged beings whom God had placed near Him. In a certain measure, Mary shares in the authority of the Eternal Father over His Son's Humanity. Jesus could say of His Mother what He said of His Father in Heaven: 'I do always the things that please her.' (St. John viii. 29)."—(Marmion: Christ, the Life of the Soul).

EXTENSION AND RECRUITING.

1. If there is one duty in the Legion which is not understood to the point of being fulfilled, it would appear to be the duty of extending the Legion. The individual Legionaries and Praesidia indeed recruit members, but not so often do they try to bring about the start of other Praesidia. Curiae almost invariably think in terms of their own areas only. Their ambitions to extend the Legion rarely take wings. They expect some higher council to think to that end across seas or continents, but they themselves are slow to cross a parochial or a diocesan boundary in the effort to set the Legion working in new territory.

Evidently there is a misunderstanding of Legionary duty in this direction. So let that duty be stated definitely. The duty of Extension is not for the higher councils alone, nor for Curia Officers alone. It is the duty of each member of the Curia. Nay more, it is the duty of each individual Legionary, and each one must be made to realise that fact and to account now and then for his stewardship. The influencing of others by interview or correspondence is an obvious method of fulfilling this duty, but special ways will suggest themselves to each one.

The impulses which have spread the Legion over the world have not proceeded from many places. One hesitates to say how few. If many centres could only be made to send forth such impulses, the Legion would soon exist in all places, and the Lord's harvest fields would be thronged with willing labourers. (St. Luke x. 2).

2. An efficient branch of the Legion will be the source of immense good. As one may suppose that this good will be doubled by the establishment of a second branch, every member (and not merely the officers) should endeavour to bring about this desirable thing.

As soon as it is found that the members' reports and other items of the agenda have regularly to be curtailed in order to anticipate the automatic closure, a stage will have been reached when division is not only desirable but necessary. If not then effected, a dropsical state will supervene, in which interest in the work and membership will diminish. The Praesidium will not only lose the power of transmitting life to another branch, but will find it difficult to preserve its own existence.

To the proposal to form an additional Praesidium in a particular locality, it may be alleged that present numbers are coping satisfactorily with the existing needs. Against this, it is to be emphasised that, as the primary purpose of the Legion is the sanctification of its own members, and of the community at large through the play of that sanctity, it logically follows that increase of membership must, for this reason alone, be also a principal aim. Possibly the provision of work for the new members may be somewhat of a problem in small places. Nevertheless, let new members be accepted and sought. The Legion must never think in terms of limitation: better material than that already within the ranks might be excluded. When the more obvious needs have been covered, look deeper. Work is necessary to enable the machine to function: therefore invent it, if needs be.

Suggestions for the working of a Praesidium in a village or rural district are set out under that head.

In places where the Legion already exists, the effort should be made to provide the officers and a fair proportion of the new members by transfer from an existing branch. Praesidia should consider it as the greatest honour to supply their best material for the formation of a new Praesidium. This is the healthiest form of pruning. A Praesidium depleted by such a gift of its members, will find its ranks quickly refill, and its apostolate attended by an added benediction.

In towns or localities where no branch of the Legion already exists, it may not be feasible to secure members with Legionary experience, in which case the founders of the new Praesidium must apply themselves all the more assiduously to the study of the Handbook and whatever commentaries may be available thereon.

In setting up the first Praesidium in a new place, it is well to diversify its work as much as possible. This will better ensure the interest of the meetings and thus promote the health of the Praesidium. Moreover the varying abilities and tastes of the members can thereby be provided for.

3. There is need for a word of caution on the subject of recruiting members. There is a real danger that the requirements may be made too severe. Naturally the standard of those, who have been members for some time, will be higher than general standards. This must be allowed for in considering new members. It would be incorrect to insist upon a standard from a new recruit which the existing members only reached after some time in the Legion.

It is very common for Praesidia to excuse a low recruiting figure on the ground that suitable material is not available, but seldom will this explanation be found justified on an examination of all the circumstances. It is suggested that the fault lies almost invariably with the Praesidium itself. Either:—

(a) No serious effort is being made to recruit; which means that there is individual and collective neglect of duty by the Legionaries; or

(b) The Praesidium is making the mistake of applying to possible recruits over-stringent tests, such as would have excluded the bulk of its original and present members.

Those responsible argue that they must not risk the entry of unsuitable material. But neither must they deny the benefits of membership to all except a tiny few. If choice has to be made between undue rigour and undue laxity, the former is the greater error, because it kills the lay apostolate for want of workers. The other course would merely breed mistakes, and these can be repaired.

The Praesidium will take a medium course, but some element of risk must needs be faced. The only certain way of ascertaining that material is suitable is by actual experiment. The real safeguard is that the unsuitable person, if he does enter, quickly drops out under the stress of the work.

Whoever hears of the raising of an army being abandoned because of the fear that inefficient material might creep in? The system of the army exists for the moulding and handling of average human material in quantity. Likewise, the Legion, being Catholic Action, must aim at a fairly large membership. It has, of course, its tests for membership, but those tests should not be such that good, average material cannot pass them. The spiritual and close-knit system of the Legion exists for the purpose of moulding and controlling persons who require moulding and discipline, not for supermen. There should be no question of taking in only a type which is so superlatively holy and discreet as not to represent the ordinary laity at all.

To sum up, therefore, the sorrow is not that so few are fit for membership, but that so few are willing to assume the burden of it. This leads to the further consideration which follows:—

(c) Eligible persons may be deterred from joining, because the atmosphere of the Praesidium is excessively staid or stiff or otherwise uncongenial to them.

The Legion does not restrict its membership to the young, but the young must be specially sought for and catered for. If the Legion does not attract them, it is largely failing in its purpose, for the movement which does not appeal to the young will never exert a wide influence. Furthermore, the young are the key to the future. Therefore, the reasonable tastes of youth must be understood and allowed for. Bright, generous, enthusiastic youth must not be kept out by setting up standards which are inappropriate to the young or which may be nothing else than kill-joy standards.

"A primary law for every religious society is to perpetuate itself, to extend its apostolic action over the world, and to reach the greatest possible number of souls. 'Increase and multiply and fill the earth' (Gen. I. 28). This law of life imposes itself as a duty upon each person who becomes a member of the Society. Pére Chaminade thus formulates this law:—'We must make conquests for the Blessed Virgin, make those with whom we live understand how sweet it is to belong to Mary, to induce many of them to join us in our onward march.' "—(Petit Traité de Marialogie—Marianiste).

FUNCTIONS.

The duty of periodically bringing together the members of the Legion in any district, in order that they may know each other and that the spirit of unity may be fostered, is imposed upon each Curia.

The following annual functions are recommended.

1. THE ACIES.

Bearing in mind the importance of devotion to Mary in the Legion system, each year there shall be a Consecration of Legionaries to Our Lady. The Consecration —which shall comprise both an individual and a collective consecration—will take place on March 25th or a day convenient thereto, and will be known as the Acies. This Latin word, meaning as it does an army ranged in battle array, is appropriate to a ceremony in which the Legionaries as a body assemble to renew their fealty to Mary, Queen of the Legion, and from her to receive strength and blessing for yet another year's battle with the forces of evil. Moreover, the word is in effective contrast with Praesidium, which contemplates the Legion, no longer drawn up in united array, but split up into its various sections, each engaged in its own particular sphere of duty.

The Acies is the great central annual function of the Legion, so that it is necessary to stress the importance of attendance on the part of every member. The essential idea of the Legion, upon which all else is built, is that of working in union with and in dependence on Mary, its Queen. The Acies is the solemn declaration of that union and dependence, the renewal—individual and collective—of the Legionary promise of fealty. Hence it is manifest that any Legionaries who can attend and yet fail to do so, have little or none of the spirit of the Legion in them. The membership of such persons is not an asset to the Legion.

The following procedure is suggested:—

On the day fixed for the ceremony, the Legionaries shall assemble—if possible in a church. At a convenient spot is placed a statue of the Immaculate Conception, suitably decorated with flowers and candles. In front of the statue will stand a large-size replica of the Legion Vexillum, which is described elsewhere in its own Section.

The proceedings commence with a hymn, followed by the Rosary and other opening prayers of the Legion. An address by a Priest on the significance of the consecration to Our Lady follows. Legionaries then proceed singly (or in pairs—if the number is great) towards the statue. On reaching the Vexillum, each Legionary pauses; then, placing the hand upon the staff of the Vexillum, he repeats vocally, as an individual Act of Consecration, the following words: "I am all thine, my Queen, my Mother, and all that I have is thine." This done, the Vexillum is relinquished, the Legionary bows slightly and passes on. If the number of the Legionaries is large, the making of the individual Act of Consecration will occupy some time. In such case it will prevent the proceedings from becoming tedious if an organ be played during the procession of the Legionaries to and from the statue.

When all Legionaries have resumed their places, an Act of Consecration to our Lady is said aloud by the Priest on behalf of all present. Following this, the Catena is recited, all present standing. Then follows, if at all possible, Benediction of the Most Blessed Sacrament; after which the concluding prayers of the Legion are recited, a Hymn is sung, and the proceedings terminate.

A sample Order of Proceedings can be obtained on application.

"Mary is an object of terror to the powers of hell. She is 'terrible as an army set in battle array' (Cant. vi. 3), for, like a wise Commander, she well knows how to dispose her power, her mercy, and her prayers for the confusion of the enemy and for the benefit of her servants."—(St. Alphonsus Liguori).

2. THE ANNUAL GENERAL REUNION.

A Reunion of all the members shall be held on a day as near as possible to the Feast of the Immaculate Conception. This begins with a Church celebration, consisting of Rosary, Legion prayers, Hymns, special Sermon, and Benediction of the Most Blessed Sacrament. There follows a musical evening, contributed to exclusively by Legionaries, and comprising some Addresses or papers of Legionary interest. The remarks made below in respect of the social and cordial character of the Praesidium function have equal application to this Reunion.

"Joyousness lent a sweet charm to the spiritual knighthood of St. Francis. As genuine Knight of Christ Francis was inexpressibly happy to serve his Liege, to follow Him in poverty and to be like unto Him in suffering; and this blissful happiness in the service, the imitation, and the suffering of Christ he announced as knightly Minstrel and Troubadour of God to the whole world."—(Felder: The Ideals of St. Francis of Assisi).

3. AN OUTDOOR FUNCTION.

An Excursion, Pilgrimage, or outdoor function should be held during the summer. As determined by the Curia, this may be either a Curia or a Praesidium function. In the latter event, two or more Praesidia may combine for the function.

"That they all may be one, as thou Father, in me, and I in thee; that they also may be one in us."—(St. John xvii. 21).

4. THE PRAESIDIUM FUNCTION.

Each Praesidium will hold a social function about the Feast of the Nativity of Our Lady. In centres where there are many Praesidia, several Praesidia may, if they desire, combine to hold such a festival.

Suitable persons, who are not Legionaries, may be invited to attend, with a view to inducing them to undertake membership.

It is recommended that the full Legion prayers (including the Rosary) be said, divided into three parts as at a Praesidium meeting. The time thus taken from the social part of the evening does not amount to many minutes, but this tribute to Our Lady will be more than repaid by the enhanced success of the function. The Queen of the Legion is the "Cause of Our Joy," and she will reply by making the occasion one of special happiness.

Interpersed among the musical items should be a few very short Legion talks. All will, thereby, learn a little more about the Legion, and, incidentally, the programme will be diversified. Mere entertainment tends to pall.

It will surely be unnecessary to remind Legionaries that formality must find no place there. This is to be specially guarded against where more than one Praesidium is participating. It must be the object to make all those present know each other better. Therefore, the programme should afford opportunity for movement and conversation. Those in charge should contrive that the members do not keep together in parties, and thus frustrate the main purpose of the function which is the fostering of the spirit of unity and affection in the Legion family.

"Francis' entire life was henceforth attuned to this basic note of joy. With imperturbable calmness and cheerfulness of mind he sang to himself and to God songs of joy in his heart. His ceaseless endeavour was to keep himself interiorly and exteriorly in a joyous mood. In the intimate circle of his brothers he likewise knew how to sound the pure key-note of joyfulness, and to make it swell to such full harmony that they felt themselves raised to an almost heavenly atmosphere. The same joyful note pervaded the converse of the Saint with his fellow-men. Even his sermons, in spite of their burden of penance, became hymns of gladness, and his mere appearance was an occasion of festive joy for all classes of people."—(Felder: The Ideals of St. Francis of Assisi).

FUNDS.

1. Every Legionary body shall make a contribution towards the maintenance of its next-highest council. Subject to this, every Legionary body has full control over its own funds and exclusive liability for its own debts.

2. The various bodies should not limit their contributions to bare minima. It is recommended that whatever surplus funds remain after the needs of the Praesidium have been met, should be sent to the Curia for the general purposes of the Legion. In this, as in all other matters, the relations of the Praesidium to the Curia should be those of a child to its mother, the latter filled with solicitude for the interests of the former, which in turn tries to afford every assistance in lightening the maternal cares.

Too often it is found that Praesidia do not sufficiently appreciate the fact that the Curiae and higher councils are dependent on their contributions. At most they meet the bare needs of Curiae, and sometimes even fail in this. As a consequence, Curiae cannot aid the higher councils to bear the heavy burden attaching to the work of extension, the starting and visitation of branches, and general running expenses. The result is

A TYPICAL PRAESIDIUM MEETING.

THE SETTING OF THE LEGION ALTAR.
The altar must not be outside the circle of the meeting.

either that this work is inadequately done, or else that the shoulders of a few bear the burden which should through the Praesidium, be the responsibility and the joy of every Legionary.

3. All proposals for novel expenditure are to be referred by Praesidia to the Curia, so that the latter may judge if anything is involved which might have faulty reactions.

4. The Curia must not assume financial responsibility in respect of any work being carried on by a Praesidium. That responsibility rests on the Praesidium itself. The necessity for this regulation is obvious. Without it, any group running a Club, Hostel, or other work could, by being constituted a Praesidium, turn the other Praesidia into collecting agencies on its behalf.

It follows from this that no Praesidium may call, otherwise than as a favour, upon any other Praesidium or upon the Curia for assistance in the collection of funds.

5. Any transfer of funds, other than by a Praesidium to its special work or vice versa, shall be a matter for Curia sanction.

6. In the event of a Praesidium or a Legionary council falling through, or ceasing to function as a Legion body, the ownership of its Vexillum and other Legionary equipment is thereupon vested in the next-highest governing body.

7. The Spiritual Director shall have no personal financial responsibility for debts which he has not himself advised.

"All mankind is one whole, a body in which each member receives and ought also to give. Life should live and circulate. It comes to all: he who would stop it, loses it. He who consents to lose it, finds it. Each soul, if it would live, should pour itself forth into another soul. Every gift of God is a force which must be passed on, in order to be preserved and multiplied."—(Gratry: The Month of Mary).

PRAESIDIA REQUIRING SPECIAL MENTION.

1. JUNIOR PRAESIDIA.

1. Praesidia for persons under 18 years may be established with the approval of the Curia and subject to any special conditions which may be deemed necessary. See Section on Praesidium, paragraph 21.

2. It is to be regarded as an essential condition that at least the President of such a Praesidium should be an adult. A second adult officer would be desirable with a view to providing for the absence of the President, and for the possibilities of expansion. If these Senior Legionaries remain members of the Senior Praesidium, the work of officering the Junior Praesidium satisfies their work-obligation. But, if they are members of the Junior Praesidium only, they must perform for it a substantial, active work proportioned to their adult capacity. These officers should, if at all possible, be experienced Legionaries, who understand perfectly the Legion system, and who are otherwise fitted to accomplish in these youthful Legionaries the purpose which the Legion has in view in setting up the Praesidium. That purpose is not primarily the doing of a certain amount of useful work, but the training and spiritualising of its members, and the preparing of them to take their place in the ordinary ranks of the Legion when schooldays are finished.

3. Obviously the Allocutio will hold a doubly important place in the system by reason of the inability of many of the young Legionaries to master the contents of the Handbook through their own reading of it. Therefore, the Spiritual Director (or in his absence the President) should base every Allocutio on the Handbook. A small section should be read, and then explained in such a detailed and simple way as to make it certain that every member fully understands it. The Handbook should be ploughed through in this way week after week, from start to finish, and then returned upon. But, indeed, the termination of Junior membership comes so rapidly that there may not be the

opportunity of covering the ground twice for the same Legionaries. Each defective Allocutio, accordingly, represents an opportunity thrown away, a loss which cannot be made good.

4. As the works adopted by Senior Praesidia will probably not be available for a Praesidium of this type, ingenuity will be required to provide each member weekly with **a substantial active task.** The works of the Praesidium should be diversified. Different works will educate in different ways. As each member cannot do all the works, the next best way of getting an all-round training is to watch all of them being done by others. Moreover the proceedings of the Praesidium gain in interest.

5. Suggestions for the work are:—

(a) Helping at home (or in the school if the Praesidium be an internal one) in the spirit of the Legion, that is of Mary at Nazareth; seeking for work instead of trying to escape it; choosing the most unpleasant tasks; putting one's heart into the doing of the least things; being always sweetness and thoughtfulness itself; working always for Jesus and preserving the sense of His presence.

Let it be borne in mind that He who was "the Sovereign Lord of men and of angels demeaned Himself in such wise as regards His parents that He might well be believed to be their servant rather than their Son, often lighting the fire, preparing their meals, washing the dishes, or carrying water from the fountain." (Gerson.)

The foregoing must be *in addition* to the ordinary weekly task. It will not serve as the task.

(b) The study of the Handbook. If this can be systematically done after the method recommended in the Section on Study, it will provide a most useful course, without being felt to be "just a school task." It will be invaluable training to these future props of the Senior Legion.

(c) Teaching the Catechism to younger children.

(d) Distribution of the Miraculous Medal after the following plan. At each meeting one or two medals (a fixed number) are served out to each Legionary. They are to regard these as a ration of ammunition, which as soldiers of Mary they must use to the greatest disadvantage of the enemy, i.e., by giving them, if possible, to non-Catholics or neglectful Catholics. This idea stirs the imagination and induces sacrifices. They should be instructed as to the manner of answering the questions which are likely to be asked and as to the utilisation of openings. A Junior Praesidium, working in an area in which no Catholic school existed, in two months brought into the Church five children and one adult. As well, it secured many cases of return to the Sacraments.

(e) Winning of Auxiliary members. This will include the instructing of their recruits in the saying of the prayers, also the periodic visitation of them so as to ensure their perseverence.

(f) Recruiting for "something Catholic," i.e., the gaining of a recruit a week for some devotion or practice: Daily Mass, a Sodality, Apostleship of Prayer, Rosarians, Holy Childhood, etc.

(g) Acting as Prefects for a Children's Sodality. If perfection is the aim, this work should comprise the notifying—by personal call to each member—of each meeting of the Sodality; also the visiting of its sick and absent members, and the methodical efforts to increase membership. Obviously many Juniors will be required for this work.

(h) Collection of literature for subsequent distribution by themselves or by other Societies.

(i) Tending of Altars, Oratories, gardens or other parts of a school or institution.

(j) Sewing for the poor or for the Foreign Missions.

(k) Superintendence of Juniors' Recreation.

(l) Visitation of children in a hospital or other institution.
(m) Visitation of the sick and the blind—specially selected cases.
(n) Bringing of young children to Mass and the Sacraments.
(o) Serving Mass.

6. It should be brought home to the members that their own holiness is not only the main object of the Legion but also the mainspring of the Legion's work. Hence, they should be encouraged to perform spiritual exercises for the intentions of the Praesidium. But these exercises should not be set to the members, and it is probably better that they should not be reported on at the meeting. It is suggested that spiritual offerings of this kind might be noted on a piece of paper and placed in the Secret Bag along with the members' money contribution. It is particularly emphasised that spiritual exercises cannot substitute for the active work. If they are performed, it must be in addition to the active work.

7. Care and thought must be given by the members to their Reports, and they should be diligently educated by their Officers in the manner of furnishing a Report. The nature of their work will not usually provide much material for an interesting or detailed report, so a special effort will be needed to render the proceedings interesting and varied.

8. Junior members will not take the Legionary Promise, nor may they wear the Legion Badge, nor sit on a Senior Curia. But in all other respects the full routine of prayers, system and meetings, inclusive of the Secret Bag Collection, must be scrupulously followed, just as in the case of Senior Praesidium.

9. It has often been suggested that the prayers should be modified so as to facilitate the membership of children. The inadmissibility of such proposals should be evident from a reading of this Section, which indicates that Junior membership should be an approximation to Senior membership. There is no question of

"Junior" meaning "trivial." High ideals of action and devotion are to be placed before the Junior members, who should, in general, be expected to play the part of leaders among other young people. It is manifest that this standard cannot be reached by any child who, after some instruction, is incapable of saying the full Legion prayers intelligently.

10. What is to be anticipated from such a Praesidium? To a certainty, a changed outlook in its members—which is equivalent to a changed world for them—a new outlook:—

(a) on the Church, once they have realised that they are its soldiers, with a definite place in its warfare, and with responsibility for its extension.

(b) on the everyday round and task. As a tiny point of light illuminates a room, so the little Legion task gives a new meaning to the whole course of the week. What the members learn and practice in the Praesidium they will live in their ordinary life.

(c) on their neighbor in whom they have been taught to see and serve Christ.

(d) on their home, which they have learned to surround with the atmosphere of Nazareth.

(e) on "duty" and "discipline." These two all-important things, which are so odious to the young because so misunderstood by them, will be made comprehensible and beautiful when linked with those other two words: "Mary" and "Legion."

(f) on prayer, when they realise that it is not a mere custom-imposed task but a source of power, the support of their work, and their valuable contribution to the Legion treasury and thence to the Church.

Analysing this, it is not too much to claim that in the proper working of a Praesidium on the foregoing lines lies one of the greatest possible educative influences which could be brought to bear on the young.

It will develop in them every quality which is proper to the Catholic character, and will serve as a mould out of which will come in number holy and reliant young people, a joy to their parents and superiors, and a mainstay to the Church.

"Religious of both sexes will render a signal service to Catholic Action by preparing for it from a tender age the boys and girls under their charge in schools and colleges. At first, the young people are to be sweetly attracted to an interest in the work of the apostolate, and then by constant and painstaking effort induced to become members of Catholic Action organisations. *Where the latter do not already exist, those Religious should themselves establish them.*

"There is absolutely no more suitable means at hand, no finer opportunity lies open, for initiating the youth into Catholic Action, than that which is afforded by schools and colleges. This training of a youth élite will be of great benefit to the whole school or institution. If, in any such place, at least the choicest amongst the pupils are thoroughly imbued with the spirit of the Christian Apostolate, it is not difficult to understand what an influence for good they will be amongst all the others. But it is the young people themselves, who are thus being trained to Catholic Action, that will benefit most. As we have often declared, in these associations providentially coming into their lives at a particularly dangerous age, they will be forewarned by heavenly doctrine and invigorated with supernatural strength. Likewise they will find in them a help and protection which will enable them to face boldly, and with invincible courage overcome the many grave dangers which beset their path in that society in which they have to live."—(Pius XI. A.A.S. Vol. xxviii. Num. 5. p. 159).

2. COLLEGE PRAESIDIA.

A Praesidium may be established in a Seminary or College. A College, especially a Teachers' Training College, which establishes and encourages such a Praesidium will do a far-reaching work. Out from its walls will go each year a number of its students destined to play a significant part in their new surroundings. If these have already received some training as Legionaries, they will of a certainty start the Legion, or join it, if already established in the place to which they go. Then what a difference of outlook! What a different moulding for the innumerable children who will pass through their hands! Is not this the hundredfold in exchange for the hour or so a week which the College Praesidium may have snatched from the time of studies?

Another, and a present gain, will lie in the fact that the sense of identity with their organisation outside in the world, fighting the Lord's battle in the cities' slums, and with many great enterprises in hand, will vitalise their own less enterprising work. The doings of their comrades in the battle-line outside will catch the imagination of these youthful Legionaries (a process which is helped by everything in the Legion system), and will preserve them, and many through them, from that bane of institutions, the disposition to regard religion as a mere routine. If the latter idea takes root in the impressionable years, harm has been done for which the most resplendent scholastic attainments will not compensate.

The only real way of learning the Legion is to work its system. Lectures are often given urging pupils to undertake the apostolate when they go out into the world, but such lectures, however excellent, are but dry bones compared with the living body of actual practice. Moreover, without some actual training, an intention or desire to begin apostolic work is of little value. Inexperience is easily intimidated, or if a beginning is made along one's own lines, it will almost assuredly end in a morass.

An effort should be made to provide the members with ordinary active work outside the College. If this proves to be impossible, the Praesidium should follow methods somewhat similar to those suggested in the preceding section on Junior membership. In particular, a thorough study of the Handbook should be undertaken.

It is in order to establish a Praesidium in a college where the students all go home for the vacations, rendering it impossible to hold meetings during that period. During that time, some of the members may be able to work in the Praesidia in their home towns.

"How shall I show my love, since love proves itself by deeds. To strew flowers is the only means of proving my love, and these flowers will be each word and look, each small daily sacrifice. I wish to make profit out of the smallest actions and do them all for Love. For Love's sake I wish to suffer and to rejoice: thus shall I strew my flowers. Not one that I see but —singing all the while—I will scatter its petals before Thee. Should my roses be gathered from amid thorns, I will sing notwithstanding, and the longer and sharper the thorns, the sweeter will grow my song."—(The Little Flower).

3. PRAESIDIA IN VILLAGES OR RURAL DISTRICTS.

1. The argument, constantly heard, that there is no scope for the Legion in small places, makes it necessary to prove its universal adaptability.

In advance, it is again stressed that no place, which does not possess a substantial apostolic leaven, can possibly be deemed to be in a healthy religious state. Therefore, apostolic organisation and the work necessary to that organisation, must be provided.

The apparently unfavourable case is here taken of a sparsely populated rural parish of many miles in area, consisting of a village, with no Convent or Hospital, a Church in the village itself with possibly a Chapel in an outlying district, and one or two Priests to minister to a congregation of farmers, agricultural labourers, and perhaps a sprinkling of fisher folk if there is a sea coast.

2. An effective beginning of Legion work could be made by conducting a methodical visitation of the area for the purpose of bringing every person into Auxiliary membership. The canvass should have in mind the ideals set out in the Section on Auxiliary Membership. It should be made less with the idea of covering ground than of deepening acquaintance.

3. In practically every Parish there is a Sodality or Confraternity which the Legionaries could increase and maintain by an active following up of lax members. In the event of the absence of a Sodality, the Parish might be organised on the basis of Auxiliary membership, with periodic Church or other meetings.

4. Distance from the Church makes it impossible for many to enjoy the privileges of Daily Mass, visits to the Blessed Sacrament, sermons, and public devotions.

The Legionaries might supply for the lack of these by bringing to the houses of the people such devotions as the Apostleship of Prayer (with its three degrees of Morning Offering, Decade of the Rosary, and Communion of Reparation), the Enthronement of the Sacred Heart, or even the practice of Nocturnal Adoration.

5. There will be scope for such works as the care of Altar linen, the decoration of Altars and the beautification of the Church, instruction of children at Sunday School and for the reception of the Sacraments. A Children's section at Mass might be arranged and shepherded.

6. The homes of the old, the bed-ridden, and the blind could be visited to prepare them for the Priest, to perform any little services they may require, or simply to shorten weary hours by talking or reading to them, and by supplying them with books and papers. Many are the instances where their rooms have been papered and whitewashed by their Legionary visitors.

7. The superintendence of motherless families (whose fathers are away at work during the day, leaving the care of the home to an elder child) would form an especially beautiful task for some Legionary able to pay a visit every day. Other cases will be discovered which require visitation on various grounds.

8. For children, the Legionaries might organise a branch of the Holy Childhood, or troops of Boy Scouts or Girl Guides; for the young people, a Church choir, a social club, concert party, or dramatic class, to relieve the monotony of rural life and to provide funds for such good works as have been already suggested.

9. They might provide what is generally so badly needed in the country—a Catholic library. Enterprises of this kind frequently fail owing to the difficulty in getting borrowers to return books. Yet, what an ideal work for the Legion. Two Legionaries might profitably make it their Legionary duty to supply and collect books at two or three homes. There they would be welcome visitors, and they could in time carry out

a thorough Legion Apostolate. Catholic papers might be sold weekly in the same way.

10. The work of Study might be added to the other activities of such a Praesidium. See the Section on Study.

11. Local conditions will suggest other works. The vista widens as one goes along. One begins to feel that one Praesidium is inadequate—even for a village, if organised on thoughtful principles. It may happen that a Priest is already carrying on some of the works. Were he to work them through the Legion and devote himself to training the Legionaries and developing their work, he would find that it would energise the religious life of the whole parish.

12. It will be less an outward religious neglect than a cynical or selfish outlook on life which the country Legionaries will encounter, and which they must confound by their voluntary service and persevering self-sacrifice.

Where a parish is good, the main work of the Legion will be to make all understand that they must not be selfishly inactive, but must stand solidly behind the Pope, praying constantly for his intentions, for the agonising, and for all kinds of sinners and problems; in a word, organising and multiplying the prayers and good works of the flock into a great flood of prayer for the triumph of the universal Church. All, old and young alike, must be made to realise that the possession of the treasures of the Faith brings with it the obligation of sharing those treasures, by every means in their power, with the infinite multitude who are in darkness and in the shadow of death.

13. Even in the smallest Praesidium all the rules of the Legion must be scrupulously observed, including that of attendance at the weekly meeting. The latter, in fact, becomes magnified in importance according as the parish becomes smaller and the work scarcer and duller. An evening meeting may not always be practicable in a country district where long distances have to be travelled. Sunday afternoon might be

substituted, or any hour which experience proves to be the most convenient for the majority of the members.

"The soul sets about its daily work. Whether it be humble and, in a material sense, insignificant work, or whether it be work of a more notable kind, is of little importance: by the soul it is performed with Jesus and for Jesus beneath the gaze of His heavenly Mother. The soul knows that she is there close at hand, watching it tenderly, at no time allowing it to go out of her sight, acting in short as a mother does in regard to her child."—(De Jaegher: The Virtue of Trust).

THE SOULS OF OUR DEPARTED LEGIONARIES.

The end of the campaigning has come and a Legionary lies nobly dead. Now at last he is confirmed in Legionary service. Through all eternity he will be a Legionary, for the Legion has shaped that eternity for him. It has been the fibre and the mould of his spiritual life. Moreover, the might of the united petition, uttered daily and earnestly by active members and Auxiliaries alike, that the Legion should reassemble without the loss of any one, has helped him through the dangers and the difficulties of the long way. What a joyful thought for all Legionaries—on his account and on their own! But for the moment, there is sorrow at the loss of friend and comrade, and there is need of prayer so that the deliverance of the departed soldier from the realm of Purgatory may be speedily accomplished.

The Praesidium should without delay have a Mass offered for the soul of each one of its Active members who may die; and each member of that Praesidium should specially recite all the Legion Prayers, inclusive of the Rosary, at least once for the same intention. But these duties do not extend to the deceased relatives of members. As many Legionaries as possible, and not those of the particular Praesidium alone, should attend the Mass and accompany the remains to burial.

It is recommended that the Rosary and other Legion prayers should be recited while the interment is actu-

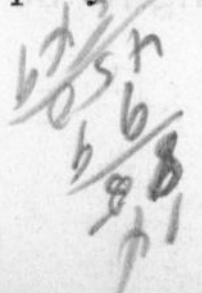

ally taking place. This could be done immediately after the official prayers of the Church. This Practice, besides being of much benefit to the deceased, will be found to be a source of deep consolation to the sorrowing relatives, to the Legionaries themselves, and to all the friends present.

It is trusted that the same prayers will have been said more than once beside the remains during the period of laying out. Nor should the duty of remembrance be deemed then to cease.

In the month of November each year, each Praesidium shall have a Mass celebrated for the souls of the Legionary Dead, not of that Praesidium alone but of all the world. In this, as on all other occasions where prayer is offered for departed Legionaries, all grades of membership are comprised.

"Purgatory forms part of the realm of Mary. There, too, are her children, who in a passing spell of pain await their birth to the glory which will never pass.

"St. Vincent Ferrer, St. Bernardine of Sienna, Louis de Blois, as well as others, explicitly proclaim Mary to be Queen of Purgatory; and the Blessed de Montfort urges us to think and act in accordance with that belief. He wishes us to place in Mary's hands the value of our prayers and satisfactions. He promises us that, in return for this offering, those souls which are dear to us will be more abundantly relieved than if we were to apply our prayers to them directly."—(Lhoumeau: La Vie Spirituelle a l'Ecole du B. de Montfort).

THE DUTY OF LEGIONARIES TOWARDS MARY

1. The honouring of the Legion devotion to Mary by serious meditation and zealous practice is placed on each member as a solemn trusteeship to the Legion. It is to be regarded as an essential part of Legionary duty, ranking before any other obligation of membership. (See Article on Legionary Devotion and Appendix II.)

The Legion aims to bring Mary to the world as the infallible means of winning the world to Jesus. Manifestly, the Legionary without Mary in his heart can play no part in this. He is divorced from the Legionary purpose. He is an unarmed soldier, a broken link, or rather as a paralysed arm—attached to the body, it is true—but of what use for work!

The study of every army (and no less that of the Legion) must be to bind the individual soldier to the leader, so that the latter's plan passes smoothly into concerted action. The army acts as one. To this end is all the elaborate machinery of drill and discipline directed. In addition, there is found in the soldiers of all the great armies of history, a devotion of a passionate sort for their leader, intensifying their union with him, and rendering easy the sacrifices which the execution of his plan called for. Of this leader it could be said that he was the inspiration and soul of his soldiers, in their hearts, one with them, and so forth. These phrases describe the operation of his influence and in a measure express a truth.

But at best such unity is only an emotional or mechanical one. Not so, the relation between the Christian soul and Mary its Mother. To say that Mary is in the soul of the faithful Legionary would be to picture a union infinitely less effective than that which actually exists, the nature of which is summed up by the Church in such titles of our Lady as "Mother of Divine Grace," "Mediatrix of all Graces." In these titles is expressed a sway of Mary over the life of the soul, so complete that even that closest of earthly unions—the mother and the babe unborn—is inadequate to describe its intimacy. Other natural processes around can help to make real to the mind this place of Mary in the operations of grace. The blood is not distributed except by the heart, the eyes are the necessary link with the world of vision, and the bird—despite the beating of its wings—cannot lift itself without the support of the air; so the soul, according to the divinely established order, cannot without Mary lift itself to God or do God's work.

Not being a creation either of the reason or of the emotions, but a Divine arrangement, this dependence on Mary exists even though it is not adverted to. But it can be, and should be, immeasurably strengthened by a deliberate participation in it. In intensity of union with her, who is (as St. Bonaventure says) the dispenser of Our Lord's Blood, lie marvels of sanctification and an incredible source of power over the souls of others. Those whom the plain gold of the apostolate could not ransom from the captivity of sin, are freed—everyone—when Mary studs that gold with the jewels of the Precious Blood which she has in her gift.

So, beginning with a fervent Consecration, frequently renewed in some phrase embodying it (for instance: "I am all thine, my Queen, my Mother, and all that I have is thine"), this thought of the ever-present influence of Mary in the soul should be reduced to such methodical and vivid practice that the soul may be said to "breathe Mary as the body breathes air."—(Grignion de Montfort.)

In the Mass, Holy Communion, Adoration, the Rosary, the Stations of the Cross, and other Devotions, the Legionary Soul must seek, as it were, to identify itself with Mary, and to meditate on the mysteries of the Redemption through that supremely faithful soul which lived them with the Saviour, and in them played an indispensable part.

And so, imitating her, thanking her tenderly, rejoicing and sorrowing with her, giving her the long study and the great love, bringing some thought of her into every prayer and work and act of the spiritual life, forgetting itself and its own resources to depend on her; the soul of the Legionary becomes so filled with the image and thought of her that the two souls are but one soul. The Legionary, lost in the depth of Mary's soul, shares her faith, her humility, her Immaculate Heart (and hence the potency of her prayer); and swiftly is transformed into Christ, which is the object of all life. While on the other hand, in and through her Legionary, Mary participates in every Legionary duty and mothers souls, so that in each of those worked for and of one's fellow-workers, not only is the person of Our Lord seen and served, but seen and served by Mary, with the same exquisite love and nurturing care which she gave to the actual body of her Divine Son.

Its members thus grown into living copies of Mary, the Legion sees itself in truth a Legion of Mary, united to her mission and guaranteed her victory. It will bring Mary to the world, and she will give light to the world and presently set it all ablaze.

"With Mary live joyfully, with Mary bear all your trials, with Mary labour, with Mary pray, with Mary take your recreation, with Mary take your repose. With Mary seek Jesus; in your arms bear Jesus, and with Jesus and Mary fix your dwelling at Nazareth. With Mary go to Jerusalem, remain near the Cross of Jesus, bury yourself with Jesus. With Jesus and Mary rise again, with Jesus and Mary mount to Heaven, with Jesus and Mary live and die."—(Thomas à Kempis: Sermon to Novices.)

2. The imitation of Mary's humility is both the root and the instrument of Legionary action.

The Legion speaks to its members in terms of an army and battles. This is fitting, for the Legion is the instrument and visible operation of Her who is like an army in battle array and who wages an intense warfare for the soul of every man. Moreover, the martial idea is one with great appeal to mankind. Legionaries, knowing themselves to be soldiers, are stimulated to impart a soldierly seriousness to their work. But the warfare of Legionaries is not of this world, and must be waged according to the tactics of Heaven. "Meek hands alone the Legion's sword of strife may rear, and ever zeal begins its life in silent thought and fear."* The fire which burns in true Legionary hearts springs only from the ashes of lowly and unworldly qualities. Particular among these is the virtue of humility, so misunderstood and despised by the world. Yet, it is noble and strong, and confers a strange nobility and strength on those who seek it and practise it.

In the Legion system, humility plays a unique part. In the first place, it is an essential instrument of the Legionary apostolate. For, the effecting and develop-

* Applying to the Legion a verse of Newman's.

ing of the personal contact, on which the Legion relies so largely in its work, call for workers with gentle, unassuming manners such as are derived only from true humility of heart. But humility is more to the Legion than a mere instrument of its external action. It is the very cradle of that action. Without humility there can be no effective Legionary action.

Christ, says St. Thomas Aquinas, recommended to us humility above all things, for thereby is removed the chief impediment to the salvation of men. All the other virtues derive their value from it. Only when humility exists, will God bestow His favours. When it fades, those gifts will be withdrawn. The Incarnation, the source of all graces, depended on it. Mary says, in the "Magnificat," that in Her God hath showed might in His arm, that is, He has exerted in her His very omnipotence. And she proclaims the reason. It was her humility which had won His regard and brought Him down to terminate the old world and begin the new.

But how could Mary be a model of humility, considering that her treasury of perfections was altogether immeasurable—touching in fact the very borders of infinity, and that she knew it? She was humble because she was likewise aware that she was more perfectly redeemed than any other of the children of men. She owed every gleam of her inconceivable sanctity to the merits of her Son, and that thought was ever vivid in her mind. Her peerless intellect was full of the realisation that as she had received more, so no other creature stood as much in God's debt as she. Hence her attitude of exquisite and graceful humility was effortless and constant.

Studying her, therefore, the Legionary will learn that the essence of true humility is the recognition and unaffected acknowledgment of what one really is before God; the understanding that one's worthlessness alone is one's own. Everything else is God's free gift to the soul: His to increase, diminish, or withdraw completely, just as He alone gave it. A sense of one's subjection will show itself in a marked preference for humble and little-sought tasks, in a readiness to bear contempt and rebuffs, and generally in an attitude towards the manifestations of God's Will which will reflect Mary's own declaration: "Behold the Handmaid of the Lord."—(St. Luke i, 38.)

The necessary union of the Legionary with his Queen requires not only the desire for that union, but the capacity for it. A person may determine to be a good soldier, but yet may never possess the qualities which will make him an efficient cog in the military machine. In consequence, that man's union with his general is an ineffective one, so that he impedes the working out of the military plan. Similarly, the Legionary may aspire to play a great part in the plan of his Queen; yet he may be incapable of receiving what Mary so ardently longs to give. In the case of the ordinary soldier this incapacity would proceed from defects of courage, intelligence, physical fitness, and the like. In the case of the Legionary, that incapacity would be caused by the absence of the virtue of humility. The purpose of the Legion is the sanctification of its members and the radiation of that sanctity in the world of souls. But there can be no holiness without humility. Moreover, the Legion apostolate operates through Mary. But there can be no union with Mary without some likeness to her, and there can be little likeness to her in default of her especial virtue of humility. If union with Mary is the indispensable condition—the root, so to speak—of all Legionary action, then the soil on which these roots depend is humility. If that soil is deficient, the Legionary life will wither.

It follows that the Legion's battle for souls must begin in the heart of the individual Legionary. Each one must wage the battle with himself, determinedly conquering in his heart the spirit of pride and self. This terrible struggle with the root of evil within one, this constant striving after purity of intention, how exhausting it is! It is the battle of a lifetime. Reliance upon one's own efforts will make it the failure of a lifetime; for self winds itself even into the attack on self. Of what use are his own muscles to one struggling in a quicksand? A firm support is necessary.

Legionary, your firm support is Mary. Lean upon her with complete trust. She will not fail you, for she is deeply rooted in that humility which is vital to you. In the faithful practice of the spirit of dependence upon her will be found a supreme, simple, comprehensive way of humility—what Grignion de Montfort terms "a little-known secret of grace, enabling us quickly and with but little effort to empty ourselves of self, fill ourselves with God, and become perfect."

Consider how this is so. The Legionary, in turning towards Mary, must necessarily turn away from self. Mary takes hold of this movement and elevates it; makes of it the supernatural dying to self which fulfils the stern but fruitful law of the Christian life. (St. John xii. 24-25). The humble Virgin's heel crushes the serpent of self, with its many heads:—

(1) of self-exaltation; for if Mary, so rich in perfections as to be called by the Church the Mirror of Justice, endowed with unbounded power in the realms of grace, is nevertheless found on her knees—the humblest handmaid of the Lord! what must be the Legionary's place and attitude;

(2) of self-seeking; for, having given himself and all his goods, spiritual and temporal, to Mary to use as she thinks fit, the Legionary continues to serve her in the same spirit of complete generosity;

(3) of self-sufficiency; for the habit of leaning on Mary inevitably produces distrust of one's own unaided powers;

(4) of self-conceit; for the sense of partnership with Mary brings realisation of one's own inadequacy. What has the Legionary contributed to that partnership but painful weaknesses!

(5) of self-love; for what is there to love! The Legionary, absorbed in love and admiration of

his Queen, is little inclined to turn from her to contemplate himself;

(6) of self-satisfaction; for in this alliance the higher standards must prevail. The Legionary models himself upon Mary and aspires to her perfect purity of intention;

(7) of self-advancement; thinking with Mary's thoughts, one studies God alone. There is no room for plans of self or reward;

(8) of self-will; completely submitted to Mary, the Legionary distrusts the promptings of his own inclinations and in all things listens intently for the whisperings of grace.

In the Legionary, who is truly forgetful of self, there will be no impediment to the maternal influences of Mary. She will develop in him energies and sacrifices beyond nature, and make of him a good soldier of Christ (2 Tim. ii. 3), fit for the arduous service to which that profession calls him.

"God delights to work on nothing; from that deep foundation it is that He raises the creations of His power. We should be full of zeal for God's glory, and at the same time convinced of our incapacity to promote it. Let us sink into the abyss of our worthlessness; let us take shelter under the deep shade of our lowliness; let us tranquilly wait until the Almighty shall see fit to render our active exertions instrumental to His glory. For this purpose He will make use of means quite opposed to those we might naturally expect. Next to Jesus Christ no one ever contributed to the glory of God in the same degree as the Blessed Virgin Mary, and yet the sole object to which her thoughts deliberately tended was her own annihilation. Her humility seemed to oppose an obstacle to the designs of God, but it was, on the contrary, that humility precisely, which facilitated the accomplishment of His all-merciful views."—(Grou: Interior of Jesus and Mary.)

3. Intensity of Effort in Mary's Service.

In no circumstances should the spirit of dependence upon Mary be made an excuse for lack of effort or for defects in system. Indeed the exact contrary must obtain. Because one works with Mary and for her so completely, it follows that one's gift to her must be the choicest that can be offered. One must always work with energy and skill and fineness. Now and then, fault has had to be found with branches or members who did not appear to be making sufficient effort in connection with the ordinary Legion work or with extension or recruiting. Sometimes this kind of answer is forthcoming. "I distrust my own powers. I rely altogether on Our Blessed Lady to bring about the right result in her own way." Often this reply proceeds from earnest persons who are inclined to ascribe to their own inactivity a sort of virtue, as if method and effort implied a littleness of faith. There may be, too, a certain danger of applying human ideas to these things and of reasoning that if one is the instrument of a simply immense power, the exact degree of one's own effort does not so greatly matter. Why, it may be argued, should a poor man who is in partnership with a millionaire, exhaust himself to contribute an extra penny to the already overflowing common purse?

It is necessary, therefore, to emphasise a principle which must govern the attitude of the Legionary towards his work. It is that Legionaries are in no wise mere instruments of Mary's action. There is question of a true co-operation with her for the purpose of enriching and ransoming the souls of men. In that co-operation each supplies what the other cannot give. The Legionary gives his action and his faculties: that is all of himself; and Mary gives herself with all her purity and power. Each is bound to contribute without reserve. If the spirit of this partnership is honoured by the Legionary, Mary will never be found wanting. Therefore, the fate of the enterprise may be said to depend entirely on the Legionary, so that he must bring to it all his intelligence and all his strength, perfected by careful method and by perseverance.

Even if it were known that Mary were going to give a desired result independent of the Legionary effort, nevertheless that effort must be exerted in its fulness, with just the same intensity as if all depended on it. While placing a limitless confidence in the aid of Mary, the Legionary's effort must always be pitched at its maximum. His generosity must always rise as high as his trust. This principle of the necessary interaction of boundless faith with intense and methodical effort is expressed in another way by the Saints, when they say that one must pray as if all depended on that prayer and nothing on one's own efforts; and then one must strive as if absolutely everything depended on that striving.

There must be no such thing as proportioning the output of effort to one's estimate of the difficulty of the task, or of thinking in terms of "just how little can I give to gain the object in view?" Even in worldly matters, such a bargaining spirit constantly defeats itself. In supernatural things it will always fail, for it forfeits the grace on which the issue really hangs. Moreover, human judgments cannot be depended on. The apparent impossibility often collapses at a touch; while, on the other hand, the fruit which hangs almost within reach, may persistently elude the hand, and at long last be harvested by someone else. In the spiritual order the calculating soul will sink to smaller and smaller things and finally end in barrenness. The only certain way lies in unrestricted effort. Into each task, trivial or great, the Legionary will throw supreme effort. Perhaps that degree of effort is not needed. It may be that a touch would be sufficient to bring the work to completion; and were the completion of the task the only objective, it would be legitimate to put forth that slight effort and no more. One would not —as Byron says—uplift the club of Hercules to crush a butterfly or brain a gnat.

But Legionaries must be brought to realise that they do not work directly for results. They work for Mary quite irrespectively of the simplicity or the difficulty of the task; and in every employment the Legionary must give the best that is in him, be it little or be it great. Thereby is merited the full co-operation of Mary, so that even miracles are wrought where they are needed. If one can do but little, and yet does it with all one's heart, Mary will come in with power and will give that feeble movement the effect of a giant's strength. If, having done all that he can, the Legionary is still a million miles from success, Mary will bridge that distance to carry their joint work to an ideal conclusion.

And even if the Legionary puts into a work ten times the intensity which is needed to perfect it, nevertheless not a particle of what he does is wasted. For is not all his work for Mary and at the service of her vast design and purpose? Mary will receive with joy that surplus effort, will multiply it exceedingly, and with it supply grave needs of the household of the Lord. There is nothing lost of anything which is committed to the hands of the careful housewife of Nazareth.

But if, on the other hand, the Legionary's contribution falls meanly short of what might reasonably be required from him, then Mary's hands are held from giving munificently. The compact of common goods with Mary, so full of unique possibilities, is set aside by Legionary negligence. O what sad loss to souls and to the Legionary himself thus to be left on his own resources!

It is useless, therefore, for the Legionary to justify insufficient effort or slovenly methods by alleging that he relies on Mary altogether. Surely that sort of reliance, which enabled him to shrink from reasonable endeavour on his own part, would be a weak ignoble thing. He seeks to transfer to Mary's shoulders a burden which his own are adequate to bear. Would any ordinary knight of chivalry serve his fair lady so strangely!

So, just as if nothing had yet been said on this subject, let this root principle of the Legionary alliance with Mary be stated once again. The Legionary must give to the utmost of his capacity. Mary's part is not that of supplying what the Legionary refuses to give. It would not be proper for her to relieve her Legionary from the effort, method, patience, thought, which he can provide, and which is due by him to the treasury of God.

Mary desires to give profusely, but she cannot do so except to the generous soul. Therefore, desirous that her Legionary children will draw deeply from her immensity, she anxiously appeals to them, in her Son's own words, for a service "with their whole heart, and with their whole soul, and with their whole mind and with their whole strength." (St. Mark xii. 30).

The Legionary must only look to Mary to supplement, to purify, to perfect, to supernaturalise the natural, to enable weak human effort to achieve what is impossible to it. But these are mighty things. They can mean that mountains will be torn from their roots and hurled into the sea, and the land will be made plain and the paths straightened to lead on to the Kingdom of God.

"We are all unprofitable servants, but we serve a Master who is absolutely economical, who lets nothing go to waste, not a drop of the sweat of our brow, any more than a drop of His heavenly dew. I know not what fate awaits this book; whether I shall finish it, or whether I shall reach even the end of the page that lies beneath my pen. But I know enough to cause me to throw into it the remnant, be it great or small, of my strength and of my days."—(Frederic Ozanam.)

4. Legionaries Should Undertake De Montfort's True Devotion to Mary.

It is desirable that the practice of the Legionary devotion to Mary should be rounded off and given the distinctive character which has been taught by the Blessed Grignion de Montfort under the titles of "The True Devotion," or the "Slavery of Mary," and which is enshrined in his two books, the "True Devotion to the Blessed Virgin" and the "Secret of Mary."

That Devotion requires the formal entry into a compact with Mary, whereby one gives to her one's whole self, with all its thoughts and deeds and possessions, both spiritual and temporal; past, present, and future, without the reservation of the smallest part or slightest little thing. In a word, the giver places himself in a condition equivalent to that of a slave possessing nothing of his own, and wholly dependent on, and utterly at the disposal of Mary.

But the earthly slave is far freer than the slave of Mary. The former remains master of his thoughts and inner life, and thus may be free in everything that matters to him. But the surrender to Mary bears with it everything: each thought, the movements of the soul, the hidden riches, the inmost self. All—on to the final breath—is committed to her that she may expend it all for God. It is a sort of martyrdom, the sacrifice of self to God, with Mary as the altar of that sacrifice. How conformed, indeed, to the sacrifice of Christ Himself, which likewise began in Mary's bosom, was publicly confirmed in the arms of Mary uplifted in the Presentation, embraced every moment of His life, and was consummated on Calvary on the Cross of Mary's heart.

The True Devotion is inaugurated by a formal Act of Consecration, but it consists principally in the subsequent living of that Consecration. The True Devotion must represent not an act but a state. Unless Mary takes possession of all the life, and not merely of minutes and hours of that life, the Act of Consecration —even though frequently repeated—has but the value of a passing prayer. It is like a tree which has been planted, but which has never taken root.

But this does not mean that the mind has to remain ever fixed upon the Consecration. Just as ones' physical life is governed by one's breathing or by the beating of the heart, even though these operations are not consciously viewed, so it is with the True Devotion. Even though not adverted to, it works incessantly on the life of the soul. It suffices if the idea of Mary's ownership is now and then made vivid by deliberate thought, by Acts and ejaculations; provided that the fact of one's dependence on her remains permanently acknowledged, always at least vaguely present to the mind, and put into force in a general way in all the circumstances of one's life.

If there is a warmth in all this, it can be a help. But if not, it does not affect the value of the Devotion.

Oftentimes, in fact, warmth makes things soft and not dependable.

Mark this well: the True Devotion does not depend on fervour or emotions of any kind. Like every lofty edifice, it may at times burn in sunshine, while its deep foundations are cold like the rock they rest on.

Reason is commonly cold. The best resolve may be icy. Faith itself can be chill as a diamond. Yet these are the foundations of the True Devotion. Set in them, the latter will abide; and the frost and the storm, which cause mountains to crumble, will only leave it the stronger.

The graces which have attended the practice of the True Devotion, and the position it has attained in the devotional life of the Church, would reasonably appear to indicate that it represents an authentic message from Heaven; and this is precisely what Grignion de Montfort claimed it to be. He attached to it immense promises, and he asserted most positively that those promises would be fulfilled if the conditions which govern them are fulfilled.

And as to the everyday experience: speak to those whose practice of the Devotion is more than a surface affair, and see with what complete conviction they speak of what it has done for them. Ask them if they may not be the victims of their feelings or imagination. Always, they will declare that there is no question of it; the fruits have been too evident to admit of their being deceived.

If the sum of the experiences of those who teach, and understand, and practise the True Devotion is of value, it seems unquestionable that it deepens the interior life, sealing it with the special character of unselfishness and purity of intention. There is a sense of guidance and protection: a joyful certainty that now one's life is being employed to the best advantage. There is a supernatural outlook, a definite courage, a firmer faith, which make one a mainstay of any enterprise. There is a tenderness and a wisdom which keep strength in its proper place. There is, too, the protectress of them all, a sweet humility. Graces come which one cannot but realise are out of the common. Frequently, there is a call to a great work, which is patently beyond one's merits and natural capacity. Yet with it come such helps as enable that glorious but heavy burden to be borne without faltering. In a word, in exchange for the splendid sacrifice which is made in the True Devotion by selling oneself into this species of slavery, there is gained the hundredfold which is promised to those who despoil themselves for the greater glory of God. To employ the vivid imagery of Newman: "When we serve, we rule; when we give, we have; when we surrender ourselves, we are victors."

The objection to making the Consecration is usually due, less to a purely selfish outlook, than to perplexity. There is difficulty in understanding how those things for which one is bound in duty to pray, such as one's family, one's friends, the Pope, one's country, etc., will fare if one makes the unreserved gift of one's spiritual treasures. Let all these misgivings be put aside, and let the Consecration be boldly made. Everything is safe with Our Lady. She is the guardian of the treasures of God Himself. She is capable of being the guardian of the concerns of those who place their trust in her. So, together with the assets of one's life, cast all its liabilities—its obligations and duties—into that great sublime heart of hers.

Here, where one is being urged to make sacrifice, is not the place to seek to prove that such a proceeding is in reality a paying proposition. For this would sap the very foundations of the offering and deprive it of the character of sacrifice on which its value depends. It will suffice to recall that once upon a time a multitude of ten or twelve thousand were in a desert, and were hungry. (St. John vi. 1-14). In all that number only one person had brought food with him. What he possessed amounted to five loaves and two fishes, and he was asked to give them up for the common good; and he did so with willingness. Then, those few loaves and fishes were blessed and broken and distributed to the multitude. And in the end all that immense throng did eat, until they could eat no more; and among them he who had given the original seven items of food. And yet what remained over filled twelve baskets, full and to overflowing! Now supposing that individual had said: "What good will these few loaves and fishes be to so great a multitude? Besides, I require them for the members of my family here with me and oppressed by hunger. I cannot give." But no! He gave, and he and his people received far more from the miraculous repast than they had contributed to it. And no doubt they had a form of claim to the twelve basketfuls, if they desired to assert it.

Such is always the way of Jesus and Mary with the princely soul which gives its possessions without reserve or stipulation. The gift avails to satisfy the wants of a vast throng. Yet, one's own needs and intentions, which had appeared to suffer, are filled to overflowing and still the Divine bounty lies scattered about.

Let us, then, hasten to Mary with our poor loaves and fishes, and press them into her arms, so that Jesus and she may multiply them to feed the souls of the millions hungering in the arid desert of this world.

The form of one's ordinary prayers and actions need not be changed as a result of the making of the Consecration. The customary paths of life may be pursued, and one still may pray for one's usual intentions and for all special purposes, but subject in future to Mary's good pleasure.

"But after all, I loudly protest that, having read nearly all the books which profess to treat of devotion to our Lady, and having conversed familiarly and holily with the best and wisest of men of these latter times, I have never known nor heard of any practice of devotion towards her at all equal to the one which I wish now to unfold; exacting from the soul as it does more sacrifices for God, emptying the soul more of itself and of its self-love, keeping it more faithfully in grace and grace more faithfully in it, uniting it more perfectly and more easily to Jesus Christ; and finally being more glorious to God, more sanctifying to the soul, and more useful to our neighbour, than any other of the devotions to her."—(B. Grignion de Montfort.)

OTHER DUTIES OF LEGIONARIES.

1. Regular and Punctual Attendance at the Weekly Meetings of the Praesidium. (See Article on the Scheme of the Legion).

(a) This duty is more difficult when one is tired than when fresh; and in bad weather than in fine; and, generally, when one is tempted to go elsewhere. Yet where is the test but in the difficulty, and where the real merit but in the conquering of difficulties?

(b) It is easier to see the value of doing a work than the value of attendance at a meeting to report on that work, yet the meeting is the prime duty. The meeting is to the work as the root is to the flower; the latter will not live without the former.

(c) Fidelity in attendance in the face of long travelling to and fro is proof of a deep supernatural vision, for natural reasoning suggests that the value of the meeting is outweighed by the waste of time involved in the travelling. But it is not time wasted. It is a part, and a specially meritorious part, of the whole work done. Was Mary's long journey in the Visitation a waste of time?

"To her other virtues Saint Thérése joined an unflinching courage. It was always a principle with her that 'we should go to the end of our strength before we complain.' How many times did she not assist at Matins suffering from vertigo or violent headaches! 'I am still able to walk,' she would say, 'and so I ought to be at my post.' Thanks to this undaunted energy, she performed acts that were heroic."—(Saint Thérése of Lisieux.)

2. Performance of the Weekly Work Obligation.

(a) This work should be **"substantial,"** that is, the Legionary should aim to spend a couple of hours a week at it. Some may not be able to give this amount of time, but on the other hand, the Legionary's gift of himself may, and frequently does, extend to many evenings in the week. The work must represent some definite active duty assigned by the Praesidium, not something dictated by the pleasure of the individual

Legionary. **Prayers or other spiritual exercises, however considerable, do not satisfy this obligation, or even supply in part the place of active work.**

(b) The work is but prayer in another form, and the rules of prayer must be applied to it. No work will persist for long without that supernatural framework. Either, a duty will be easy, in which case it will become monotonous; or if interesting, it will most probably be difficult, and marked by rebuffs and seeming failure. In either event, human considerations will quickly urge its abandonment. Instead, the Legionary must be trained to look through the mists of human sentiments, which obscure every work, for its true outline which is the supernatural. The more that work is like a Cross, the more it is to be esteemed.

(c) The Legionary is a soldier, and duty should not be a less virile thing to the Legionary than it is to the soldiers of earthly causes. Everything that is noble and self-sacrificing and chivalrous and strong in the soldierly character should be found at its height in the true Legionary of Mary, and of course reflected in that Legionary's work.

Soldierly duty may variously mean death, or the monotony of a sentry beat, or the scrubbing of a barrack-floor. But in each case, duty alone is looked to, not what comprises that duty. In all circumstances is found the same fidelity, and defeat or victory do not affect duty. No less solid must be the Legionary's conception of duty: no less thorough its application to each item of work, the most insignificant as well as the most difficult.

(d) The Legionary work is to be done in closest union with Mary. But, in addition, it must be regarded as an essential aim of that work to instil into those, who are the object of it, a knowledge of Mary and a true love of her, which will cause those souls to undertake some form of service of her. An understanding of Mary and a devotion towards her are necessary to the health and development of souls. "For she is a partner in the Divine mysteries and may indeed be described as their guardian. On her, as on the most noble foundation after Jesus Christ, rests the faith of all generations." (Pius X.: Ad Diem Illum). The consideration of Legionaries is invited to other thought-provoking words of Pius X.: "As soon as devotion to the august Mary has driven deep its roots into souls, then—and not till then—will he who labours for those souls see proceed from them fruits of virtue and sanctity corresponding to his toils on their behalf."

"Remember, you are fighting a winning battle, like our Lord on Calvary. Do not be afraid to use the arms He sharpened, nor to share the wounds He bore. Whether the victory should come in your generation or in the next, what is that to you? Carry on the tradition of patient toil; and let the Lord take care of the rest, for it is not for us to know the time nor the moments which the Father has appointed in His power. Take heart and bear the burden of your knighthood with the unflinching courage of the high-souled men who went before you."—(T. Gavan Duffy: The Price of Dawning Day).

3. Legionary Courage.—Each profession calls for its own particular type of courage, and counts as unworthy the member without that courage. The Legion's demand is especially for moral courage. Nearly all of its work consists in the approaching of persons with intent to bring them nearer to God. Occasionally, this will be met by resentment or lack of understanding, which will show itself in various ways, less deadly than the missiles of warfare, but—as experience shows—less often faced. For the thousands who brave the hail of shot and shell, hardly one can be found who will not shrink from the mere possibility of a few jeers, or angry words, or criticism, or even amused looks, or from a fear that he may be thought to be preaching or making an affectation of holiness.

"What will they think? What will they say?" is the chilling reflection, where instead should be the Apostles' thought on the joy of being deemed worthy to suffer contempt for the name of Jesus (Acts v. 41).

Where this timidity, which is commonly called human respect, is allowed free play, all work for souls is reduced to triviality. Look around and see the tragedy of this. Everywhere the Faithful are living in the midst of great communities of pagans or non-Catholics or lapsed Catholics. Five per cent. of these would be won by the first serious effort which presented the Catholic doctrines to them individually. Then that five per cent. would be the thin end of the wedge to conversions on a great scale. But that effort is not made. Those Catholics would wish to make it. Yet they do nothing, because their powers of action are paralysed by the deadly poison of human respect. For different people the latter assumes different labels: "common prudence," "respect for the opinions of others," "hopelessness of the enterprise," "waiting for a lead," and many other plausible phrases; but all of which end in inaction.

It is told in the life of St. Gregory Thaumaturgus that when he was about to die, he enquired of those about him how many unbelievers there were in the city. The reply came quickly: "Seventeen only." The dying Bishop meditated a while on the figure stated, and then remarked: "Exactly the number of believers whom I found when I became Bishop here." Finding seventeen believers, he left seventeen unbelievers. Wonderful! Yet the grace of God has not been exhausted by the passage of the centuries. Faith and courage could draw on it as freely to do the same today. Faith is ordinarily not lacking, but courage is.

Realising this, the Legion must set itself to a deliberate campaign against the operation in its members of the spirit of human respect. Firstly, by opposing to its action the force of a sound discipline. Secondly, by educating its Legionaries to look upon human respect as a soldier would upon cowardice. They must be taught to act in the teeth of its impulses, and brought to realise that love and loyalty and discipline are after all poor things if they do not bring forth sacrifice and courage.

A Legionary without courage! What can we say about such except to apply the expression of St. Bernard: "What a shame to be the delicate member of a Thorn-crowned Head!"

"If you fought only when you felt ready for the fray, where would be your merit. What does it matter even if you have no courage, provided you behave as though you were really brave. If you feel too lazy to pick up a bit of thread, and yet do so for love of Jesus, you gain more merit than for a much nobler action done on an impulse of fervour. Instead of grieving, be glad that, by allowing you to feel your own weakness, Our Lord is furnishing you with an occasion of saving a greater number of souls."—(St. Thérése of Lisieux.)

4. Furnishing at the Meeting a Verbal Report of Work done.—This is a very important duty, and one of the chief exercises which help to sustain interest in the work of the Legion. It is for this latter purpose as much as for the supplying of information to the meeting that the report is intended. A good test of the efficiency of the Legionary is the attention bestowed on the reports, and the manner of presenting them. Each report is a brick in the edifice of the meeting, and the integrity of the latter depends upon the perfection of the reports. Each report missing or defective is a blow at the meeting, which is the source of life.

An important part in the training of the member should lie in the learning of the methods of other members, as disclosed through their reports, and in the hearing of the comments which one's own reports elicit from experienced Legionaries. It follows that if a report gives only meagre information, it cannot be the means of helping either the member who makes it or those who listen to it.

For fuller consideration of the report and the manner of making it, see paragraph 8 of the Section, "Order of the Praesidium Meeting," and paragraph 15 of the Section, "The Meeting and the Member."

"Bear in mind the insistency with which S. Paul calls on Christians to succour, and to be mindful of, and to pray for 'ALL MEN; for God will have all men to be saved . . . for Christ gave Himself a redemption for all' (I Tim. II, 6). And this principle of the universality of duty and of the object of it comes also into this sublime saying of St. John Chrysostom: 'Christians, you will render an account not of yourselves alone but of the whole world.' "—(Gratry: Les Sources).

5. Inviolable Confidence must be Preserved by the Legionaries in regard to what they hear at their meetings or in the course of their visitation. This knowledge comes to them because they are Legionaries, and it would be an intolerable treachery to the Legion for them to divulge it. Reports must, of course, be made to the Praesidium meeting, but even here there must be circumspection. This question is more fully discussed in paragraph 19 of the Section "The Meeting and the Member."

"Keep that which is committed to thy trust."—(I Tim. vi. 20).

6. Every Member should have a Notebook in which will be kept a brief record of cases. (a) It is due to the work to attack it in a business-like way; (b) past and unfinished cases will not be lost sight of; (c) without its aid a suitable report will not be made; (d) it will form a training in habits of order; (e) this tangible record of work done will prove a valuable corrective in that inevitable hour when present failure casts its hue over past performance.

This record should be of a guarded character (i. e., a species of code should be devised), so as not to disclose delicate information to eyes other than those of the Legionary. It should never be entered up in the presence of the persons concerned.

"Let all things be done decently and according to order."—(I. Cor. xiv. 40).

7. The daily recitation by each Legionary of the Catena Legionis (Chain of the Legion), composed principally of the Magnificat, Mary's own prayer, the evening hymn of the Church, "the most humble and grateful, the most sublime and exalted of all the Canticles,"—(B. Grignion de Montfort.)

As the name implies, this is the link between the Legion and the daily life of all its members—Active and Auxiliary and the bond which unites them one to another and to their Blessed Mother. The name is suggestive, too, of the obligation of daily recitation.

Let the idea of a chain, composed of links—each link vital to perfection—be to each Legionary an admonition against forming a broken link in the Legion's chain of daily prayer.

Legionaries whom circumstances have forced to relinquish active membership (and even those whom less worthy reasons have caused to forsake the ranks), should still keep up this beautiful practice and preserve at least this bond with the Legion unbroken during life.

"When I converse familiarly with Jesus, each time I will do this in Mary's name, and partly in her person. Through me she desires to re-live those hours of sweet intimacy and of ineffable tenderness which she spent in Nazareth with her beloved Child. With my aid, she would once more talk delightedly with Him; thanks to me, she would embrace Him and press Him to her bosom, as once she did at Nazareth."—(De Jaegher: The Virtue of Trust).

8. The relations between members. Legionaries are ready enough to honour in a general way the duty of loving their fellow-members, but sometimes do not remember that it must include an attitude of kindliness towards seeming shortcomings. Failure in this direction will deprive the Praesidium of grace, and may have the calamitous consequence of causing others to discontinue membership.

And on the other hand, all should be sensible enough to realise that their membership is something quite independent alike of the fact that they have a President or colleague whom they find pleasant or the reverse; and of real or imagined slights or lack of appreciation or of disagreements, or rebukes, or of other accidental circumstances.

Self-suppression must be the basis of all work in common. Without it even the best workers may threaten the organisation. Those serve the Legion best, who moderate their own individuality, and adapt themselves most completely and most harmoniously to the system. On the other hand, he that says something or does something that departs from the sweetness which should characterise the Legion, may be opening an artery that will result fatally. Let all, then, watch that they do those things which fall to the centre, not from it.

When discussing the attitude of Legionary to Legionary there is special need to refer to what are lightly, but incorrectly called the "petty jealousies." Jealousy is seldom petty in itself. It means acid in the individual heart. It enters all but universally into human relations, poisoning them. In the malevolent, it is a fierce and maddening force which can perpetrate most dreadful things. But likewise it tempts the unselfish and the pure of heart through their sensitive and loving natures. How hard it is to see oneself displaced by others, outpaced in virtue or in performance, put aside in favour of the young! How bitter is the contemplation of one's own eclipse! The best of souls have felt that secret pang, and have learned from it their own amazing weakness. For that bitterness is really smouldering hate, and near to bursting into destructive flame.

Relief may lie in trying to forget. But the Legionary must aim at higher things than such a peace. He must be satisfied with nothing less than victory, a vastly meritorious conquest over stark nature arrayed in battle, the transformation of the half-hate of envy wholly into Christian love. But how can such a wonder be achieved? It will be done by putting into force the fulness of Legionary duty to his fellow-members and to those around him, in each of whom he has been taught to see and reverence his Lord. Each sting of jealousy must be met by this reflection: "That person, whose increase has caused my pain, is none other than the Lord. My feelings, therefore, must be those of John the Baptist. My joy is filled that Jesus is exalted at my expense. He must increase, but I must decrease."

That outlook is heroically holy. It is the raw material for a destiny. What glorious scope it gives to Mary to free from every stain of vanity a soul through which the light will shine unto others (St.

John i. 7), for her fashioning of yet another selfless envoy to prepare the way before the Lord! (St. Mark i. 2).

A precursor must always desire his own eclipse by him whom he announces. An apostle will always see with joy the growth of those around him, and will never think to measure their uprise against his own. He is no apostle who wishes growth to all, except when that growth casts shadow on his own! That jealous thought would show that self is first when self is touched, whereas self in the apostle must be always last. Nay more! the spirit of envy cannot co-exist with true apostleship.

"With her first words of respect and loving salutation, Mary imparts that first sanctifying impulse which purifies those souls, regenerating John the Baptist and in the same moment ennobling Elizabeth.

"But if those first words have worked such great things, what is to be thought of the days, the weeks, the months which followed? Mary is giving all the time. . . . And Elizabeth receives—and why not say it boldly out—receives without jealousy. That Elizabeth, in whom God has likewise effected a miraculous maternity, bows before her young cousin without the slightest secret bitterness at not having been herself the one chosen by the Lord. Elizabeth was not jealous of Mary; and later on, Mary will be incapable of feeling jealous of the love her Son will give to His Apostles. Nor, will John the Baptist have a jealousy of Jesus, when his own disciples leave him for Jesus. Without a trace of bitterness, he will see them go from him, his only comment being: 'He that cometh from above, is above all. . . . He must increase but I must decrease.' (St. John iii, 30, 31)."—(Perroy: L'Humble Vierge Marie).

9. The relations between co-visitors. Legionaries owe an especial duty to their co-visitors. Here is the mystic number "two"—the symbol of charity, upon which all fruitfulness depends: "Two and two He sent them before His face." But "two" must not signify merely two persons who happen to be working together, but a unity such as that of David and Jonathan, whose souls were knit one with the other. Each loved the other as his own soul.—(I. Kings xviii. I.)

The approach to the harvest in this spirit will be truly blessed, so that returning "they shall come with joyfulness, carrying their sheaves."—(Ps. cxxv.)

It will be in small details that the union of co-visitor with co-visitor will be shown and developed. Broken promises, missed appointments, unpunctuality, failures in charity of thought or word, little discourtesies, airs and graces: these dig a trench between the two. No unity is possible.

"Next to religious discipline, the most precious guarantee of blessings and of fruitfulness for a religious society is found in fraternal charity, in harmonious union. We must love all our brothers, without exception, as the privileged and chosen sons of Mary. What we do to each of them, Mary regards as done to herself, or rather as done to her Son Jesus—all our members being called by their vocation to become, with Jesus and in Jesus, the very son of Mary."—(Petit Traité de Marialogie—Marianiste.)

10. Extension of the Legion. Part of the duty of every Legionary shall be the winning of new members. "Thou shalt love thy neighbour as thyself"; hence if the Legion is a blessing to oneself, shall not one seek to bring that blessing to others? If one sees souls lifted by its work, should one not aspire to extend that work?

And finally can any Legionary not strive to gather in new members, if he reflects that the Legion cannot but advance them in the love and in the service of Mary? This, after Jesus Himself, is the greatest blessing which can enter a life. For God has made her—in dependence on Christ and inseparable from Him—the root and the growth and the flowering of the supernatural life.

If not approached and urged thereto, innumerable persons will never think to enter upon the High Way, for which they inwardly yearn, and which would lead on to such wonderful things for themselves, and, through them, for other souls.

"To every man there openeth
A way, and ways, and a way.
And the High Soul climbs the High Way,
And the Low Soul gropes the Low,
And, in between, on the misty flats,
The rest drift to and fro.
And to every man there openeth
A High way and a Low,
And every man decideth
The Way his soul shall go."
—(John Oxenham).

11. Study of the Handbook. It is imperative that every member should, according to capacity, study the Handbook thoroughly. It is the official exposition of the Legion. It contains in briefest possible compass what it is important that every properly equipped Legionary should know of the principles, the laws, the methods, and the spirit of the organisation. Members—and in particular, Officers—who do not study the Handbook cannot possibly work the system properly; while, on the other hand, increased knowledge will always bring increased efficiency. The unusual feature will be presented of interest growing with time, and quality with quantity.

The cry "too long!" is not uncommonly heard, and sometimes, by a strange disproportion, from persons who each day give to the perusal of the newspapers an amount of time adequate for the reading of the major part of the Handbook.

"Too long! too much detail!" Would the serious student of his country's laws, or of medicine, or of military science, apply such words to a text-book of only similar size which embodied all that he was expected to know concerning the particular science he was studying? Far from saying or thinking so, he would in a short week or two have committed to memory every idea, every word even, contained in such a treatise. Verily, "the children of this world are wiser in their generation than the children of light."—(St. Luke xvi. 8.)

And the objection is made that "the Handbook is full of difficult ideas and advanced matters, so that many of our younger and simpler members can hardly understand it. So why not have a simplified Handbook for such as them?" It should not have to be pointed out that such a suggestion is contrary to the first laws of education which require that the student be gradually led on into unknown territory. There is no education at all if a person understands a thing fully in advance. Why should a Legionary expect to understand the Handbook right off, any more than a schoolboy be expected to understand at first sight an Algebra or his first Latin Book? It is the function of the class and the whole idea of education to make clear what was not clear and to implant it as knowledge.

Similarly, it must be the aim of the Praesidium to **educate** its members in the Handbook. This will be done through the spiritual reading, through the Allocutio, and by stimulating the Legionaries in a systematic reading and study of the Handbook.

The learning of the Handbook might fittingly be made a part of the work-obligation of every member during the probationary period, and from time to time should be returned upon to keep knowledge fresh. All of the Handbook should be made the subject of such a study. For even sections such as "Junior Praesidia," "Objections," etc., contain things which bear on the everyday work and on the principles governing the Legion.

"Although he held knowledge to be the result of interior illumination, Saint Bonaventure, nevertheless, was well aware of the labour which study entails. And so, quoting St. Gregory, he put forward as an illustration of study the miracle at the marriage at Cana of Galilee. Christ did not create the wine out of nothing, but bade the servants first fill their pitchers with water. In the same manner the Holy Ghost does not grant spiritual intelligence and understanding to a man who does not fill his pitcher—that is his mind—with water—that is with matter learnt from study. There can be no illumination without effort. An understanding of eternal truths is the reward of the labour of study which no man can avoid."—(Gemelli: The Franciscan Message to the World.)

12. To be in a sense always on duty. As far as prudence will dictate, the Legionary must aim at bringing the spirit of the Legion to bear on all the affairs of daily life and must ever be on the alert for opportunities to promote the general object of the Legion, viz., to destroy the empire of sin, uproot its foundations, and plant on its ruins the standard of Christ the King.

Duty means discipline. Being always on duty means unrelaxed discipline. Therefore, one's speech, and dress, and manners, and general conduct, however simple they may be, must never be such as to disedify. Persons will look for fault in those whom they observe to be active in the cause of religion. Failings, which in others would hardly attract notice, will, in a Legionary, be considered unworthy, and will largely spoil his efforts to do good to others. Nor is this unreasonable. Is it not just to require a goodly standard from those who are urging others on to higher things?

But there must be here, as in all things, right reason. Those who are well-intentioned must not be deterred from apostolic effort by the sense of their own deficiencies. For that would mean the end of all apostleship. Neither are they to think that perhaps it would be hypocritical for them to counsel a perfection which they do not possess. "No," says St. Francis de Sales, "it is not being a hypocrite to speak better than we act. If it were, Lord God! where should we be? We would have to remain silent."

"Mary shows us her Divine Son and addresses to us the same invitation that she did of old to the serving-men at Cana: 'Whatsoever He shall say to you, do ye.'—(St. John ii, 5.) If at her command we pour into the vessels of Charity and Sacrifice the tasteless water of the thousand details of our everyday actions, the miracle of Cana is renewed. The water is changed into a delicious wine, that is to say, into choicest graces for ourselves and for others."—(Cousin.)

13. The making of an enclosed Retreat. Every Legionary should, if at all possible, make an enclosed Retreat once every year. Having personally experienced the benefit of such a Retreat, Legionaries should organise for them, spread abroad the idea of them, and where they are not yet established, aim to have this done.

This is the recommendation of His Holiness Pius XI, in the Encyclical quoted below, to those "companies of pious lay people who ambition to serve the Apostolic Hierarchy by the works of Catholic Action. In these sacred Retreats they will see clearly the value of souls and be inflamed with the desire of helping them; likewise they will learn the ardent spirit of the apostolate, its diligence, its deeds of daring."

Legionaries need not be deterred from trying to cast abroad the benefits of a Retreat by reason of the fact that there is no possibility of providing sleeping accommodation. Practical experience has proved that a form of Retreat, with manifest fruits, can be made by those who spend a single day from morning to night in the making of the Spiritual Exercises: indeed there is no other way of bringing them to the masses. Almost any sort of premises with some grounds attached can be converted to this use for a day, and the expense of providing a few simple meals will not be great.

"The Divine Master Himself was wont to invite His Apostles to the friendly silence of retreat: 'Come apart into a desert place, and rest a little' (Mark vi, 31); and when He left this earth of sorrows to go to heaven, He willed that these same Apostles and His disciples should be polished and perfected in the upper chamber at Jerusalem, where for the space of ten days 'persevering with one mind in prayer' (Acts I, 14), they were made worthy to receive the Holy Spirit: surely a memorable retreat, which first foreshadowed the Spiritual Exercises; from which the Church came forth endowed with virtue and perpetual strength; and in which, in the presence of the Virgin Mary Mother of God, and aided by her patronage, those also were instituted whom we may rightly call the precursors of Catholic Action."—(Pius XI: Encyclical, Mens Nostra, Dec. 20, 1929.)

14. The Legionary must pray as well as work. Though the recital of the Catena Legionis is the only daily duty imposed by the Legion on its Active members, the latter are earnestly urged to include all the prayers of the Tessera in their daily programme. The Auxiliary members' duty requires those prayers, and it would be a reproach to the active units were they to fall short of what the Auxiliaries, in countless numbers, are contributing. It is true that the Auxiliary does not perform the active work. Nevertheless, it is certain that the Auxiliary is of greater service to the Legion's Queen than the Active member who works but does not pray. This is the reverse of the intention of the Legion, which conceives the Active membership as the spearhead of its attack and the Auxiliaries as the haft only.

Moreover, the fervour and perseverance of the Auxiliaries will depend in great measure upon their conviction that they are supplementing a self-sacrificing and in fact heroic service—one far beyond their own. For this additional reason, the Active member must constitute a model and an inspiration to the Auxiliary. But, a genuine inspiration he can hardly be, if his service of prayer falls below that demanded from the Auxiliary, leaving a doubt as to who serves the Legion the better.

Every Legionary, Active and Auxiliary, should enrol in the Confraternity of the Most Holy Rosary. The benefits attaching to membership are immense. See the relative Appendix.

"Of all prayers, the Rosary is the most beautiful and the richest in graces; of all, it is the one which is most pleasing to Mary, the Virgin Most Holy. Therefore, love the Rosary and recite it every day with devotion: this is the testament which I leave unto you so that you may remember me by it."—(Pius X.)

15. Lastly, the Legionary must be devoted to the Eucharist, which is—to use the words of Pius XI.—"the very source and the perpetual inspiration of Catholic Action." To the member who has the interests of the Legion deeply at heart, there is commended the consideration of the Section on the Eucharist which follows, and of the Section on Praetorian membership, and of the Appendix on the Archconfraternity of Mary, Queen of our Hearts.

"The life of man upon earth is a warfare."—(Job vii. 1.)

"Our Lady protects and defends her children and faithful servants. She puts herself round about them, and she accompanies them, like an army in battle array."—(B. Grignion de Montfort.)

THE LEGIONARY AND THE EUCHARIST.

HOLY MASS.

Already it has been stressed that the sanctification of the member is the first object of the Legion. It is moreover, the primary means of action, for only in the measure that the Legionary possesses grace can he be the channel of it to others. Hence it is that the Legionary begins his membership by a request to be filled, through Mary, with the Holy Spirit and to be used as an instrument of His power which is to renew the face of the earth.

The graces, which are thus asked for, flow one and all from the sacrifice of Jesus Christ on Calvary. By means of the Mass, the Sacrifice of the Cross is continued amongst men. The Mass is not a mere symbolic representation of the past, but places really and actually present in our midst that supreme action which Our Lord consummated on Calvary, and which redeemed the world. The Cross was not worth more than the Mass, because the two are but one and the self-same Sacrifice, time and space being pushed aside by the hand of Omnipotence. The Priest and the Victim are the same, the setting alone is different. The Mass contains everything that Christ offered to God, and all that He acquired for men; and the offerings of those who assist at Mass become one with the great offering of Christ.

Therefore to the Mass must the Legionary have recourse if a plenteous sharing in the gifts of Redemption is desired for oneself and for others. By reason of the fact that opportunities and circumstances differ so much, the Legion does not impose any obligation on its members in this matter. Nevertheless, solicitious for them and their work, it urges and implores each one of them to assist frequently—every day if at all possible—at Mass, and at that Mass to receive Holy Communion.

Legionaries are bound to perform their actions in union with Mary. Especially does this apply to the great act of assisting at Mass. Our Blessed Lord did not begin His work of Redemption without the consent of Mary, solemnly asked and freely given. Likewise He did not complete it on Calvary without her presence and her consent, "From this union of sufferings and of will between Mary and Christ, she merited to become most worthily the Restorer of the lost world and the Dispenser of all the graces Jesus purchased by His death and by His Blood." (Pius X.) She stood by the Cross of Jesus on Calvary, representing all mankind there, and at each new Mass the offering of the Saviour is accomplished subject to the same conditions. Mary is present, as ever co-operating with Jesus—**the Woman,** foretold from the beginning, crushing the serpent's head. A loving attention to her ought, therefore, to form part of every Mass rightly heard.

And also with Mary on Calvary were the representatives of a Legion, the Centurion and his men, who took a mournful part in the offering of the Victim, though indeed they did not know they were crucifying the Lord of Glory (1 Cor. II, 8). And, wonder of wonders! grace burst upon them! "Contemplate and see," says St. Bernard, "how piercing is the glance of faith. Consider attentively what lynx-eyes it possesses. On Calvary it enabled the Centurion to see life in death, and to recognise in a dying breath the sovereign spirit." Looking upon their dead and disfigured victim, the Legionaries proclaimed Him to be the very Son of God (St. Matt. xxvii. 54).

These fierce rude converts were the fruits, swift and unexpected, of Mary's prayers. They were strange children that the Mother of Men first received on Calvary, yet they must have ever made the name of Legionary dear to her. So, who can doubt that when her own Legionaries—united to her intentions, part of her co-operation—come to the Daily Mass, she will gather them to her, and give to them the "lynx-eyes" of faith and her own overflowing heart, so that they will enter most intimately (and with surpassing profit) into that continuation of the sublime sacrifice of Calvary.

When they see the Son of God lifted up, they will unite themselves to Him to be but a single victim, for the Mass is their sacrifice as well as His sacrifice. Then they should receive His adorable Body; for this partaking, with the Priest, in the flesh of the immolated

Victim is essential, if the fulness of the fruit of the Divine Sacrifice is to be gathered.

They will understand the essential part of Mary, the new Eve, in those holy mysteries—such a part that "justly may it be said that with Christ she has redeemed the human race." (Benedict XV.) And when they come away, Mary will be with her Legionaries, giving them a share and part in her administration of graces, so that on each and all of those they meet and work for are lavished the infinite treasures of Redemption.

"In the Sacrifice of the Mass we are not merely reminded of the Sacrifice of the Cross in a symbolical form. On the contrary, the Sacrifice of Calvary, as a great supra-temporal reality, enters into the immediate present. Space and time are abolished. The same Jesus is here present who died on the Cross. The whole congregation unites itself with His holy sacrificial will, and through Jesus present before it, consecrates itself to the heavenly Father as a living oblation. So Holy Mass is a tremendously real experience, the experience of the reality of Golgotha. And a stream of sorrow and repentance, of love and devotion, of heroism and the spirit of sacrifice, flows out from the altar and passes through the praying congregation."—(Karl Adam: The Spirit of Catholicism.)

HOLY COMMUNION.

The whole purpose of the Legion of Mary consists in the making of its members holy so that they in turn may bring holiness to the other members of the Mystical Body. Now the Eucharist is the centre and source of grace: therefore, it must be the very keystone of the Legionary scheme. The most ardent activity will accomplish nothing of value if it forgets for a moment that its main object is to establish the reign of the Eucharist in all hearts. For thereby is fulfilled the purpose for which Jesus came into the world. That purpose was to communicate Himself to souls so that He might make them one with Him. The means of that communication is chiefly the Holy Eucharist. "I am," said Christ, "the living Bread which came down from Heaven. If any man eat of this Bread, he shall live for ever; and the Bread that I will give is My Flesh for the life of the world." (St. John vi. 51-52.)

The Eucharist is the infinite good. For in that Sacrament is Jesus Himself, as much present as He was in His home at Nazareth or in the Upper Room at Jerusalem. The Holy Eucharist is no mere symbol of Him, or instrument of His power, but is Jesus Christ Himself substantially. So that she, who had conceived Him and nurtured Him, "found again in the adorable Host the blessed fruit of her womb, and renewed in her life of union with His Sacramental presence the happy days of Bethlehem and Nazareth." (Eymard.)

Many who think Jesus little better than an inspired man, are found to yield Him reverence and imitation. If they thought Him to be more, they would render Him more. What, therefore, should proceed from the Household of the Faith? How inexcusable are those Catholics who believe, but do not practise that belief. That Jesus whom others admire, Catholics possess—ever living in the Eucharist. They have free access to Him and can, and should, receive Him even daily as the food of their souls.

Considering these things, one sees how sad it is that such a splendid heritage should be neglected: That persons having the faith of the Eucharist should nevertheless permit sin and thoughtlessness to deprive them of this vital need of their souls, which Our Lord had in mind for them from the first moment of His earthly existence. Even as a new-born Babe in Bethlehem (which means the House of Bread), He lay on that straw of which He was the Divine Wheat: destined to be made into the heavenly Bread which would make men one with Him and with each other in His Mystical Body.

Mary is the Mother of that Mystical Body. As she once anxiously attended to the wants of her Christ-Child, so now she yearns to feed that Mystic Body, of which she is, no less, the Mother. How her heart is anguished at seeing that her Babe, in His Mystical Body, is hungry—even starving—by reason of the fact that few are nourished as they should be with the Bread Divine, while many receive it not at all. Let those, who aim to be associated to Mary in her maternal care of souls, share her maternal anguish, and strive, in union with her, to allay that hunger of the Body of Christ. Every avenue of Legionary action must be availed of to awaken knowledge and love of the Blessed Sacrament and to dissipate the sin and indifference which keep men from it. Each Holy Communion brought about is truly an immeasurable gain. Through the individual soul, it nourishes the entire Mystical Body of Christ, and causes it to advance in wisdom and growth and grace with God and men.—(St. Luke ii. 32.)

"What! Mary not know in advance, Mary not comprehend the mystery of the Eucharist: when her Son was born at Bethlehem, the House of Bread: when she laid Him on that straw, of which He was the Divine Wheat! Oh! let us elevate our ideas, let us entertain sentiments worthy of this incomparable creature in whom all is marvellous.

" 'The Mother of Jesus,' says Pére de Machault, 'knew that He had come to be the Saviour of men, as much by the instruction that she had received from the Angel, as by the interior light of the Holy Spirit. She knew that one of the principal means that He would employ for our salvation would be to make Himself the Eucharist, the Bread of our souls; consequently she desired to give Him to us in that quality.' This was the sweet meditation of St. Augustine, who contemplating Jesus in His early infancy at His Mother's breast, addressed to her this devout prayer: 'O Virgin, suckle thy Son, nourish our Bread. That infant sheltered in thy arms, whom thou dost press to thy bosom, thou knowest will be our Bread. He is as yet too young. He must reach maturity. He must attain full growth. Take care, then, to feed Him. Give Him the breast that He may grow. Reflect that by suckling and feeding thy Son, thou art suckling and feeding all the faithful whose milk and nourishment He will one day be in the Eucharist!' "—(Tesniére: Our Lady of the Blessed Sacrament.)

THE LEGIONARY AND THE MYSTICAL BODY OF CHRIST.

1. LEGIONARY SERVICE IS BASED ON THIS DOCTRINE.

At the very first meeting of Legionaries the supernatural character of the service, which they were undertaking, was stressed. Their approach to others was to be brimful of kindness, but their motive was not to be that merely natural one. In all those whom they served, they were to see the Person of Jesus Christ Himself. What they did to those others—even the weakest or lowest—they were to remember that they did it to Our Lord Himself, according to his own words: "Amen, I say to you, as long as you did it to one of these my least brethren, you did it to me."—(St. Matt. xxv. 40.)

As at the first meeting, so ever since. No effort has been spared to bring home to Legionaries that this motive is to be the basis of their service, and likewise that the discipline and internal harmony of the Legion rest chiefly upon the same principle. In their officers and in each other they must recognise and reverence Christ Himself. In order to ensure that this transforming truth will remain impressed on the minds of the members, it is incorporated in the Standing Instruction which is read monthly at the Praesidium meeting. In addition, the Standing Instruction emphasises the other Legionary principle that the work must be done in such a spirit of union with Mary that it is she working through the Legionary, who really performs it.

These principles, upon which the Legion system is built, are a consequence of the doctrine of the Mystical Body of Christ. This doctrine forms the main theme of the Epistles of St. Paul. This is not surprising, for it was a declaration of the doctrine which converted him. There was light from Heaven. The great persecutor of the Christians was thrown, blinded, to the ground. Then he heard those overwhelming words: "Saul, Saul, why persecutest thou me?" And St. Paul rejoined: "Who art thou Lord?" And Jesus replied: "I am Jesus whom thou persecutest." (Acts ix. 4-5.) What wonder that these words burnt themselves into the Apostle's soul, so that he must always speak and write the truth which they expressed.

St. Paul describes the union which exists between Christ and the Baptised as being like the union between the Head and the other members of the human body. Each part has its own special purpose and work. Some parts are noble and some are less so; but all are dependent one upon the other, and the same life animates them all. All are put to loss by the failure of one, as all profit by the excellence of one.

The Church is the Mystical Body of Christ and His fulness (Eph. i. 22-23). Christ is its Head, its chief, indispensable, and perfect part, from which all the other members of the body derive their powers, their very life. In Baptism we are attached to Christ by the most intimate ties imaginable. The very limbs of our body are less part of us than we are part of Christ. Realise therefore that mystical does not mean unreal. To use the vehement expression of Holy Scripture, "we are members of His body, of His flesh, and of His bones" (Eph. v. 30). Sacred obligations of love and of service are set up between the members and the Head, and between the members themselves. (I Ep. St. John iv. 15-21.) The image of the body helps to a vivid realisation of those obligations, and this is half-way to the fulfilment of them.

This truth has been described as the central dogma of Christianity. For, in fact, all the supernatural life, all the graces conferred on man, are a fruit of the Redemption. The Redemption itself is based on the fact that Christ and the Church form together but a single mystical person, so that the satisfactions of Christ the Head, the infinite merits of His Passion, belong to His members, who are all the Faithful. This is the reason why Our Lord could suffer for man and expiate faults which He had not Himself committed. "Christ is the Saviour of His Body." (Ephes. v. 23.) The activity of the Mystical Body is the activity of Christ Himself. The faithful are incorporated into Him, and then live, suffer, and die in Him, and in His resurrection rise again. Baptism only sanctifies because it establishes between Christ and the soul that vital connection by which the sanctity of the Head flows into its members. The other Sacraments, and above all the Divine Eucharist, exist for the purpose of intensifying the union between the Mystical Body and its Head. In addition, that union is deepened by the operations of faith and charity, by the bonds of government and mutual service in the Church, by labour and suffering rightly submitted to, and generally by every act of the Christian life. Especially will all of these be effective when the soul acts in deliberate concert with Mary. Mary forms an eminent bond of union, due to her position as Mother of both Head and members. "We are members of His Body, of His Flesh, and of His Bones" (Eph. v. 30), and hence, with equal reality and fulness, children of Mary His Mother. The sole purpose of Mary's existence is to conceive and bring forth the whole Christ, that is the Mystical Body with all its members perfect, and fitly joined together (Eph. iv. 15-16), and one with its Head, Jesus Christ. Mary accomplishes this in co-operation with, and by the power of the Holy Ghost, who is the life and soul of the Mystical Body. It is in her bosom and subject to her maternal care that the soul grows up in Christ and comes to the age of His fulness. (Eph. iv. 13-15.)

"In God's scheme of Redemption, Mary plays a principal part, unlike any other. Among the members of the Mystical Body, she holds a special place of her own, the first after the Head. In the divine organism of the whole Christ, Mary performs a function which is intimately bound up with the life of the entire body. She is its Heart. . . . More commonly, the role of Mary in the Mystical Body is (following St. Bernard) likened to that of the neck, which joins the head to the rest of the body. This comparison exemplifies fairly well the universal mediation of Mary between the Mystical Head and His members. However, the neck does not exemplify as effectively as the heart the idea of the all-important influence exercised by Mary, and of her power, second only to God, in the workings of the supernatural life. For the neck is no more than a connecting link. It plays no part in the initiating or influencing of life. The heart, on the contrary, is a reservoir of life, which first receives into itself the richness which it has then to distribute to the whole body."—(Mura: Le Corps Mystique du Christ.)

2. MARY AND THE MYSTICAL BODY.

The various offices which Mary fulfilled, of nourishing, tending, and loving the actual Body of her Divine Son, are still her offices in regard to each member of the Mystical Body, the least brethren as well as the most honourable. So that, when "the members are mutually careful one for another" (I Cor. xii. 25), they do not act independently of Mary, even when, through thoughtlessness or ignorance, they fail to recognise her presence. They but join their efforts to Mary's efforts. It is already her work, and she has been exquisitely busied on it from the time of the Annunciation to this very day. Hence it is that Legionaries do not really bring Mary to help them in their service of the other members of the Mystical Body. She it is who summons them to assist her. As it is her special and proper work, no one is able to take part in it save by her gracious permission. Let those who attempt to serve their neighbour, and who yet narrow down the place and privileges of Mary, give a thought to this logical consequence of the doctrine of the Mystical Body. Still more, this doctrine has its lesson for those who profess to receive the Scriptures, but who at the same time ignore or decry the Mother of God. Let such persons recall that Christ loved His Mother and was subject to her (St. Luke ii. 51), and that His example obliges the members of His Mystical Body. "Thou shalt honour . . . thy Mother." (Exodus xx. 12.) By divine command, they must render her a filial love. All generations are bound to bless that Mother. (St. Luke i. 48.)

As no one can even attempt the service of his neighbour other than in the company of Mary, similarly, no one can discharge this duty worthily except by entering to some degree into the intentions of Mary. It follows that the more close the union with Mary, the more perfectly is fulfilled the divine precept of loving God and serving one's neighbour. (I John iv. 19-21.)

The special function of Legionaries in the Mystical Body is to guide, console, and enlighten others. That function cannot be adequately discharged without a realisation of the position of the Church as the Mystical Body of Christ. The place and privileges of the Church, its unity, authority, growth, sufferings, miracles, triumphs, its conferring of grace and forgiveness of sin, can only be appreciated by understanding that Christ lives in the Church and through it continues His mission. The Church reproduces the life of Christ and all the phases of His life.

Each member of the Church is summoned by Christ its Head to play its part in the work of the Mystical Body. The more important parts of the Mystical Body are set out by St. Paul as being the rulers, apostles, pastors, and those generally on whom the main burden falls of feeding and building up the Mystical Body (I Cor. xii. 28). The Faithful who are privileged to engage in the apostolate "are not too far removed from this office. They lend a helping hand to the Church and in a measure complete its pastoral ministry." (Pius XI). Thus they rank among the more honourable members with whom Christ is the more intimately united. If their office in the Mystical Body is to be defined, can it not be said of them that they are not too far removed from its heart: that organ whose action sends the blood of Christ coursing through the veins and arteries of the Mystical Body, bringing life and growth with it? But this is Mary's special role. She is indeed the very heart of the Mystical Body, so that to tell Legionaries to immerse themselves in their work is but the same thing as to urge them to bury themselves in Mary.

"The eye cannot say to the hand: I need not thy help, nor again the head to the feet: I have no need of you." (I Cor. xii. 21.) Out of this let the Legionary learn the importance of his share in the apostolate. Not only is he one body with Christ and dependent upon Christ, but likewise Christ, who is the Head, is in a true sense dependent on him; so that even Christ, Our Lord, must say to the Legionary "I need thy help in My work of saving and sanctifying souls." It is to this dependence of the Head on the Body that St. Paul refers when he speaks of filling up in his own flesh what is wanting of the sufferings of Christ. (Coloss. i. 24.) This striking expression does not suggest that Christ's work was in any way imperfect, but simply emphasises the principle that each member of the body must give what it can give towards the working out of its own salvation and that of others.

Let this teach the Legionary his sublime vocation in the Mystical Body. It is to supply what is wanting to the mission of Our Lord. What an inspiring thought for the Legionary: that Christ stands in need of him to bring light and hope to those in darkness, consolation to those who are afflicted, life to those who are dead in sin. It goes without saying that it must be the Legionary's place and duty to imitate in a quite especial manner the surpassing love and obedience which Christ the Head gave His Mother, and which the Mystical Body must reproduce.

"As St. Paul assures us that he fills up the sufferings of Christ, so we may say in truth that a true Christian, who is a member of Jesus Christ and united with Him by grace, continues and carries to completion, by every action performed in the spirit of Jesus Christ, the actions which Jesus Christ Himself performed during the time of His peaceful life on earth. So that when a Christian prays, he continues the prayer of Jesus during His life on earth. When he works, he makes up what was wanting to the life and conversation of Jesus. We must be like so many Jesus' upon earth, continuing His life and His actions, doing and suffering all in the spirit of Jesus, that is to say in holy and divine dispositions."—(St. John Eudes: Kingdom of Jesus.)

3. SUFFERING IN THE MYSTICAL BODY.

The mission of the Legionaries brings them into close touch with humanity, and especially with suffering humanity. Therefore, they should possess insight into what the world insists on calling the problem of suffering. There is not one who does not bear through life a weight of woe. Almost all rebel against it. They seek to cast it from them, and if this be impossible, they lie down beneath it. Thus are frustrated the designs of Redemption, which require that suffering must have its place in every fruitful life, just as in weaving the woof must cross and complement the warp. While seeming to cross and thwart the course of man's life, suffering in reality gives that life its completeness.

For, as Holy Scripture teaches in every page, it is for us "not alone to believe in Christ, but also to suffer for Him" (Philip i. 29); and again: "If we be dead with Christ Jesus, we shall live also with Him. If we suffer, we shall also reign with Him." (2 Tim. ii. 11. 12.)

That moment of our death in Christ is represented by a Cross, all dripping with Blood, upon which our Head has just finished His work. At the foot of that Cross stands a figure, so desolate that it seems impossible for her to continue to live. That woman is the Mother alike of the Redeemer and of the redeemed. It was first from her veins that the blood was drawn which now lies scattered cheaply about, but which has ransomed the world. That Precious Blood will henceforth flow through the Mystical Body, forcing life, so to speak, into every crevice of it. But all the consequences of this flowing must be understood, so that they can be applied. That precious stream brings to the soul the likeness of Christ; but it is the Christ complete: not merely the Christ of Bethlehem and Thabor—the Christ of joy and glory, but as well the Christ of pain and sacrifice—the Christ of Calvary.

Every Christian should be made to realise that he cannot pick and choose in Christ. Mary realised this fully even in the joyful Annunciation. She knew that she was not invited to become only a Mother of Joys, but the Woman of Sorrows as well. But she had always given herself utterly to God, and now she received Him completely. With full knowledge, she welcomed that Infant Life with all it stood for. She was no less willing to endure anguish with Him than she was to taste bliss with Him. In that moment, those Sacred Hearts entered into a union so close as to approach identity. Henceforth, they will beat together in and for the Mystical Body. Thereby Mary has become the Mediatrix of all Graces, the Spiritual Vessel which receives and gives Our Lord's Most Precious Blood. As it was with Mary, so shall it be with all her children. The degree of man's utility to God will always be the closeness of his union with the

Sacred Heart, whence he can draw deeply of the Precious Blood to bestow it on other souls. But that union with the Heart and Blood of Christ is not to be found in a phase of His life, but in the life entire. It is as futile, as it is unworthy, to welcome the King of Glory and to repulse the Man of Sorrows, for the two are but the one Christ. He who will not walk with the Man of Sorrows has no part in His mission to souls, nor share in its sequel of glory. Consider, therefore, and it will be seen that suffering is always a grace. When it is not to bestow healing, it is to confer power. It is never merely a punishment for sin. The sufferings of the sinner are united to Our Lord's own sufferings, and become of priceless worth; while on the other hand, the Passion of Our Lord overflows, as an inestimable privilege, into the bodies of the sinless and the saintly in order to conform them ever more perfectly to His own likeness. This interchange and blending of sufferings is the basis of all mortification and reparation.

A simple comparison with the circulation of the human body will make this place and purpose of suffering more vivid. Consider the hand. The pulse which throbs in it is the beat of the heart. The warm blood from the heart courses through it. That hand is one with the body of which it forms part. If the hand grows cold, the veins contract and the flow of the blood is impeded. As it grows colder, the flow diminishes. If the chill is such that the movement of blood ceases, frost-bite sets in, the tissues begin to die, the hand becomes lifeless and useless. It is as a dead hand, and if left in that condition, gangrene will result. Those stages of cold illustrate the possible states of members of the Mystical Body. These may become so unreceptive of the Precious Blood flowing through that Body, that they are in danger of dying, like the gangrenous limb which must be cut off. It is plain what must be done in the case of a chilled limb. The blood must be induced to circulate again in order to restore it to life. The forcing of the blood through the shrunken arteries and veins is a painful process; yet that pain is a joyful sign. The majority of practising Catholics are as limbs not actually frost-bitten. Scarcely even (in their self-satisfaction) do they regard themselves as chilled. Yet they are not receiving the Precious Blood to the degree that Our Lord wills for them. So He must force His life upon them. The movement of His Blood, dilating their reluctant veins, gives pain; and this makes the sorrows of life. Yet, when this idea of suffering is grasped, should it not turn sorrow into joy. The sense of suffering becomes the sense of Christ's close presence.

"Jesus Christ has suffered all that He had to suffer. No more is anything wanting to the measure of His sufferings. His Passion then is finished? Yes: in the Head; but there remains the Passion of His Body. With good reason, therefore, does Christ, still suffering in His Body, desire to see us share in His expiation. Our very union with Him demands that we should do so. For as we are the Body of Christ and members one of the other, all that the Head suffers, the members ought to endure with it."—(St. Augustine.)

DUTIES OF OFFICERS OF PRAESIDIA.

THE SPIRITUAL DIRECTOR.

As the Legion judges its success entirely according to the spiritual qualities developed in its members and brought to bear by them on their work, it follows that the Spiritual Director, on whom the duty primarily falls of inspiring the members with these qualities, is the very mainspring of the Praesidium. He will attend its meetings and he will, together with the President and the other Officers, take care that the rules are kept, and the Legion system carried out both in the spirit and the letter. He will guard against all abuses, and he shall uphold all due Legionary authority.

If his Praesidium is worthy of the name, he has within it the special zeal and possibilities of his parish. But it depends on him for its work, which should be of a worthy and difficult kind. It depends on him for spurring on, because interior reluctances and external barriers have to be broken down. It looks to him to be the animating principle of its spirituality. So much in fact depends on him that Pius XI. puts it thus: "My fate is in thy hands." It would be a sorrow if even in a single case that sense of trust should be misplaced; if even one little band, wishful to do its best for God and Mary and souls, should be left straying, truly a flock without its shepherd! What would the chief shepherd say of such a one, to whom he also had looked to be "the soul of the association, the inspiration for all good undertakings, the source of zeal"? (Pius XI.)

The Spiritual Director (or to describe more accurately the varied part he is called upon to fill—the Director) will regard his Praesidium as a novice-master would those placed under his care, and will seek incessantly to develop their spiritual outlook and to elicit in them acts and qualities proper to a Legionary of Mary. It will be found that these spiritual qualities will rise to the heights to which they are summoned, so that the Spiritual Director need not fear to make his call one to heroic virtue, or to place before his members work requiring heroic qualities to perform. But likewise he shall insist upon an unvarying fidelity in the minor details of their duty as the essential foundation for great achievement. Though character may be shown in the big moments, it is in the small moments that it is made.

He will see to it that his members do not approach their work in a spirit of self, and will thus ensure that they return neither elated by success nor depressed by apparent failure, prepared, if bidden, to return a thousand times to the most disagreeable or most depressing duty.

He will see that they supplement a fearless and thorough execution of their active work by prayer for it and by acts of self-sacrifice, and he will teach them that it is just at the time when all ordinary means have failed, when things are humanly speaking hopeless, that the Queen of the Legion, their Mother, can be turned to with most certain confidence, and will grant them the victory.

Essentially it will be the duty of a Spiritual Director of the Legion of Mary to fill all his members with an enlightened and most intense love of the Mother of God, and in particular for those privileges of hers which the Legion specially honours.

As a member of the Praesidium, the Spiritual Director will take part in its transaction of business and in its various discussions, and will be "as necessity demands, teacher, counsellor, and guide." (Pius X.) He should, however, be careful that he does not find himself assuming as well the duties of President. Should there be a tendency in this direction, it will not be for the good of the Praesidium. If to his prestige as Priest, and his infinitely wider knowledge of life, is added the taking and conducting of the business by him, the effect upon the meeting will be overwhelming. It will be found that the consideration of each case will take the form of a dialogue between the Spiritual Director and the Legionary concerned, in which the President and the members at large will play no part, remaining silent from a feeling (especially to be counted on in the case of women) that their intervention would bear the complexion of an effort to interfere with the judgment of the Spiritual Director. With the discontinuance of its free and home-like discussion of cases, the meeting will have lost what is at once its chief element of attractiveness, its principal educative force, and its greatest source of health. Such a Praesidium will do no work on the occasion of the absence of the Spiritual Director, and may collapse in the event of his departure.

In case a Praesidium undertakes the work of study, the Spiritual Director will supervise the choice of books to be read. He will exercise a vigilant censorship on this work, and he shall allow no doctrines to be proposed to the members but such as are in full accord with the authentic principles of the Church.

Immediately after the recitation of the Catena, a short talk, preferably by way of commentary on the Handbook (see Order of Meeting—Allocutio) should be given by the Spiritual Director. In the event of his absence, this duty devolves upon the President.

Immediately after the conclusion of the Final Prayers of the Meeting, he shall impart his Blessing to the members.

"Christ actually did appoint a Priesthood, which should not only represent Him and stand for Him, but should in a certain sense be Himself—that is to say, that He should exercise divine powers through its agency; and that devotion and reverence towards the priest should be a direct homage to the Eternal Priesthood of which the human minister is a partaker."—(Benson: Friendship of Christ.)

THE PRESIDENT.

1. The chief duty of the President shall be to attend at the meetings of the Curia to which the Praesidium is attached, and by this and by other means to keep the Praesidium firmly united with the main body of the Legion.

2. In the meetings of the Praesidium, the President shall occupy the chair and conduct the business. He shall allocate the work and receive the members' reports on their work. He shall remember that he is there as the Legion's trustee for the faithful carrying out of the system in all its details. Default in this trusteeship is an act of infidelity to the Legion. The armies of the world would call it treachery and would visit the offender with the severest penalties.

3. He shall be primarily charged with the responsibility of seeing that the room of meeting is ready (i. e. as regards light, heat, seating, etc.) for the meeting to begin at the due time.

4. He shall begin the meeting punctually at the appointed hour, interrupt the proceedings at the ordained time for the recitation of the Catena, and bring the meeting to a conclusion at the prescribed time. In this connection, it is suggested that the President keep a watch before him on the table.

5. He shall give the Allocutio in the absence of the Spiritual Director.

6. He shall instruct and supervise the other officers in the performance of their duties. But it is not to be thought that these latter duties are confined to the special responsibilities of their own offices. It should be obvious that the things here set forth as Presidential duty could not possibly be discharged by the President unaided. Therefore the presidential responsibility and initiative must be shared with others. The ideal is that **all** the officers should combine as a team to run the Praesidium, between them covering perfectly what has to be done. The President must train the other officers in this ideal.

7. He shall ever be on the look-out for members of special merit, whom he can recommend to the Curia in connection with vacant officerships in his own Praesidium or elsewhere. As the efficiency of a Praesidium depends on the excellence of its officers, it should be the glory of a President to raise up worthy ones, and thus provide for the future of the Legion.

8. He shall set a high level of spirituality and zeal to all his fellow-Legionaries, but not in such a way as to take upon himself work which his members should be doing. Were the President to do the latter, he might indeed show zeal, but he would not set example; for he is preventing those, for whom the example is intended, from following his lead.

9. He shall remember that whispered or indistinct reports are the enemy of the meeting, and during the latter he must himself speak in a tone of voice which will ring throughout the room. If he relax in this he will find his members delivering reports which can only be heard with an effort, and at once will the meeting languish.

10. It shall be his duty to see that each member makes an adequate report, to lead on by judicious questioning the inexperienced or shy members, and on the other hand to moderate those reports which, though excellent in themselves, threaten to absorb too great a proportion of the time available.

11. He shall cultivate the spirit of fraternity in the Praesidium, knowing that when this is gone all is gone. He shall himself safeguard it by exhibiting the deepest affection for each and every one of his members, and in general by setting the example of a great humility. He shall receive Our Lord's words: "He that will be first among you shall be your servant."—(St. Matt. xx. 27.)

12. He shall encourage his members to express their views and volunteer their help in cases not their own, and thus develop in them a lively sense of interest in all the work of the Praesidium.

13. He shall satisfy himself that the work of each Legionary is being done:—

(a) in the right spirit;
(b) along the right lines;
(c) that all the good which the Legion would wish to see reaped in each case is in fact achieved;
(d) that old work is from time to time returned upon, and
(e) that an enterprising spirit is kept alive in the members by the regular breaking of new ground, where possible.

14. He shall secure from the members the degree of effort and self-sacrifice of which they are capable. To require from a Legionary of good capacity some petty task, is to do a great injustice to that Legionary, whose eternity is being shaped. There are none who will not take things easily if they are encouraged to do so. Thus the President must goad them on to God, who wants from each one of His creatures the maximum of its capacity.

15. A President, who feels that the Praesidium is drifting into careless ways or loss of spirit, should consult privately with the Curia (i. e. with its Officers) as to the proper course to be adopted, and if his own transfer to ordinary membership is recommended, he should most humbly abide by that decision which will be full of blessings for him.

16. He shall, like every other member, satisfy the

obligations of membership by doing the ordinary work of the Praesidium. It would appear superfluous to enunciate this rule in the case of a President, did not experience prove the contrary.

17. Finally, he must never be found wanting in those things which a leading authority on Catholic Action (Card. Pizzardo) insists must characterise in a very special manner every leader in that movement: the virtue of docility to ecclesiastical authority, the spirit of self-denial, of charity and harmony with other organisations and with the individuals belonging to those organisations.

"From the moment I was given the charge of souls, I saw at a glance that the task was beyond my strength, and quickly taking refuge in Our Lord's arms, I imitated those babes who when frightened hide their faces on their father's shoulder: 'Thou seest, Lord,' I cried, 'that I am too small to feed Thy little ones, but if through me Thou wilt give to each what is suitable, then fill my hands; and without quitting the shelter of Thy arms, or even turning my head, I will distribute Thy treasures to the souls who come to me asking for food. When they find it to their liking, I shall know that it is not to me they owe it, but to Thee; while if on the contrary they complain, finding fault with its bitterness, I shall not be at all disturbed, but shall try to persuade them it comes from Thee, and will take care to give them none other.' "—(Autobiography of St. Thérése of Lisieux.)

THE VICE-PRESIDENT.

1. It shall be the duty of the Vice-President to attend the meetings of the Curia, and to preside at the Praesidium meeting in the event of the absence of the President. It is, however, to be understood that the post does not carry any right of succeeding to a vacant presidency.

The following advice, adapted from the Manual of the St. Vincent de Paul Society, has equal application to the Vice-President of a Praesidium: "When the President is absent, especially for some time, it should be understood that the Vice-President has all his powers and stands entirely in his place. An Association should never stand still for want of a member, and this would be the case if the members did not venture to do anything in the President's absence. It is therefore not alone his right, but it is a conscientious duty on the part of the Vice-President to supply fully the place of the President when absent or prevented from attending, in order that, when the latter returns, he may not find that everything has been languishing for want of him."

2. He shall generally assist the President in the management of the Praesidium and the carrying through of business. Too often it is supposed that this duty only begins when the President is absent. This is an error which will prove disastrous both to the Vice-President and to the Praesidium. The correct view is that the Vice-President should co-operate intimately in the presidential action. The pair should be in relation to the Praesidium much as the father and mother are to the home, or as the Commander-in-Chief and Chief-of-Staff are to an army. The Vice-President supplements the President. He is meant to be an active officer, not a reserve officer, or a passive one. During meetings, his special function is to supervise the innumerable things which are outside the attention of the President, but on which may depend the proper working of the Praesidium.

3. In particular the Vice-President is charged with the duty of looking after membership. He should make the acquaintance of new-comers on the occasion of their first attendance, and welcome them to the Praesidium; introduce them to the other members before or after the meeting; see that they are assigned to work, instructed in the obligations of membership (including that of daily recitation of the Catena), and made aware of the existence and details of the Praetorian degree of membership.

4. He shall keep and mark up the Praesidium rolls of membership; take necessary action when the time of probation comes to an end; note the fact that a member may be absenting himself from the meetings; and then, by writing or otherwise, endeavour to prevent a complete falling away from membership.

It is obvious that between those whose membership is never in doubt and those who drop out at once through unsuitability, there must be a large intermediate class whose perseverance in membership will depend upon external or accidental circumstances, and whom the special care of a kindly membership officer would preserve in membership. Be it remembered, too, that the keeping of a member is more important to the Legion than the gaining of a new member. Thus the work of this officer, if faithfully carried through, would be directly responsible for a multitude of good actions and spiritual victories, would rapidly lead to the formation of new Praesidia, and would in itself be an apostolate of quite a special kind.

5. He shall see to it that the duty of prayer for the deceased members is not neglected. That duty is defined elsewhere in a special section.

6. He shall visit the Sick members, or secure that they are visited by other Legionaries.

7. He shall supervise the other members in their efforts to gain and to keep in touch with Auxiliary members, and shall look after the Probation and Auxiliary Registers.

"The knowledge that it was impossible to do anything of myself greatly simplified my task, and confident that the rest would be given me over and above, the one aim of my interior life was to unite myself more and more closely with God. Nor has my hope been ever deceived: each time I have needed sustenance for the souls under my charge I have always found my hands filled. Had I acted otherwise, and relied upon my own strength, I should very soon have been forced to surrender."—(Autobiography of St. Thérése of Lisieux.)

THE SECRETARY.

1. On the Secretary devolves the responsibility of keeping the minutes of the Praesidium. Considerable care should be bestowed upon the preparation of the minutes, which should be read in distinct tones. The minutes play a most important part, both from the manner of reading and from their substance. Well-read minutes, neither too long nor too short, which have

obviously cost the Secretary considerable trouble, set a good headline for the rest of the meeting, and will in no small measure conduce to its efficiency.

2. The Secretary must have regard for his instruments, if he wishes to produce good results. It is a fact, dependent on the structure of the human mind, that even a good Secretary, writing with a pencil or a broken pen on inferior paper, will not ordinarily produce a worthy record. Therefore, the minutes should be written in ink and in a book of good quality.

3. The Secretary does not discharge his work-obligation to the Praesidium by the performance of his secretarial duties alone.

4. He shall attend the meetings of the Curia.

5. He shall punctually furnish all information and all returns which may be required by the Curia, and shall generally be responsible for the correspondence of the Praesidium. The Secretary shall also see that the stationery supplies of the Praesidium are kept at a proper level.

6. Portions of the Secretary's duty may, however, be delegated by the President to other members of the Praesidium.

"In the abstract it seems easy to do good to souls, to make them love God more, and to mould them to one's own ideas. But, when we put our hands to the work, we quickly learn that without God's help it is as impossible to do good to them, as to bring back the sun when once it has set. Our own tastes, our own ideas must be put aside, and in absolute forgetfulness of self we must guide souls, not by our way, but along that particular path which Our Lord Himself indicates."—(Autobiography of St. Thérése of Lisieux.)

THE TREASURER.

1. The Treasurer shall be responsible for the making and receiving of all payments by and to the Praesidium, and for the keeping of full and properly written accounts thereof.

2. He shall see to it that the Secret Bag collection is made at each meeting.

3. He shall pay money only on the direction of the Praesidium, and shall lodge funds in hand to the credit of the Praesidium in such manner as the latter may direct.

4. He shall bear in mind the recommendation as to accumulated funds which is contained in the Article on Funds, and shall from time to time bring the matter before the Praesidium.

5. He shall attend the meetings of the Curia.

"Your little lambs find me severe, I know, Mother, and if they were to read these lines they would say that, so far as they can see, it does not in the least distress me to run after them, and to point out how they have soiled or torn their beautiful white fleece. But whatever they may say, they know in their hearts that I love them with a very great love, and they need have no fear of my imitating 'the hireling . . . who seeth the wolf coming and leaveth the sheep and flieth." (St. John x. 12.)"—(Autobiography of St. Thérése of Lisieux.)

THE TRIBUNE.

1. The Tribune shall attend the meetings of a Women's Praesidium, and shall assist it in its work.

2. He shall especially be charged with the duty of furthering co-operation with other organizations, and of obtaining, through them and other appropriate channels, assistance for those who are found to be in need of it, but which the Praesidium is not itself empowered to give.

To this end he should make himself familiar with the local charitable and welfare system.

3. He shall attend the meetings of the Curia.

"I am ready to lay down my life for my novices, though my affection is so disinterested that I would not have them know it. By God's help, I have never tried to draw their hearts to myself. I have always known that my mission was to lead them to Him, and to you, Mother, who on earth hold His place in their regard, and whom, therefore, they must love and respect."—(Autobiography of St. Thérése of Lisieux.)

ADDITIONAL GRADES OF MEMBERSHIP.

In addition to the ordinary active membership, the Legion recognises three other grades of membership:

1.—MEMBERS LAUREATE.

An honorary or Laureate* degree of membership may be conferred on non-members who have rendered eminent services to the Legion. Councils may recommend names to the Concilium, but to the latter alone belongs the right of conferring the degree.

Laureate members shall share in all the prayers and works and privileges of the Legion.

It cannot be too strongly urged that Laureate membership must constitute a jealously guarded privilege. The greatest thing that the Legion has to offer is its ordinary (including Praetorian) membership, but the Laureate membership is an approximation to it. Now it slights the dignity of ordinary membership, with its regular and laborious weekly round of duty and prayer, to raise to a degree of kinship with it a person who has conferred some ordinary or passing service upon the Legion, or who has merely given a generous subscription.

The services upon which the Laureate membership follows must be really notable. They should indeed be such that it can be declared that they have contributed to the building of the Legion, thereby placing the entire Legion under a lasting debt of gratitude, which can only be acquitted by associating the person in question with the life of the Legion in the capacity of member, and by the bestowing of a permanent share in its works and prayers.

Names of persons deemed worthy of Laureate membership should in the first instance be proposed privately to the Officers of the Concilium and, only if approved by them, then mentioned to the Concilium for decision.

It is trusted that Laureate members will be able to intensify their union with the Legion by taking on the duties defined in the following section.

***Or laurel crowned, having reference to the Roman custom of decking with laurel those whom it was sought to honour.**

"Naturally, she will be more disposed to give to those who give to her. Here is a battle of generosity! But on this field Mary cannot be vanquished. On those good souls who have done anything for her, she lavishes a hundredfold return."—(Texier.)

2.—AUXILIARY MEMBERSHIP.

This membership consists of those who are unable or unwilling to assume the duties of active membership, but who undertake to give the Legion the priceless backing of their prayers. Auxiliary membership is subdivided into two degrees.

One is for Priests, those in Major Orders, and Religious only. These are more particularly designated Adjutores Legionis, or Adjutorians. The other is for the lay-members, who are simply styled "Auxiliaries." This twofold Auxiliary membership is to the Legion what its wings are to a bird. With these wings widely expanded by possession of many Auxiliaries, and beating powerfully under the rhythmic drive of their faithful prayer, the Legion can soar into the higher air of supernatural ideal and effort. It flies swiftly whithersoever it wills, and even the mountains cannot stay its course. But if those wings are folded, the Legion hobbles awkwardly and slowly along the ground, brought to a stop by the slightest obstacle.

A. Adjutorian Membership.

This, the right wing of the praying Legion, is reserved, as stated above, to Priests, those in Major Orders, and Religious. How earnestly the Legion desires union with this consecrated class, which has been specially deputed to lead lives of prayer and close intimacy with God, and which forms in the Church a glorious power-station of spiritual energy! Effectively linked up with that power-station, Legionary machinery would pulsate with an irresistible force. Hence, in the urgent interest of the Legion, appeal is to be made to every Priest and Religious to place a little of themselves in the service of this crusade of Mary. They have it in their power to become its driving-force.

Consideration of the conditions of membership will show how sweet a burden they assume; one so light that the fullest day will not feel it; which conflicts with no duty of Rule; which indeed does nothing more than prudently offer the superintendence of their spiritual treasures to Her whom God has already appointed His own Treasurer. Where is the room for misgiving?

"Give me," said Archimedes of old, "a lever and a support for it, and I will lift the Earth itself." United to Mary and to an active Apostolate which lives by her, the Adjutorians will find therein that essential support on which to rest the long lever of their holy prayers, which then become omnipotent to uplift the burdened souls of the entire world and move away its mountainous problems.

It is recognised that the prayers of Priests and Religious are often subject to so many obligations that the fulfilment of the definite prayer-obligation of the ordinary Auxiliaries would be difficult or the cause of scruple. Hence, the Adjutorian is allowed the option of fulfilling his obligations of membership in either of two ways: (1) by the performance of the definite service of prayer prescribed for ordinary Auxiliary membership at (B) below; or (2) in a manner less definite, but nevertheless one from which the greatest blessings will flow to souls through the Legion, that is by the daily recitation of the Catena Legionis (i. e., the Magnificat with Antiphon, Versicle, Responsory, and Prayer of Our Lady Mediatrix of all Graces), together with the following Formula of Offering in substance or in intention: "Mary Immaculate, Mediatrix of all Graces, I place at your disposal such portion of my daily Masses, Communions, prayers, works, and sufferings as is permitted to me."

It will be observed that in the above Formula, Adjutorians do not make their offering directly for the Legion, but only indirectly through the Intentions of Our Blessed Lady. The Legion is satisfied with what may come to it through this channel, and it does not press for any more.

Mary's Intentions are the interests of the Sacred Heart. They take in every need of the Church. They cover the whole apostolate. They extend the whole world over. They descend also to the Holy Souls abiding their time in the abode of Purgatory. Zeal for Mary's intentions is comprehensive care for the needs of Our Lord's Body. For she is no less the solicitous Mother now than she was in the days of Nazareth. Conformed to her intentions, one goes straight to the goal, which is God's Will. But making one's own approach, what a tortuous route results: will it ever bring one to the journey's end?

It will be noticed that the daily recitation of the Legion Proper Prayer (i. e. the prayer beginning with the words: "Confer, O Lord, on us") is not obligatory on Adjutorians who fulfil their Legionary service under method (2) above. But obviously it will strengthen the alliance of the Adjutorian with the Legion if this distinctive item of Legionary prayer is taken on.

The Adjutorians are welcome at all Legion functions.

The question is sometimes asked if an Adjutorian can also become a Praetorian. The answer is in the negative. For the Praetorian membership is a degree of Active membership. Moreover, as the daily prayer of the Adjutorian includes (with the possible exception of the Legion Proper Prayer) every item of the Praetorian prayer-duty, there would be no purpose in the Adjutorian's assuming the additional title of Praetorian.

The considerations, set out at (C) below, apply in their measure to the Adjutorian membership, and should be read along with the foregoing.

"In the Cenacle, where by the outpouring of the Holy Ghost the Church was definitely founded, Mary begins to exercise visibly, in the midst of the apostles and the disciples gathered together, a role which she will continue ever after to exercise in a more secret and intimate manner: that of uniting hearts in prayer and

of giving life to souls through the merit of her all-powerful intercession: 'All these were persevering with one mind in prayer with the women, and Mary the Mother of Jesus and with His brethren. (Act. I, 14.)"—(Mura: Le Corps Mystique du Christ.)

B. The Auxiliary Degree for Lay-members.

This degree is the left wing of the Legion's praying army. Its members are simply styled "Auxiliaries." Their Legionary service consists in the daily recitation of the prayers comprised in the Tessera, namely: the Invocation and Prayer of the Holy Ghost; five Decades of the Rosary and the invocations which follow them; the Catena; and the prayers described as "Concluding Prayers." These may be divided throughout the day, as convenient.

This Auxiliary service is to be offered for the intentions of Our Blessed Lady.

Persons, whose daily Rosary is already firmly bound to particular intentions, may become Auxiliaries without obligation to say an additional Legion Rosary.

The value of this Auxiliary service will be greatly enhanced if the Auxiliary will, **in addition to the obligations already prescribed,** make the daily Formula of Offering which is prescribed above for the Adjutorians.

There are no age-limits in the case of Auxiliary membership.

"He who prays helps all the souls of men. He helps his brethren by the saving and powerful magnetism of a soul that believes, knows, and wills. He supplies what S. Paul demands from us above all things: prayers, supplications, and acts of thanksgiving on behalf of all men. 'Cease not to pray and to make supplication at all times in the Holy Ghost.' (I Tim. ii, I). And does it not seem that if you cease to watch, to insist, to make efforts, to hold fast, everything will relax, the world will relapse, your brethren will feel in themselves less strength and support? Yes, surely it is so. Each one of us in a measure bears up the world, and those who cease to work and to watch overburden the rest."—(Gratry: Les Sources.)

C. General Considerations affecting both Degrees of Auxiliary Membership.

(a) Supplementary Service. The Legion appeals to Auxiliaries of both degrees to regard the essential conditions of membership, not as limits of service, but as a minimum, which they will chivalrously supplement by many other prayers and acts made specially with this intention.

It is suggested to Priest-Adjutores that they should in all their Masses make a special memento, and even occasionally offer the Holy Sacrifice, for Mary's intentions and the Legion. Other Auxiliaries might, even at the expense of some sacrifice, find it possible to have an occasional Mass offered for the same intention.

However generously the Auxiliary may give to the Legion, nevertheless he receives one hundredfold, one thousandfold, one millionfold in return. And how is this? It is because the Legion teaches its Auxiliaries—no less than its Active members—how great is Mary, enlists them in soldierly service for her, and makes them love her properly. All this is something so great that words like millionfold do not measure the gain. It raises the spiritual life to a higher plane, and thereby assures a higher eternity.

(b) Who can refuse to Mary the gift defined in either division above? For she who is the Queen of the Legion is, as well, Queen of the World and of all its departments and concerns, so that to give to her is to give where the need is greatest, where one's prayers will accomplish most.

It will be observed that Auxiliaries are not called upon to make their Offering on behalf of the Legion, but in favour of Our Blessed Lady to do with as she thinks fit. As their offering to her is made in their capacity as Legionaries, it is probable that in the distribution of the treasure placed at her disposal, she will have regard to the needs of the Legion. But it is also conceivable that the Legion might receive nothing; nor does the Legion desire to receive anything which would do more good elsewhere.

(c) In administering the store thus placed in her hands, Mary Immaculate will have regard to the requirements of one's ordinary life and duties and to all existing obligations. And so the question may arise: "I would wish to join, but I have already given everything to Mary with complete abandon, or to the Holy Souls, or to the Missions. Everything is gone. There is nothing left over for the Legion, so of what use am I to its Auxiliary ranks?" The Legion answers: It is of greatest benefit for the Legion to gain so unselfish a person. This anxiety to help the Legion is in itself an additional prayer, a proof of special purity of intention, an irresistible call upon the limitless generosity of the guardian of the Divine treasury. Certain it is that if you join she will respond, and that the new intention will gain while the old intentions will not lose. For it is the art of this most wonderful Queen and Mother that though she has availed of our offer and helped others liberally from our spiritual treasures, yet we ourselves have grown strangely richer. Her intervention has meant the doing of an extra work. A marvellous multiplication has taken place: what Grignion de Montfort calls a secret of grace and thus describes: "Inasmuch as our good works pass through the hands of Mary, they receive an augmentation of purity and consequently of merit and of satisfactory and impetratory value. On this account they become more capable of solacing the Souls in Purgatory and of converting sinners than if they did not pass by the virginal and liberal hands of Mary."

Every life has need of the magic of this admirable transaction, where what we have is taken, placed at usury, accomplishes its work, and then returns with increment. This magic can be found in the gift to Mary of a faithful Auxiliary membership.

(d) Possibly because of the number of souls in stress with which it is in touch, Mary seems to have given to her Legion some little of her own irresistible appeal to the heart. Legionaries will not find it difficult to enlist their friends in this auxiliary service so vital to the Legion, and so valuable to the Auxiliaries themselves who are thereby associated to Legion membership, with share in all the prayers and works of the Legion.

(e) The discovery, too, has been made that the

membership of the Legion's Auxiliary or praying ranks has the same power to catch the imagination that active membership possesses. Persons who otherwise would not think of saying the Rosary every day, are found to be faithfully carrying out the obligations of Auxiliary membership, which demands the daily recitation of all the prayers on the Legion prayer-card, already detailed. Numbers in workhouses and other institutions, who had lost heart, have gained an interest in life through joining the Legion Auxiliaries, while multitudes in villages, and living otherwise in circumstances which tend to make religion a tame thing, if not a matter of routine, have through their Auxiliary membership realised that they are of importance to the Church; nay, have found themselves taking a proprietary interest in the Legion, reading with intense interest any scrap of news about it they chance to see. They feel themselves to be part of its most distant battles for souls. They realise it to be dependent upon their prayers. Word from the Praesidia winning souls in some wildwest mining-camp or Red Indian village fills their drab lives with the throb of those far-distant doings. Their existences have become transformed by that most inspiring of ideas, the sense of participation in a crusade. And even the holiest of lives require the stimulation of such an idea.

(f) It should be the object of every Praesidium to bring every Catholic in its area into Auxiliary Membership. Thereby a favourable soil is provided for the working of other aspects of the Legion apostolate. A visitation for this purpose, implying a compliment, will be universally well received and a goodly response may be anticipated.

(g) It is the world-wide adventure and battle for souls of the Legion, rather than the local needs, which are to be represented to the Auxiliaries as the object of their service of prayer. The conception should be placed before their minds that though they are not in the fighting ranks, nevertheless they play an essential part, comparable to that of the munition workers and the supply services, without which the fighting forces are powerless.

(h) Persons should not be lightly accepted as Auxiliaries. In advance they should be made fully acquainted with the obligations, and there should be reasonable assurance that they will be true to them.

(i) With a view to intensifying the interest of the Auxiliaries in the service undertaken by them, and thus (1) in the present, improving its quality and ensuring its perseverance; and (2) in the future, leading them on to full membership; they should be given an insight into the work of the Legion.

(j) The keeping in touch with the Auxiliaries, for the purpose of preserving their membership and interest will be necessary, and will provide admirable work for certain of the Legionaries whose ideal should be the leading on still further of their charges. See the relative Article in Section on Works, which defines the spirit in which this visitation is to be undertaken.

(k) Every Auxiliary should be made aware of the great benefits attaching to membership of the Confraternity of the Most Holy Rosary. As the Auxiliary is already saying more than the amount of prayer required by the Confraternity, the only additional obligation entailed by joining the latter is the registration of name and blessing of one's beads by a Priest having the necessary faculties.

(l) Likewise, in the interest of the full development of the Auxiliary Soldiers of Mary, the "True Devotion" —or entire consecration of one's life to Mary—should at least be explained to them. Many of them might be glad to undertake this fuller service of her.

Lest some should be inclined to think that this Devotion can be practised only by persons of advanced spirituality, it is important to record that it was to souls just emerging from the bondage of sin, and to whose darkened memory it was necessary to recall the elementary truths of the Catechism, that the Blessed Grignion de Montfort spoke of the Rosary, of devotion to Mary, and of the Holy Slavery of Love.

(m) It may be possible, and considered desirable, to set up amongst the Auxiliaries some loose form of organisation comprising meetings or rallies of its own. Such a network in the community would tend to permeate it with the apostolic and prayerful ideals of the Legion, and generally to carry the principles of Catholic Action to the whole population.

(n) In particular, a Parish Society based on Auxiliary membership would be nothing less than any other Society. But in addition, it would be the Legion, with all the Legion's warmth and colour. The periodic meetings of such a Society would keep its members in touch with the spirit and needs of the Legion and ensure fidelity to their obligations as Auxiliaries.

(o) Auxiliaries must not be employed on ordinary active Legion work. Proposals to utilise them in this way are at first sight attractive. It seems a good thing to lead on the Auxiliaries. But consideration will show that what is really at stake is the doing of Legionary work without the Legion meeting, in other words the setting aside of the vital condition of active membership.

(p) Where deemed desirable or possible, Auxiliaries may participate in the Acies, which in such circumstances forms an admirable function for them and brings them into intimate touch with the Active Legionaries. Auxiliaries who are prepared to make the individual Act of Consecration, should make it after the Active Legionaries.

(q) The Invocation to be inserted on the Tessera for Auxiliary members shall be "Mary Immaculate, Mediatrix of all Graces, pray for us."

(r) The Legion's call to the Active member to be "ever on duty for souls" is addressed likewise to the Auxiliary.

(s) The Auxiliary, just as much as the active member, must strain every nerve to bring others into Legionary service, so that presently the Catena Legionis will truly link parish to parish and envelop the whole world in a golden network of prayer.

(t) It is frequently suggested that the prayers of the Auxiliary service should be reduced or changed to meet the case of blind or illiterate persons or of children. Apart from the fact that an obligation is inclined to lose its binding force according as it becomes less definite, the impossibility of administering such a concession should be manifest. It could not and would not long be withheld from the less illiterate, the partly blind, or the very busy. In time, the relaxation would become the ordinary practice.

No! The Legion must insist upon the performance of the standard service. If this is beyond the powers of certain persons, they cannot be Auxiliaries. But they can give invaluable help by praying for the Legion in their own way, and they should be encouraged thereto.

(u) It is allowable to require the Auxiliary to defray the cost of the Tessera and of a certificate of membership. But otherwise no subscription shall be payable in respect of Auxiliary membership.

(v) A Roll of its Auxiliary members, containing names and addresses, and subdivided as to Adjutorians and ordinary Auxiliaries, shall be kept by each Praesidium and shall be submitted periodically to the Curia or to its authorised visitors. This Roll shall be examined carefully with a view to seeing that it is being properly kept, that new members are being zealously sought for, and that existing members are being visited occasionally to keep them in mind of their obligations.

(w) Membership of the Auxiliary degree is effected by the entry of name upon the Auxiliary Roll of any Praesidium. This Roll shall be in the care of the Vice-President.

(x) Names of candidates for the Auxiliary degree shall be placed on a provisional list until three months Probation has been served. Then the Praesidium must satisfy itself that the obligations of membership have been faithfully discharged before placing the candidate's name on the Auxiliary Roll.

"What recompense will our good Jesus give us for the heroic and disinterested action of making a surrender to Him, by the

hands of His holy Mother, of all the value of our good works? If He gives a hundredfold, even in this world, to those who for His love quit outward and temporal and perishable goods, what will that hundredfold be which He will give to the man who sacrifices for Him even his inward and spiritual goods?"—(Bl. Grignion de Montfort.)

3.—THE PRAETORIANS.

The Praetorian* degree is a higher grade of Active membership, consisting of those who to the ordinary obligations of membership undertake to add:—(1) the daily recitation of all the prayers comprised in the Tessera of the Legion; (2) Daily Mass and Daily Holy Communion. No one should be deterred from undertaking the Praetorian degree by fears that he will not succeed in attending Mass or receiving Holy Communion absolutely every day. No one can be certain of such exact regularity as this. Anyone, who does not fail normally more often than once a week, may register with confidence as a Praetorian; (3) the daily recitation of some form of Office approved by the Church, such as the Little Office of the Blessed Virgin, the Little Office of the Immaculate Conception, the Franciscan Office (if Tertiaries), or a substantial portion (i.e. Matins and Lauds or the Day Hours) of the Divine Office.†

The following, however, is to be understood:—

(a) This is only a degree of membership and not a separate unit of organisation. Thus, separate Praesidia of Praetorians shall not be set up;

(b) the Praetorian degree of membership is to be regarded as no more than a private contract of the individual Legionary;

(c) nothing implying the smallest degree of moral compulsion is to be resorted to for the gaining of Praetorians. Thus, while Legionaries may,

*The Praetorian Guard was the picked regiment of the Roman Army.

†An edition in English of the Roman Breviary has been compiled by the Benedictines of Stanbrook, and published in quarterly parts of convenient size by Burns, Oates, and Washbourne, London.

and should, frequently be recommended to undertake this degree, no names are to be taken or mentioned publicly;

(d) membership is effected by the entry of name on a special Roll which shall be kept by the President of the Praesidium.

(e) Spiritual Directors and Presidents shall endeavour to increase their Praetorian membership, but shall, as well, keep in touch with existing members to see that obligations continue to be fulfilled.

If the Spiritual Director were willing to allow his name to be inserted in the Praetorian Register, it would intensify his Legionary membership, and bind him still more strongly to his Praesidium. As well, it could not but react favourably upon the growth of the Praetorian membership of the Praesidium.

The Legion anticipates much from the Praetorian degree. It will lead many members on to a life of closer union with God through prayer. The recognition of this degree means the incorporation in the Legion system of a heart of prayer; in which more and more Legionaries will tend to bury themselves; which will inevitably affect the whole spiritual circulation of the Legion; make the Legion more and more instinct with the spirit of reliance upon prayer in all its works; and cause it to realise ever more completely that its chief and true destiny is to spiritualise its members.

"Grow you must; I know it; it is your destiny; it is the necessity of the Catholic name; it is the prerogative of the Apostolic heritage; but a material extension without a corresponding moral manifestation, it is almost awful to anticipate."—(Cardinal Newman: Present Position of Catholics.)

ORDER OF THE PRAESIDIUM MEETING.

1. The Setting of every Meeting shall be uniform. The members should sit around a table, at one end of which for the purpose of the meeting a small temporary altar is erected. On a white cloth of sufficient size is placed a statue of the Immaculate Conception (in the attitude of the distribution of Graces), of height about two feet—flanked by two vases of flowers and two candlesticks with lighted candles. A little to the right of the statue, and a little in advance of it, should be set the Vexillum, which is described in its own Section.

Photographs of the setting of the altar and of the Vexillum will be found elsewhere in this Handbook.

As the idea is that the statue represents the Queen present among her soldiers, the altar must not be separated from the meeting-table or so placed as to remove the statue outside the circle of the members.

Filial love towards our Heavenly Mother dictates that the equipment and the flowers should be as good as possible. Preferably the vases and candlesticks should be of silver. As the expense of the equipment is not a recurring item, no Praesidium will find this a burdensome provision. It should be regarded as an honourable duty on the part of some Legionary to keep the Vexillum and the vases and candlesticks clean and bright, and duly provided with flowers and candles at the expense of the Praesidium.

The words "Legio Mariae" may be worked upon the cloth, but not the name of the Praesidium. Points of unity, not of distinction, should be stressed.

"Early in 1921 it was learned that the Pope had just approved of the Feast of Mary, Universal Mediatrix of the divine graces. . . . The comprehensive affirmation: 'Every grace comes to us through Mary' seems to be beyond dispute, so that we may portray Mary just as she was seen by Soeur Catherine Labouré in 1830 in the chapel of the Sisters of Charity, Rue du Bac, Paris. Thereby the Blessed Virgin is effectively shown in her role as dispenser of grace. With her foot she crushes the serpent. Her arms she extends and lowers towards our earth. From her hands, laden with rings and precious stones, proceed luminous rays. 'Behold in these,' said Mary, 'the symbol of the graces which I shower on those who ask them from me.' "—(Plus: Marie dans notre Histoire Divine.)

2. Punctually at the appointed time, the members shall be in their places, and the meeting shall begin. But a punctual start (so necessary for the efficiency of the Praesidium) will not be possible unless the Officers are in attendance some time in advance in order to make the requisite preparations.

No meeting of the Legion should ever be commenced without a written agenda. In the case of the ordinary Praesidium meeting, this will take a more or less stereotyped form, and be termed the **"Work Sheet."** From it the President will call the business. In the Work Sheet should be set down in detail all the work being done by the Praesidium, and opposite to each item, the names of the members assigned to it. The various items need not necessarily be taken in the same order at succeeding meetings, but every member's name appearing should be called and a report taken from each one, even though they may be working in parties of two or more.

"Idealism, however fervent and absorbing, must never be an excuse for vague and unpractical emotion. As already pointed out the genius of St. Ignatius consisted in his careful and methodic exploitation of religious energy. Steam is of no use, rather a nuisance, until we have a cylinder and piston for it. How much spiritual fervour goes to waste, without a particular examen and definite applications! A gallon of petrol might be misused to blow a car sky-high; with care and inventiveness it can be employed to propel it to the top of the hill." (Alfred O'Rahilly: Life of Father William Doyle.)

3. The meeting opens with the Invocation and Prayer to the Holy Ghost, Who is the source of that Grace, that Life, that Love, of which we rejoice to regard Mary as the channel.

"From the moment when she conceived the Son of God in her womb, Mary possessed, so to speak, a certain authority or jurisdiction over every temporal procession of the Holy Ghost, in such sort that no creature receives any grace from God except through her mediation. . . . All the gifts and virtues and graces of the same Holy Spirit are administered by her, to whom she pleases, when she pleases, and in the quantity and manner she pleases."—(St. Bernardine: Sermo de Nativitate.)

4. There follow five Decades of the Rosary, of which the Spiritual Director shall initiate the first, third, and fifth, and the members the second and fourth. No member is to act as if the Rosary were a silent prayer. The same measure of dignity and respect should be imparted to its recitation as if the gracious personage to whom it is addressed, were visibly present in the place of the statue representing her.

The Rosary, playing, both by rule and by recommendation, such an important part in the life of the Legionary each one is urged to register in the Rosary Confraternity. (See Appendix V.) Without entailing obligations more than are ordinarily assumed, this will enhance the benefits of recitation of the Rosary and will multiply exceedingly the Indulgences to be gained therefrom. The fact that the greater part of these rich Indulgences depend upon the devout saying of the Holy Name in the Ave should be a reminder, if one is needed, that the proper recitation of the Ave requires that the second part should not begin until the first has been finished, and the Holy Name of Jesus reverently pronounced.

"Of the magnificent treasure of grace brought to us by Christ, nothing according to the Eternal designs is to be distributed to us except through Mary. Hence it is through her we must go to Christ almost in the same way as through Christ we approach our Heavenly Father."—(Leo XIII: Encyclical on the Rosary, 1891.)

5. The Rosary is immediately followed by Spiritual Reading. A series of 53 Spiritual Readings, one for each week of the year, is to be prepared by the Concilium,* and that one prescribed for the particular week shall be used at the meetings of the Praesidium. These readings will be returned upon in due order in the succeeding years. On them, become familiar by repetition, the Legion relies in no small measure for the training of its members in their duties, for the instructing of them in the science of the Legion, and for generally informing them and encouraging them.

On the conclusion of the reading, it is the custom for the members to make, together, the Sign of the Cross.

***Not yet ready. In the meantime the choice of Spiritual Reading is free, but should be limited to about five minutes duration.**

"As to the attitude and occupation of Mary at the moment the angel entered, authorities are not agreed. It is usual to exhibit her as kneeling in prayer, or reading with a large book open on a desk before her. St. Bernard says that she was studying the book of the prophet Isaias, and as she recited the verse, 'Behold, a Virgin shall conceive and bear a son,' she thought within her heart, in her great humility, 'How blessed the woman of whom these words are written! Would I might be but her handmaid to serve her, and allowed to kiss her feet!'—when, in the same instant, the wondrous vision burst upon her, and the holy prophecy was realised in herself."—(Jameson: Legends of the Madonna.)

6. The minutes of the previous meeting are read, and, if approved by the members present, are signed by the President. The minutes should strike a sensible mean between excessive and inadequate length, and shall designate each meeting by its proper serial number.

The importance of the minutes has already been stressed under the head of the Secretary's duties. The minutes, being the first item of the ordinary business of the meeting, hold, as it were, a strategic position. By their quality and the manner of reading them, they may set the tone, for better or for worse, of all that follows.

Good minutes are like good example. Poor minutes are like bad example; and it is necessary to insist that well-written minutes, badly read, rank as poor minutes. That example has compelling force upon the members. Their alertness, their reports, are affected, so that the meeting may be good or bad simply because the minutes were good or bad. And the quality of the work will follow the quality of the meeting.

So let the Secretary, when engaged on the hidden work of preparation of the minutes, reflect on these things; and let the Praesidium, in the interest of its own efficiency, oversee them.

"It would indeed be shameful if in this matter Christ's saying should be verified, that 'the children of this world are wiser than the children of light' (Luke 16, 8). We can observe with what diligence they look after their affairs; how often they balance their credit and debit; how accurately they make up their accounts; how they deplore their losses and so eagerly excite themselves to repair them."—(Pius X: Exhortatio ad Clerum Catholicum.)

7. Standing Instruction. The following Standing Instruction is to be inserted on the Work Sheet (or otherwise placed so as to ensure that it will not be overlooked at the proper time) and read out by the President at the first meeting of each month, immediately after the signing of the minutes:—

"Legionary duty requires from each Legionary:—

First, the punctual and regular attendance at the weekly meetings of the Praesidium, and the furnishing there of an adequate and audible report on the work done;

Second, the daily recitation of the Catena;

Third, the performance of a substantial active Legionary work, in the spirit of faith, and in union with Mary, in such fashion that in those worked for and in one's fellow-members, the Person of Our Lord is once again seen and served by Mary, His Mother;

Fourth, the preservation of an absolute secrecy in regard to any matter discussed at the meeting or learned in connection with the Legionary work."

"Through me, Mary desires to love Jesus too in the hearts of all those whom I can kindle with love as the result of my apostolate and my perpetual prayers. If I wholly identify myself with her, she will so flood me with her graces and with her love, that I shall come to resemble an ever-brimming stream, that in its turn will flood the souls of others. Because of me, Mary will be enabled to love Jesus and to fill Him with joy, not only through my own heart but also through the countless hearts that are united with mine."—(De Jaegher: The Virtue of Trust.) [This quotation is not to be read out as part of the Standing Instruction.]

8. Reports of the members are received. Members should remain seated while delivering their reports, which should be verbal, though members may aid themselves by notes.

The President should not take the non-performance of the Legionary duty as a matter of course. When members have been validly prevented from performing their work, they should (if possible), furnish some explanation. The absence of a report, if unexplained, conveys the impression that neglect of duty is in question and constitutes a bad example for every member.

If members are attaching a reasonable degree of seriousness to their work, the necessity for excuse will arise but seldom, and happily so, for in an atmosphere of excuses zeal and discipline wither away.

The report, though addressed to the President, should be delivered in a tone of voice which will reach every part of the room. A report, however full and faithful, which is inaudible to many of those present is — having regard to its depressing effect on the meeting — worse than no report. Whispering is no sign of modesty or gentleness as some apparently imagine. Who so modest, who so gentle as Mary? Yet could anyone imagine her mumbling her words, or talking in such a fashion that those close to her could not hear what she was saying? O Legionaries! Imitate your Queen in this, as in all other ways.

Presidents must refuse to accept reports which require an effort to hear. But first let them be above reproach themselves. The President sets the tone for all the members. Usually, the members speak less loudly than the President. If the latter speaks only in a moderate or conversational tone, the members' reports will come back in whispers. For, members speaking clearly when the President is speaking softly, will imagine themselves to be shouting, and will reduce their tones to inaudibility. Members must insist upon the President speaking out; and let the Spiritual Director stimulate all of them in this direction.

"Some Christians see little more in Mary than a creature infinitely pure and exquisite, the tenderest and gentlest Woman that ever existed. Therein, they run the risk of having for her only a sentimental devotion, or—if they are of a forceful character—of feeling but little attraction towards her. They have never realised that this Virgin so tender, the Mother so gentle is, as well, the Woman above all the most indomitable, and that never was there man so full of character as this Woman."—(Neubert: Marie dans le Dogme.)

9. The recitation of the Catena Legionis. At the fixed time, which experience has shown to be approximately mid-way between the signing of the minutes and the end of the meeting (that would be an hour after the opening of a meeting which usually lasts an hour and a half), the Catena Legionis (see Prayers of the Legion) is recited, all standing.

The antiphon is recited by all present: the Magnificat in alternate verses by the Spiritual Director (in his absence, by the President) and by the members: the Prayer by the Spiritual Director (or President) alone.

There is nothing in the Legion more beautiful than this united recitation of the Catena. Whether it finds the Praesidium immersed in joy or disappointment or treading wearily the way of routine, it comes like a breeze from Heaven, all steeped in the fragrancy of her who is the Lily and the Rose, refreshing and gladdening most wonderfully. No mere picturesque description this—as every Legionary knows full well!

"I lay special stress on the Magnificat because it seems to me that it may be considered, in a way perhaps not commonly realised, a document of outstanding importance in its bearing on Mary's motherhood of grace. The most holy Virgin, identified with Christ, as we know her to have been from the moment of the Annunciation, proclaims herself the representative of the entire human race, intimately associated with 'all generations,' and bound up with the destinies of those who are truly her own. This canticle of hers is the song of her spiritual maternity."—(Bernard, O.P.: Le Mystére de Marie.)

10. The Allocutio.* When the members resume their seats, a short talk shall be given by the Spiritual Director. Except in special circumstances, this should take the shape of a commentary upon the Handbook with the object of eventually making the members completely familiar with every point contained therein. The Allocutio will be greatly appreciated, and it will play an all-important part in the development of the members. Responsibility for the latter exists, and it would be an injustice both to them and to the Legion

***The Allocutio was the Roman General's address to his Legionaries.**

not to draw out all their possibilities. To do this it is essential that they be given a perfect knowledge of their organisation. The study of the Handbook will greatly help towards this end, but must not be considered to be a substitute for the Allocutio. Legionaries will believe that they have studied the Handbook when they have read it attentively two or three times. But even ten or twenty readings would not bring the degree of knowledge which the Legion desires. This will only be imparted by a systematic verbal explanation and expansion of the Handbook week after week, year after year, until the members have become completely familiarised with every idea it contains.

In the event of the absence of the Spiritual Director, the commentary should be made by the President or by any member designated by the President. It is stressed that a mere reading from the Handbook does not suffice for the Allocutio.

If there is a press of business, the Allocutio should not occupy more than five or six minutes.

The difference between the Praesidium where the Allocutio has been thoroughly done, and the Praesidium where it has been badly done, will be precisely the difference between a trained and an untrained army.

"I have long had the feeling that, since the world is growing so rapidly worse and worse and God has lost His hold, as it were, upon the hearts of men, He is looking all the more earnestly and anxiously for big things from those who are faithful to Him still. He cannot, perhaps, gather a large army round His standard, but He wants every one in it to be a *Hero*, absolutely and lovingly devoted to Him; if only we could get inside that magic circle of generous souls, I believe there is no grace He would not give us to help on the work He has so much at heart, our personal sanctification."—(Alfred O'Rahilly: Life of Father William Doyle.)

11. On the completion of the Allocutio, the Sign of the Cross is made by all present. Then the taking of the Reports and other business of the meeting is continued.

"If we wish this transformation of our life into that of Jesus Christ to be complete and true, and to meet with no obstacle in its perfection, the love we have towards Our Saviour must radiate around us and shine forth upon all mankind. This is what St. John points out to us when he sums up all Christian life in these words: 'And this is (God's) commandment, that we should believe in the Name of His Son Jesus Christ—and that we love one another.' (St. John iii, 23.)"—(Marmion: Christ, the Life of the Soul.)

12. Secret Bag Collection. Immediately after the Allocutio, a Secret Bag Collection is made, to which every member shall contribute according to means. The purpose is the defraying of the various expenses of the Praesidium and the contributing to the Curia and the higher councils. (See Section on Funds.)

The meeting is not to be interrupted for the making of this collection. The bag should be passed unostentatiously from member to member, and each one should place his hand in the bag even though he may not be contributing anything to it.

A proper bag should be provided for the purpose of receiving the members' offerings. A glove or a paper bag is not a proper receptacle.

The collection is secret because it is necessary to place those who have resources, and those who have not, on precisely the same level before the Praesidium. Therefore, the principle of secrecy should be respected, and one member should not disclose to another what his contribution is. In the second place, all should appreciate that not alone the Praesidium, but also the main running of the whole Legion, depends on what is put into the Secret Bag by the individual Legionary. Accordingly, the latter is not to view the matter as a mere formality, to be passed over with the giving of something which signifies nothing to him. On the contrary, the act of contributing to this Fund is one for the exercise of the sense of responsibility and generosity.

It is only the individual gift which is secret. The total amount may be announced, and of course it must be properly entered up and accounted for.

"When Jesus praises the offering of the widow 'who gives not of her abundance but of her indigence' (St. Luke xxi, 3-4), we suspect that His thought is of Mary, His Mother."—(Orsini: History of the Blessed Virgin.)

13. The Meeting ends with the concluding prayers of the Legion (see the relative Section), and the Priest's Blessing.

"Again I say to you that if two of you shall consent upon earth concerning anything whatsoever they shall ask, it shall be done to them by my Father who is in Heaven. For where there are two or three gathered together in my name, there am I in the midst of them."—(St. Matt. xviii. 19, 20.)

THE MEETING AND THE MEMBER.

1. Respect for the meeting. Everywhere in the natural order, the transmission of power depends on the making or the breaking of a connection. Similarly in the Legion system there can be a vital interruption at one point. A member may attend the meetings, and yet receive little or no communication of that inspiration, devotedness, and strength, which has been pictured above as the Legion life. There must be a union between meeting and member, and this union is not effected by a mere mechanical attendance on the part of the latter. An element must enter in to make that attendance an efficacious link between meeting and member, and this element is **respect.** On this respect (manifesting itself in obedience, loyalty, esteem) of member for meeting, everything in the Legion system depends.

2. The Praesidium must be worthy of this respect. A body, which does not in its standards rise above the average of its members, lacks the first essential of a guide, and will not long hold their respect.

3. The Praesidium must respect the Rules. Proportionately as the Legionary gives that respect to the Praesidium, will a communication of Legionary life be made to the Legionary; and as the essence of the Legionary spirit is the effort to achieve excellence, the Praesidium must set itself to win in the highest degree the respect of its members that it may correspondingly influence them. A Praesidium seeks to build upon sand, which claims from its members a respect which it does not itself give to the code under which it works; a fact which explains the insistence, throughout this Handbook, on the necessity for exact adherence to the order of meetings and the general procedure as laid down.

4. The Praesidium to be a model of steadiness. The Legion requires that the voice and action of its meetings shall be an example even to the most zealous member, and its multifold life enables it to play this part. The individual Legionary may be prevented by illness holidays or other unavoidable circumstances from performance of the duties of membership, but the Praesidium, being composed of many who will not all be so hindered at the same time, will thus be able to rise above the limitations of the individual. The weekly meeting should not be omitted for any cause short of actual inability to hold it. Should the customary day of meeting be definitely obstructed, the meeting should be transferred to another day. The fact that a great number of its members will be absent constitutes no reason for not holding the meeting. It is better to hold a meeting of a few members than to drop it altogether. It is true that little business will be transacted at such a meeting, but at least the Praesidium will have acquitted itself of its most important duty, and the business of its future meetings will gain immeasurably from the enhanced respect which its members will instinctively have for something which goes on almost in spite of those who compose it, which stands steady in the midst of their weaknesses, mistakes, and miscellaneous engagements, thus reflecting in some faint fashion the chief characteristic of the Church itself.

5. Heat and light. The room should be well-lighted and of comfortable temperature. Defects in this direction will convert to a penance the meetings that should be a pleasure, and will prejudice fatally the prospects of the Praesidium.

6. Seating accommodation. Chairs, or at least benches, should be provided for seating purposes.

If the members are scattered around on school-desks or on other improvised seating-accommodation, an air of disorder will be created, in which the Legion spirit which is a spirit of order, will not thrive.

7. Evening meetings desirable. The Legion wishes its Praesidia to hold their meetings in the evening, if at all possible. Ordinarily, morning or afternoon meetings (except, of course, those held on Sunday) will exclude from membership all but the leisured, and thus amount in effect to the setting up of the sectional Praesidia deprecated elsewhere in these pages. Howver, the Legion recognises that circumstances may possibly exist which require otherwise, and allows to Curiae a dispensing power. But this power shall only be used on the production of convincing reasons.

8. Duration of meeting. The meeting shall not last longer than one hour and a half from the appointed time for opening, unless by special permission of the Curia, which should not be lightly given. If it is found that the business is frequently cut short, or unduly rushed, by the automatic closure, it should be taken as a sign that the Praesidium has too much to do, and the formation of another Praesidium should be considered.

9. Inadequate length of meetings. There is no minimum duration prescribed, but if meetings habitually last less than about an hour (of which the prayers, spiritual reading, minutes and Allocutio occupy a half-hour), it looks as if there is inadequacy in some direction. Whether it lies in the number of members or in the quantity of the work, or in the quality of the reports, it should be rectified. In industrial circles it would be deemed a grave fault of system to neglect to work machinery to full capacity, if there is a market for the output. Similarly, the Legion system should be worked to the utmost. No one can suggest that there is not a need for the highest possible spiritual output.

10. Late arrival or early departure. Legionaries

arriving late for the opening prayers shall kneel down and recite privately the prayers (on the Tessera) which precede the Rosary and the invocations which follow it. But the loss of the Praesidium Rosary cannot be repaired. Similarly, members obliged to leave before the conclusion of the meeting should first ask the permission of the President, and then kneel and recite the Prayer—*We fly to Thy patronage,* etc. and the invocations which follow it on the Prayer-card.

Only on production of adequate reasons can persistent late-coming or early departure by a member be permitted. It is true that the work may be done and reported upon, but indifference to the missing of the opening or concluding prayers may well be believed to denote a cast of mind alien to or even hostile to the real spirit of the Legion, which is a spirit of prayer. Harm, not good, would be the fruits of such a membership.

11. Good order the root of discipline. Upon (a) the setting of the meeting faithfully according to rule; (b) the orderly succession of duty to duty; (c) the punctual taking of business as prescribed, does the Legion rely for the development in its members of the spirit of discipline, without which the meeting is as a clear head on a paralysed body, powerless either to restrain its members or to drive them on, or to form them in any way. Without discipline, the members will be at the mercy of the natural human tendency to work alone, or with as little control as possible, at the work dictated by the whim of the moment, and in the manner one pleases—and out of which no good will come.

On the other hand, in a voluntarily-assumed discipline, devoted to religious ends, lies one of the most potent forces in the world. That discipline will prove irresistible, if (and may not this follow naturally from its use as an instrument in the Marian, Legionary scheme) it operate unwaveringly, yet at the same time without admixture of grimness, and in hearty responsiveness to Ecclesiastical Authority.

12. Prayers to be one with the meeting. From time to time it has been suggested that the Rosary might be recited before the Blessed Sacrament, the members then proceeding to their meeting-room. This proposal is not allowable on the general principle that the unity of the meeting is essential to the whole Legion system. With the meeting one, all the business takes a distinctively prayerful character (producing eminent fruits of heroism and effort), which it would lose were the bulk of the prayers to be said elsewhere. Such a change would alter the whole character of the meeting, and hence of the Legion itself, which is built upon the meeting. In fact the resulting organisation, however great its merits, would not be the Legion of Mary at all. Having said this, presumably it is unnecessary to state that the actual omission of the Rosary or any other part of the prayers is—no matter what the circumstances may be—still less admissible. What the breathing is to the human body, the Rosary is to the Legion meetings.

13. Church Devotions and Meeting. As a variant of the above proposal, it may be urged that sometimes it happens that the Legionaries are morally bound to attend Church Devotions (comprising the Rosary) which coincide with the day of their meeting. In such event, the Legionaries should of course attend the Devotions; but what valid reason is there that they should not also carry out their meeting in its fulness according to rule? Surely Legionaries will consider it worth while saying an additional five Decades of the Rosary on that day for the purpose of observing the Legion rule and of keeping intact the Legion system! Innumerable persons say fifteen Decades of the Rosary every day of their lives.

14. Special Prayers at Meeting. It is frequently asked if it is permissible to offer the prayers of the meeting for special intentions. As many applications for such prayers are made, it becomes necessary to define the position:—(a) If it is a question of offering the ordinary Legion prayers of the meeting for a special intention, the ruling is that those prayers should be offered for the intentions of Our Blessed Lady, the Queen of the Legion, and not for any other intention; (b) if it is a question of supplementing the Legion prayers by some other prayers for special intentions, the ruling is that the existing prayers are already long enough, and should not ordinarily be added to. It is recognised, however, that from time to time items of exceptional Legionary concern may call for special prayer; and in that case, some short prayer may be added to the ordinary prayers of the meeting. It is emphasised that such additions must be of rare occurrence; (c) it would, of course, be allowable to recommend special intentions to the members for inclusion in their private devotions.

15. The Meeting dependent on the Reports. The meeting should be bright and cheerful. Therefore the reports should be such as will interest the members as well as inform the meeting. It is impossible to believe that the Praesidium is healthy if the meeting is deadly dull, and undoubtedly it will repel young members.

Some classes of work are so full of variety that it is easy to make a good report. Other works do not afford the same possibilities, so that each unusual feature, however small, should be remembered for mention in the report. Reports simply must not be allowed to develop into a sort of formula. A tendency in that direction shows that neither the President nor the member is doing his duty, either to themselves or to the meeting, or to the work.

Moreover, it is impossible to exercise supervision over work where the reports do not fully disclose what is being done, what is being attempted, and the methods being used. Sometimes the work is so difficult, that members, if not stimulated by the minute consideration of their efforts by the meeting, may be inclined to spare themselves. This must not be. They are in the Legion to do as much good as possible; and probably it will be in those very cases where the natural repugnances assert themselves most, that the greatest need for their work exists. It is mainly through the meeting that the Legionary discipline is exerted which overcomes those weaknesses and drives the member on to accomplishment. But if the report gives little indication as to what the Legionary is really doing, then the Praesidium can exert only a vague control over that member's actions. It will not stimulate him. It will not safeguard him. Legionary discipline then loses its grip on that member, with unhappy results both for him and for the the Praesidium.

16. Does the report offend against humility? Members have been known to justify a valueless report by saying that they felt it to be contrary to humility to parade the good which they were doing. But here is such a thing as a pride which imitates humility, and the poets have termed it the Devil's favourite sin. Those members, therefore, should beware lest in that thought of theirs may lie the subtle workings not of humility but of pride itself, and not a little of a desire to exempt their actions from minute control by the Praesidium. For surely, true humility would not urge them to set a false headline, which if imitated by the other members, would ruin the Praesidium? No, to a certainty, Christian simplicity would impel members to avoid singularity, to submit themselves sweetly to the rules and observances of their organisation, and to play fully their individual but none the less essential parts in the building up of the meeting, of which each report forms, as has been said, a brick.

17. Harmony the expression of unity. Harmony, being the outward manifestation of the spirit of love in the meeting, must reign supreme; and efficiency, in the Legion sense of the word, never excludes the idea of harmony. Good accomplished at the expense of harmony is a doubtful gain; while those failings which are in their essence opposed to it, must be shunned in the Legion like a veritable plague. One refers to things like self-assertiveness, fault-finding, ill-temper, acrimony, cynicism, and airs of superiority, at whose entry to the meeting harmony forthwith departs.

18. Work of each one a concern of all. The meeting begins with prayer in which all realise that they have participated equally. This feeling of equal participation by all should characterise each item of the subsequent business of the meeting. Hence conversation or laughter between individual members must find no place there. Members should be taught that each case is a concern not merely for the one or two members who may be engaged upon it, but for all present, in such a degree that each one pays a spiritual visit to every person or place recounted as having been the subject of visitation. Without this realisation, members will follow with a mere attention the reports and consideration of the work of others, whereas every moment must be full, not merely with the attention which one gives to an interesting account of work done, but with a sense of intimate contact, of personal concern.

19. Secrecy of paramount importance. The Standing Instruction, dinned into the ears of the members month after month, should bring home to them the all-important place of secrecy in the Legion's scheme of things.

Lack of courage in a soldier is accounted shameful, but treachery is infinitely worse. It is treachery to the Legion to repeat outside what is learned at the Praesidium meeting. At the same time, there must be reason in all things. A species of intemperate zeal is now and then encountered, which urges that the interests of charity require that the visitors should withhold from the Praesidium all names or reports in cases of neglect. In this apparently plausible suggestion lies an error, and a threat to the Legion's life. For the Praesidium could not work under such conditions:—

(a) The adoption of this course would be contrary to the general practise of Societies, all of which are accustomed to discuss their cases;

(b) Taken to its logical conclusion, the proposal would mean that the co-visitors should preserve secrecy even against each other;

(c) The unit of action and knowledge and charity is neither the individual member nor the pair of co-visitors. The Praesidium is that unit, and the detail of all ordinary cases is due to that unit. To withhold the reports is to dissolve the unit. Under the plea of charity the real interests of charity are prejudiced;

(d) There is no analogy with the case of the Priest, whose sacred functions put him on a different plane to the Legionary. The latter learns in visitation little more than any other respected person would, and what is often common property in the tenement house or district;

(e) To remove from members the obligation to furnish adequate reports is also to remove that sense of minute control which means so much in the Legion system. Moreover, the education and safeguarding of the members, which are based on the reports, are rendered impossible. Do away with the intimate weekly stocktaking of the members' work, and the door is opened wide for every sort of indiscretion;

(f) Strangest of all, the bond of secrecy itself becomes loosened. For the guarantee of Legionary secrecy (so wonderfully honoured at present) is the Praesidium grip upon the member. If this grip is weakened, the bond of secrecy weakens with it. In a word, the Praesidium is not only the unit of charity and secrecy, but is also their mainstay.

The reports to the meeting are to be regarded as being in the same category as a family's discussion of its secrets, and should partake of the same freedom until it is demonstrated that leakage is taking place. And even then, the remedy is not to limit reporting, but to expel the traitor.

It is recognised, of course, that exceptional cases will

be encountered, in which the circumstances will suggest an absolute privacy. Recourse should at once be had to the Spiritual Director (or, if he be unavailable, to some other competent adviser) who will decide the point.

20. The Meeting the mainstay of membership. It is the human tendency to be impatient for visible results, and then to grow dissatisfied with whatever is obtained. Again, visible results are an uncertain test of successful work. One member secures them at a touch, while the heroic perseverance of another remains barren. A sense of wasted effort is followed by abandonment of the work, so that the work, which is valued purely from the aspect of results, is a quicksand which will not support for long the ordinary membership. Such a support is essential. Legionaries will find it in the wealth of prayer, the ritual, the distinctive atmosphere, the week's reports of duty done, the blessed comradeship, the magnetism of discipline, the lively interest, and the very orderliness, which each week go to make up their Praesidium meeting.

No thought there of waste of effort, to unloosen membership, but everything to bind it fast! As meeting succeeds meeting in regular succession, there comes the sense of smoothly running machinery surely attaining the end for which it was contrived, and giving that fixed assurance of successful working upon which a persevering membership depends.

21. Mary's instrument of power. Let the Legionaries cast their thoughts a little further, and see in this mechanism Mary's engine of war for the extension of her Son's dominion. They are its parts. Its working depends upon the manner in which they lend themselves to it. Their faithful membership means its perfect working, which Mary utilises to achieve the results which she desires. These will be perfect results, for "it is Mary alone who knows perfectly where lies the greatest glory of the Most High."—(B. Grignion de Montfort.)

"Put thy feet into her fetters, and thy neck into her chains. Bow down thy shoulder and bear her; and be not grieved with her bonds. Come to her with all thy mind; and keep her always with all thy power. . . . Then shall her fetters be a strong defence for thee, and a firm foundation, and her chain a robe of glory. For in her is the beauty of life: and her bonds are a healthful binding."—(Ecclesiasticus vi. 25-31, applied to Our Lady by the Church. Applicable by Legionaries to the Legion system and especially to the meeting.)

SUGGESTIONS AS TO WORKS.

In this Section are set down methods, shown by general experience to be especially fruitful, of employing the work-obligation of the Legion. They represent, however, only suggestions, and particular needs may call for particular works. It is urged that enterprising and difficult work be not withheld from the Legion, which is admirably adapted to the doing of such work. Trivial tasks will react unfavourably on the spirit of the Legionaries.

1.—VISITATION OF HOSPITALS.

The visitation of a hospital ward in a city Poorhouse was the first work the Legion ever undertook and for a while it did no other. It teemed with blessings for the infant organisation, and the Legion desires that this work will ever be the first attended to by its Praesidia. The following, written in those early days, exemplifies the spirit which must always characterise it:—

"Then a name was called and a member began her report. It concerned the visitation of a hospital. It was brief, yet showed great intimacy with the patients. She admitted with some confusion that the patients knew the names of all her brothers and sisters. She is succeeded by her co-visitor. Evidently work is done in pairs. It occurs to me that apart from there being apostolic example for this, the practice prevents procrastination in the making of the weekly visitation.

"Report follows report. In some wards there is something new and there is an extended account, but most reports are short. Many are amusing, many touching, and all are beautiful in the obvious realisation shown of Whom it is that is visited in the poor patient. There is evidence of it in every report. Why, many people would not do for their own flesh and blood what is here recounted as done, simply and naturally, for the least elements in our population. The exquisite care and tenderness of the visits are supplemented by the performance of many commissions—the writing of letters, the looking up of the neglectful friends or relatives, the running of errands. It is plain that nothing is too disagreeable or too trifling to look after.

"One letter from a patient to her visitors was read over at the meeting. A phrase from it ran: 'Since you came into my life.' It rang of the twopenny romance, and all laughed. But later I thought back to a lonely person in a poorhouse bed, to whom those words meant a great deal, and the thought filled me with emotion. I reflected, too, that though said of one, it could apply to all. Thus wonderful is the power of association which can bring together many persons into one room and thence send them out on angelic missions into the lives of thousands who have dropped out of the recollection of the outside world."—("Legionary Foundations.")

It will be a commonplace of Legionary visitation that it be used to educate the poor patients to a true conception of their sufferings, that they may bear them in the proper spirit.

(a) They must be persuaded that what they regard as so intolerable is in reality a moulding to the likeness of Christ, and as such a great favour. "No greater favour," says St. Teresa, "can His Majesty bestow on us than to give us a life such as was led by His beloved Son." It is not difficult to bring home to people this aspect of suffering which, when once grasped, deprives it of half its sting.

(b) To make them realise the greatness of the spiritual treasures which they can acquire, repeat often to them the exclamation of St. Peter of Alcantara to one who had long endured a most painful illness with admirable patience:—"O happy patient, God has shown me how great a glory you have merited by your illness. You have merited more than others can gain by prayer, fasting, vigils, scourging, and other penitential works."

(c) It is desirable that the spending of these spiritual treasures should possess a variety which is lacking in the earning of them. Moreover, a gathering for self will not exercise so potent an appeal. So the Legionary will unfold the idea of the apostleship of suffering. The patients should be taught to busy themselves in the spiritual affairs of the world, offering the treasures of their sufferings for its myriad needs, and conducting a campaign whose force must be irresistible because it is at once prayer and penance.

"Such hands, raised to God," cries Bossuet, "break through more battalions than those that strike."

(d) It will aid towards perseverance if the patients feel a personal interest in what they are praying for, so that it is important that particular needs and works (notably the Legionary's own) be singled out and described to them. Presumably, the Legionary will enlist them in the Legion Auxiliaries, a step which will intensify the intimacy between visitor and visited, and secure for the Legion the powerful support of their prayers and sufferings.

(e) This new view of life opened up to them, the poor patients, who had touched the depths of misery in the thought of being so useless and a burden, will taste the supreme joy of feeling that they are of use to God.

"'I am Christ's wheat,' said St. Ignatius of Antioch, 'and that I may be made into bread worthy of God, I must needs be ground by the teeth of lions.' Never doubt that the best of crosses, the safest, the most divine is always that one which Jesus Himself ordains without consulting us. Increase your faith in this doctrine so dear to saints cast in the mould of Nazareth. Adore, bless and praise God in all the contradictions and trials which come directly from His Hand and, conquering the repugnance of your nature, say with all your heart '*fiat*,' or still better, '*Magnificat*'!"—(Mateo Crawley-Boevey.)

2.—WORK FOR THE MOST WRETCHED AND DEJECTED OF THE POPULATION.

This will involve the visitation of their haunts; and of lodging-houses, hotels, jails, and in poorhouses; and, it may be, the conducting of hostels staffed by Legionaries, resident and outdoor.

As soon as the Legion in any centre is in possession of members of sufficient experience and calibre, this work for the least of the least ones of Christ is to be undertaken. Too often it is to be found neglected, with consequent reproach to the Catholic name.

There should be no depths to which the Legion will not penetrate in its search for the lost sheep of the House of Israel. False fears will be the first obstacle. But false or founded, **someone must do this work.** If capable and trained Legionaries, safeguarded by their prayerful and disciplined system, cannot essay it, then no one can.

Till the Legion in any centre can say with truth that its members know personally, and are in touch in some way, with each and every individual member of the degraded classes, its work must be regarded as being still in a stage of incomplete development, and efforts in this direction must be intensified.

No searcher after the rare and precious things of the earth must pursue his heart's desire more earnestly than the Legionary pressing after these unfortunates of the world. His search may be their only chance of life eternal. Frequently they are so inaccessible to good influences that prison represents for them a blessing in disguise.

Moreover, the outlook of a campaigning soldier must be brought to bear on this work. Obvious inconveniences will face the Legionaries. Perhaps to the stings and arrows of outrageous words, worse things may be added. The 'rifle-fire' of blows or the 'artillery' of injuries may be turned upon them. Such things may humiliate and pain, but they must not intimidate; they should hardly even disconcert. Here lies the test of the solidity of the soldierly professions which have so often passed through the mind of the Legionary and have so many times been uttered by him. He has spoken of a warfare; here are its strikings and its wounds. He has talked of seeking for the worst of people; now that he has found them, it would be inconsistent of him to complain. Why should it cause surprise to see that the bad behave badly, and that the worst act vilely!

In short, in every circumstance of special difficulty, or in face of danger, the Legionary should remind himself: "A war is on"! This phrase, that nerves a war-ridden people to sacrifice, should steel the Legionary in his warfare for souls and hold him to his work when most others would desist.

The masculine pronoun has been used throughout, but only for convenience' sake. These recommendations have just the same application to the woman Legionary as they have to her brother-in-service. The Church has been producing woman-martyrs for two thousand years, and Legionaries were displaying heroism for eight years before a men's Praesidium was formed. Therefore, to the woman in the Legion ranks is likewise addressed the stern warning that if there is any reality in the talk of precious and eternal souls, there must be readiness to pay a price of some sort for them. What price, and by whom paid? The answer is that if ever lay-persons are to be asked to face a risk, who are they to be—if not those who are striving to be worthy of the title of Legionaries of Mary? If ever great sacrifices are to be required from lay-Catholics, from whom—if not from those whose hearts' desire it is to be soldiers of quality of the Peerless Queen? Surely they will never fail, if called upon!

But leadership may fail, through a mistaken solicitude for those led. Therefore, Spiritual Directors and all Officers are exhorted to set up standards which have some slight relation to those of the Colosseum. This word may ring unreal in these calculating days. But the Colosseum was a calculation, too: the calculation of many lovely people—no more strong, no more weak than Legionaries of Mary—who said to themselves: "What price shall a man give for a soul?" The Colosseum only summarises in a word what many words go to say in the Section of the Handbook labelled "Legionary Service," and that Section is not intended to express mere sentiment.

Work for the derelict or abandoned classes will always be a difficult, long-drawn-out one. Its keynote must be a supreme patience. A type is being dealt with which will only rise after many fallings. If discipline be put first in dealing with them, nothing will be accomplished. In a short time the rigid system will have lost all the subjects it was constituted to treat, and will have as patients those who least require treatment. Therefore, the work must proceed upon the principle of values reversed, that is, it shall concern itself especially with those whom even the optimist would term utterly hopeless cases, and whose warped minds and initial insensibility to appeal would seem to justify this description. The vile, the malevolent, the naturally hateful, the rejects and black-listed of other societies and people the refuse of cities, shall all be determinedly persevered with in spite of rebuffs, utter ingratitude, and apparent failure. Of these a considerable proportion will form a life-long task.

Obviously such a work, carried on according to such ideas, calls for heroic qualities and a purely supernatural vision. The compensation for toil so great will lie in the seeing of the objects of that toil eventually die in the friendship of God. Then what joy to have co-operated with

"Him who from the mire, in patient length of days,
Elaborated into life a people to His praise!"

(Newman: Dream of Gerontius.)

This particular activity has been considered at length because it really concerns the whole spirit of the Legion. In addition, it holds, amongst services done to the Church, a key position. For it constitutes a special assertion of the Catholic principle that even the lowest of human beings hold in relation to us a position which is independent of their value or agreeableness to us; that in them Christ is to be seen, reverenced, loved.

The proof of the reality of this love is that it be manifested in circumstances which test it. That vital test consists in loving those whom mere human nature bids one not to love: those who are poor in human esteem. Here is the acid-test of the true and the false love for humanity. It is a pivot of faith, a crucial-point of Christianity, for without the Catholic ideal this sort of love simply cannot exist. The very notion would be fantastic, if divorced from the root which gives it meaning and life. If humanity for its own sake is to be the gospel, then everything must be judged from the angle of its apparent utility to humanity. Something which would admittedly be valueless to humanity must logically, under such systems, be viewed just as sin would be viewed in the Christian dispensation, that is as something to be eliminated at any cost.

The logic of this is that in a devoted and universal attention to the "down and out," "hopeless," "impossible" and unlovely elements of the population lies the confounding of those protestations of love of humanity which are the stock-in-trade of the materialistic systems. The latter indeed strut along creditably, until the shoe begins to pinch. Then it will be seen that their love (or the appearance of it) is lavished only on those who definitely are not marked with the symbol "minus." It does not fare well with those persons whom some government department has thought fit to grade as useless or noxious. In fact, the precise position in the modern materialistic State is that there is no love wasted on the "minus" classes—the "least ones"; and altogether the outlook is so far removed from the true Christian outlook on this matter, that it is not possible for it to produce even a decent counterfeit of true Christian love. Those who, by their self-sacrificing demonstrations of that love in its highest forms, prevent men from being deceived by its counterfeit, do a supreme service to the Church.

"It is hard, you say, to put up with the evil-doer. But just for that very reason, you should devote yourself lovingly to him. Your set purpose must be to wean him from his sinful ways and to lead him on to virtue. But you retort that he does not mind what you say, nor follow your advice. How are you so sure of this? Have you appealed to him and tried to win him round? You reply that you have often reasoned with him. But how often? Frequently, you say, time and time again. And do you look on that as often? Why, even if you had to continue for a whole lifetime, you should neither relax your efforts nor abandon hope. Do you not see the way in which God Himself keeps on appealing to us through His Prophets, through His Apostles, through His Evangelists? And with what result? Is our conduct all it should be? Do we set ourselves to obey Him in all things? Alas! such is far from being the case. Yet in spite of that, He never ceases to pursue us with His pleadings. And why? It is because there is nothing so precious as a soul. 'For what doth it profit a man if he gain the whole world, and suffer the loss of his own soul.' (St. Matt. xvi. 26)."—(St. John Chrysostom).

3.—VISITATION OF THE HOMES OF THE PEOPLE.

Various expedients for the gaining of entrance to these may be utilised. It will be found that the propagation of the devotion of the Enthronement of the Sacred Heart in the home provides a specially favourable introduction and avenue to the friendship of families.

The ideals and the methods which are to characterise that approach are considered in detail in the Section on the Legion Visitation. Therein, it is sufficiently stressed that as far as possible no home should be passed over, and that in each home loving and persevering effort is to be directed towards the inducing of each person, young and old without exception, to ascend at least one step in the spiritual life.

Those detailed to this work may take to themselves in fulness the Twelve Promises of the Sacred Heart. Even the tenth: "I will give to priests the grace to touch the most hardened hearts," belongs in a measure to those who go as the priest's representatives.

Specially encouraged by this thought, the Legionaries will go with perfect confidence to grapple with the cases branded "hopeless."

The Enthronement visitation forms the most fruitful of all introductions, striking the right note of simple piety from the very commencement, facilitating acquaintance and hence repeated visits, and rendering easy the development of the Legion Apostolate.

As it is the mission of Mary to bring about the reign of Jesus, so there is a special appropriateness (which should attract the special graces of the Holy Ghost) in the Legion of Mary propagating the Enthronement.

"If your ambition is that Jesus reign in individuals or in families: first of all bring Mary to them as Queen. The salvation of the world down through the ages can come from no other source than that from which it first proceeded. The human race was saved in the moment of the Incarnation by the Blessed Virgin, and this order changeth nevermore."—(Texier).

4.—THE MAKING OF THE PARISH CENSUS.

There is no more excellent way of getting in touch with the Catholics who need attention or who have drifted into the category of the "lapsed," i.e., those who have lost all association with the Church. Going in the name of the Priest, visitation should, if possible, be from door to door. It is taken as a matter of course by the persons visited that particulars as to religion should be asked, and as a rule they are cheerfully given. Included in what is learned is much that will form subject for long-continued effort on the part of Priest and Legionaries. For example, one Praesidium, in the first year of its life, discovered in a suburban area 77 cases of lapsed Catholics.

But discovery is only the preliminary, and the easiest, step. To restore to the fold each one of those so found must be regarded as being in a measure a trusteeship conferred upon the Legion by God—one to be entered upon with joy and pursued with indomitable spirit. Let not the Legion, through any cause in its own power, fail in the fulfilment of that trust, no matter how long-drawn-out the battle, how arduous the labours, how great the rebuffs, how hardened the cases, how hopeless the prospect.

In addition, it is repeated that not merely the indifferent, but all, shall be the subject of an affectionate attention.

"We have, in the Church's field of apostolic endeavour, an official mission, a providential mode of action, a special weapon of our own. It is that we go to souls not only in the name of Mary and under the auspices of Mary, but also, and above all, that we labour with all our might to fill those souls with child-like love for her."—(Petit Traité de Marialogie.)

5.—THE DISSEMINATION OF CATHOLIC LITERATURE.

"Everything you do for the good Press, I will consider as having been done for me personally"; and again: "It is not enough that a Catholic paper be printed. There must be active propaganda in its support—propaganda from man to man, from house to house. Mark it well, propaganda in favour of the Catholic Press is as necessary as the very writing of Catholic matter itself." These words of Pius XI. show forcibly the importance of action directed to this end.

The foul or anti-religious Press is one menace. The ordinary non-Catholic Press is another and wider one. Convincingly written and attractive, containing nothing openly objectionable, it enters as a universal deluge into every home, and there saturates the minds of the old and young with an outlook which is at bottom the very opposite of the Catholic outlook. To exclude this Press would appear to be impossible, so that there is absolute necessity in each home for a good Catholic weekly, in which, like another ark, their souls may find food and safety.

Moreover, this work can be made to serve as an introduction to homes when other keys are not effective. Especially does this apply to the homes of those who are comfortably circumstanced. Difficult of access to the apostolic worker approaching them on a purely devotional mission, these homes may readily be entered on the literature crusade. In part spoiled by excessive pleasures, preoccupied with the pursuit of money, and with their faith cooled by social intercourse with heresy and unbelief, these homes require the warm sun of Catholic devotion more (yet remain more aloof from its rays) than the homes of the poor. Now, to place in them a Catholic periodical is, as Pius X. has said, to preach to them a perpetual mission. But here again, the Legion wishes the methods of its general apostolate to be brought to bear, and as a *modus operandi* the following is suggested:—

A pair of Legionaries, provided with sample copies of the periodicals adjudged suitable, should proceed methodically from home to home over a district assigned to them. By arguments which should have been the subject of serious consideration beforehand, they should seek to induce each family to become regular readers of one of the papers in question. An annual or even a quarterly subscription should not be sought for, as this will deter many. The Legionaries should themselves arrange to deliver and obtain payment for the paper weekly; and in places where work is not so abundant, it would be useful work to continue permanently the delivery. Otherwise, after an interval sufficient to attain all the objects of their visitation, the delivery of the paper should be transferred to a local newsagent or, better still, to a Junior Praesidium, for which it would form admirable work. The Senior Legionaries will then proceed to break new ground.

During the period of visitation the Legionaries will endeavour to pursue an apostolate directed towards the influencing of every member of the family. Rebuffs in this work may be expected, but such will come more often from surprise and the sting of conscience than from malice, and will readily be turned aside. In many of the cases no results will be obtained; in many others, the primary object of the visitation (i.e., the new subscribers) will be secured, but nothing more; while in a certain number of cases acquaintance will develop and the Legion apostolate may be thoroughly worked.

The subjects of the Enthronement, Confraternity and Sodality membership, the frequentation of the Sacraments, the various Devotions and religious Associations, the Foreign Missions, etc., may be judiciously introduced. Eager listeners will be found in plenty, and the gaining of new members for the Active and Auxiliary ranks of the Legion itself, or for other organisations, may result.

Especially resourceful Legionaries should be assigned to this work, which can be made most fruitful. Where success is achieved it will be of the highest order.

Another method of disseminating Catholic publications is described in the next Section relative to the conducting of a Book-barrow on the streets.

"It was not without special reason that Jesus Christ willed that Mary should stand at the foot of the Cross, and there be shown present at His death as the chief witness to the divinity of the blood which He was shedding for the salvation of the world. Thus the Cross depends upon Mary as much as Mary depends upon the Cross. 'Take Mary away, and the Cross falls down,' said St. Cyril at the Council of Ephesus."—(Mgr. de Ségur).

6.—THE BOOKBARROW.

Legionaries might conduct a Book-barrow in a public place, preferably in or near some busy street. Experience has shown the immense value of this as a Legionary work. There is no more efficacious way of carrying on a comprehensive apostolate directed to the good, the mediocre, and the bad, or of bringing the Church to the notice of the unthinking many. Therefore the Legion earnestly desires that in every large centre there should be at least one such Book-barrow.

A photograph of an actual Barrow in operation will be found facing page 65.

This barrow should be made so as to afford the greatest possible display of titles. It should be stocked with an abundant supply of inexpensive religious publications. Legionaries would form the staff.

Besides those whose primary purpose is to look through the stock with a view to purchase, almost every type of person will be drawn towards such a Barrow. Catholics desirous to talk with their co-religionists; the thoughtless and the indifferent, killing time or led by curiosity; the mildly-interested who are not of the Church, and who would be reluctant to place themselves more directly in touch with it. All these will enter into conversation with the gentle and sympathetic Legionaries in charge, who should be trained to look upon the enquiries and purchases as so many openings for the establishment of friendly "contact." The latter will be utilised to lead on all of those encountered to a higher plane of thought and action. Catholics would be induced to join "something Catholic." Non-Catholics would be helped towards an understanding of the Church. One person will leave the Barrow determined to undertake Daily Mass and Holy Communion; another to become a Legionary, Active or Auxiliary; a third to make his place with God; another bearing in his heart the seeds of conversion to the Church. Visitors to town will be interested in the Legion (which they would not otherwise see), and may be induced to start it in their own places.

It should be unnecessary to remind Legionaries that the persevering following up of the introductions and friendships initiated at the Barrow is a necessary part of the whole work.

The proposal to start a Barrow will always elicit the objection that exceptionally well-versed Catholics would be required to staff it, and are not available. It is true that special knowledge of Catholic Doctrine would be most useful. But the lack of this need not deter from starting the work. For the personal appeal will be the great consideration. As Newman says: "persons influence us, voices melt us, deeds inflame us. We are not converted by syllogisms." In a word, earnestness and sweetness are more important than deep knowledge. The latter is inclined to lure those who possess it into deep water and tortuous channels which lead nowhere, whereas a candid confession of one's weakness: "I do not know": will keep discussion on bedrock.

It will be found that the vast bulk of the difficulties, which are voiced, spring from a great ignorance, and that the ordinary Legionary is well able to deal with them. Less simple points will be brought to the Praesidium or to the Spiritual Director.

Attacks on the Church on the score of evil-doing, persecution, and lack of zeal could be argued indefinitely, and hopelessly confuse the issue. An element of truth may underlie some charges, and thus add complication to confusion. To satisfy the hostile critic on these and all other minor points of dispute is completely impossible, even if great erudition is enlisted in the task. The course to be taken by the Legionary must be that of persistently reducing the discussion to its very simplest elements: that of insisting that God must have left to the world a message—what men call a religion: that such religion, being God's voice, absolutely must be one, clear, consistent, unerring, and must claim divine authority.

These characteristics are to be found only in the Catholic Church. There is no other body or system which even claims to possess them. Outside the Church, there is only contradiction and confusion, so that, as Newman crushingly puts it, "either the Catholic religion is verily the coming of the unseen world into this, or else there is nothing positive, nothing real in any of our notions as to whence we come and whither we go."

There must be a true Church. There can be only one true Church. Where is it, if it is not the Catholic Church? Like blows, ever directed to one spot, this simple line of approach to the Truth has overwhelming effect. Its force is manifest to the simple. It is unanswerable in the heart of the more learned, though he may continue to talk of the sins of the Church. Remind such a one briefly but gently that he proves too much. His objections tell at least as much against any other religious system as they do against the Church. So that if he proves the Church to be false, by proving that Churchmen did wrong, then he has only succeeded in proving that there is no true religion in the world.

"The world can find no helper more powerful than thee. It has its apostles, prophets, martyrs, confessors, virgins, good helpers to whom I pray. But thou, my Queen, art higher than all these intercessors: that which they can all do with thee, thou alone canst do without them. And why? Because thou art the Mother of our Saviour. If thou art silent, none will pray, none will help. If thou prayest, all will pray, all will help."—(St. Anselm).

7.—WORKS FOR THE YOUNG.

If the preservation of the young in faith and innocence can be assured, how glorious the future! Then, like a giant refreshed, the Church could throw itself into its mission of converting the pagan world, and make short work of it. As it is, the great bulk of its effort is absorbed by the painful treatment of internal sores.

Furthermore, it is easier to preserve than later on to restore. The Legion will attend to both, for both are vital. But certainly it should not neglect the easier work of the two—that of preservation. Many children can be saved from disaster for the trouble it will later take to remake one debased adult.

Some aspects of the problem are as follows:—

(a) **Children's Mass Attendance.** A bishop, delivering a programme of work to Legionaries, placed as the item of first importance the conducting of a Sunday Mass Crusade amongst children. Mass missing by children he held to be one of the chief sources of all later trouble. A Sunday morning visitation of the homes of children (whose names would be ascertained from school rolls, etc.) will be found to be of sovereign efficacy.

Incidentally, it is to be borne in mind that children are seldom bad of themselves. Where they are found to be exempting themselves from this elementary Catholic requirement, it can be taken as certain that they are the victims of parental indifference and bad example, and the Legion apostolate should proceed mindful of this additional evil.

In the case of children, more even than in other directions, a spasmodic or short-term visitation will accomplish little or nothing.

(b) **Visitation of the homes of children.** In connection with the visitation of children in their own homes, stress is laid upon an important consideration. It is that an entry to families which otherwise would be, for various reasons, inaccessible to religious workers, may readily be secured when the stated purpose is the approaching of the children of that family. For it is a fact, springing from the natural relation of parent to child, that zeal for the child is above zeal for self. Ordinary parents have regard for the interests of their child even when they are forgetful of their own. The hardest heart softens somewhat at the thought of its own child. Persons may be dead to religion themselves, but deep-rooted impulses bid them not to wish their children the same fate, and instinctive joy is felt at seeing the movements of grace in their children. As a consequence, one who would repulse rudely and even violently those who seek to approach him directly on a spiritual mission, will tolerate the same workers when their mission is to his children.

Competent Legionaries, once admitted to the home, will know how to make **all** the members of that family feel the radiation of their apostolate. A sincere interest in the children will usually make a favourable impression on the parents. This can be skilfully utilised to cultivate in them the seed of the supernatural; so that, as the children had been the key to their parents' home, likewise they will prove to be the key to their parents' hearts and eventually to their souls.

(c) **Teaching Christian Doctrine to Children.** This supremely valuable work should be supplemented by the visitation of the homes of the children whose attendance is not satisfactory, or generally for the purpose of manifesting personal interest in the children, and of getting in touch with the other members of the families. Visitation of this kind is as necessary to the well-being and the extension of Catechism classes as it is in the case of a sodality. Incidentally, the Legion can serve the purpose of local branch of the Archconfraternity of Christian Doctrine. See the relative Appendix.

The following instance shows the efficacy of the application of the Legion system to the Sunday Catechism classes in a populous parish. Despite earnest efforts of the Priests, including appeals from the pulpit, the average attendance of children had fallen to fifty. At this stage a Praesidium was formed which added to the work of teaching, the visitation of the homes of the children. A year's work was sufficient to bring the average attendance at the classes to 600. And this surprising figure does not take count of the spiritual benefits conferred on innumerable careless relatives of the children.

In all works, the Legionary watchword should be: "How would Mary view and treat these, her children?" In this work, even more than in others, that thought should be vivid. There is a natural tendency towards impatience with the children. But a worse fault would lie in the imparting to the instruction of a mere business-like and secular tone, in such a way that these classes would only be regarded by the children as additional hours of school. If this comes to pass, nine-tenths of the harvest will be left unreaped. So once again consider: "How would the Mother of Jesus instruct those children, in each one of whom she sees her own Beloved?"

(d) **The non-Catholic or State School.** The life of the child who is not attending a Catholic school is all a crisis, and it may be hard to prevent it developing in later years into one of the problems. Such measures of remedy as have been approved by the Ecclesiastical Authorities of each place will be taken up by the Legion and applied with all its might.

(e) **Sodalities for the Young.** For children who have been at good schools, the crisis comes at school-leaving age. They are then emancipated from school with its sound influences, its protective restraints, its minute safeguards. Sometimes they were entirely dependent upon that support by reason of the fact that their homes did not provide religious or controlling influences.

There is the further complication that the withdrawal of these things occurs about the age of greatest moral difficulty, and unfortunately, too, when those young people have ceased to be children without becoming adults. Naturally, appropriate provision for that twilight stage is difficult, and accordingly is frequently lacking. Then, when that transition period passes, and the adult safeguarding system opens its arms to them, it usually does so unavailingly. The perilous charms of liberty have been tasted.

Therefore, the supervision which was maintained in school must in some measure be carried on when those children leave. A method which is recommended is that of forming, under the auspices of the Legion, Juvenile Sodalities or at least special juvenile sections in the ordinary Sodalities. Before the children are due to leave school, those in authority will see that the names of such children are supplied to the Legionaries. The latter will then call to their homes to make their acquaintance and to persuade them to join the Sodality. The children, who cannot be induced to join, should be made the subject of special visitation, as also those who attend irregularly.

Each Legionary would be allocated a certain number of the young Sodality members, for whom he or she will be held responsible. Before each Sodality meeting, those members will be called upon to remind them of their duty to attend. An Annual Retreat (enclosed, if possible) and an annual entertainment should form part of the system.

There is no better way, in fact there is no other definite way, of ensuring a regular frequentation of the Sacraments by the young during the post-school period.

The case of young people discharged from Industrial Schools or Orphanages requires special attention in the above direction. Sometimes they are without parents altogether; sometimes they are the victims of bad parents.

(f) **Defective attendance at School.** The signal degree of success, which has already been obtained in this direction, suggests the application of the Legionary visitation to the case of children whose attendance at school is faulty but not yet fit subject for the intervention of a school-attendance officer This officer will be successful in compelling attendance, but he will not so readily get to the root of moral or character defects which will frequently be present in such cases.

It would be the Legionary aim to win the affection of the child, and by interest and encouragement to seek to remove the circumstances which are militating against attendance at school. An unsatisfactory attendance is ordinarily the forerunner of grave disorders later on.

(g) **The conducting of Children's Clubs, Boy Scout and Girl Guide Troops, J. O. C. units, Sewing Classes, branches of the Holy Childhood, etc.** Probably these would be carried on rather as the employment of the work-obligation of part of the membership of a Praesidium than as the whole work of a Praesidium. But it would be quite in order that a Praesidium should devote itself solely to some special work, such as those mentioned. In this case, however, it must be understood that a distinct Praesidium meeting shall be held and carried out fully according to rule. It will not supply the place of the meeting if, as has been suggested, the members are gathered together, as an item of the evening's Special Work, for the purpose of reciting the prayers, reading the minutes, and rushing through a few reports. Possibly in this manner the essentials of a meeting might be conformed to, but a reading of the Section on the Scheme of the Legion will show how little of the spirit of the rules is reflected in such an expedient.

It is the desire of the Legion that during each session of a Special Work of the above type, the Legion prayers should be recited at the opening, intermediate, and concluding stages. If it is not possible to include the Rosary, at least the remainder of the Tessera prayers should be said.

(h) **The use of the "Merit Card" System.** In dealing with Works affecting the young, e.g., a Club, Catechism Class or the like, the Merit Card will be found invaluable for the purpose of preserving and stimulating attendance.

The Merit Card is a small form which contains, in addition to some printed particulars of the work in question, a number of blank lines into which is to be written (a) the name of the child (in order to prevent interchange of cards); (b) the name of the teacher or supervisor (so that a child may not change its class or group without permission); and (c) the date of the particular session.

Presumably an attendance roll will be kept in respect of each session, but in addition a Merit Card, properly filled up, will be given to each child present. This tangible result of its attendance appeals to the child-mind and to its instinct for acquisition. This by itself would aid attendance. But the Merit Card has a more definite grip. Periodically, an entertainment will be given by way of reward for those possessing a stipulated number of Merit Cards It is urged that the system be strictly administered, i.e., that the qualifying number of cards be fixed high (say at 80 per cent. of the maximum possible), and not departed from because plausible excuses are presented, or out of an eleventh-hour sense of pity for those found wanting. For even the youngest are clever to exploit the weaknesses of any system; and if they succeed, it will collapse.

"It would be easy to dwell upon the many lessons of the extraordinarily active life of St. John Bosco. I select only one, because of its extreme and lasting importance, namely, his view of the relations which should exist between teachers and taught, superiors and subjects, masters and pupils, in school, or college, or seminary. He rightly held in extreme abhorrence the spirit of aloofness, of keeping at a distance, of exaggerated dignity which, sometimes on principle, sometimes from thoughtlessness, at times from pure selfishness, makes superiors and masters almost inaccessible to those whose training and formation God has entrusted to them. Blessed John Bosco never forgot the words 'Have they made thee ruler? be not lifted up: be among them as one of them: have care of them.' (Ecclesiasticus xxxii)."—(Cardinal Bourne).

8.—STUDY.

Study could advantageously be carried on by some or all of the members of a Praesidium as an addition to their other work. Certain types of Praesidia should undertake it as a matter of course, e.g., Internal and Junior Praesidia and those which specialise in the giving of instruction.

The intense spirit of prayer and the devotional system of the Legion secures an admirable approach to such study and averts the disadvantageous possibilities which sometimes attach. The self-sufficient, the knowledge-proud, and such like, who would enter only to disturb and to drop out, will be repelled by the system. On the other hand, the latter will hold to membership those whom the quickly-spent novelty of study would not retain.

Moreover, the success of the study will be guaranteed by its being undertaken in a spirt of union with her whose seeking of light was so humble, so simple, that it forms ever the perfect model for its pursuit: "How shall this be done?" (St. Luke i. 34). Then to her He was given who is the Divine Wisdom, the Eternal Truth, the True Light. She remains the guardian of this treasure. To her must come those who wish to draw from it. Those Legionaries will see in their weekly Praesidium meeting a clustering round their lovely Mother, a twining of their hands in hers, so full of the treasures of knowledge they seek.

Thus, the salient characteristic is that the Legionary approaches his work of study from the angle of devotion rather than as an intellectual exercise. Another distinctive feature is that the study is not based on a lecture system; partly because the latter could not be accommodated to the Praesidium system; but still more, because it is a human tendency to relax in the face of a situation where one or a few assume all the work and all the responsibility, as the lecturer does. Moreover, in practice, a lecture is graded to the maximum intelligence of the audience, and hence presents difficulties to the bulk of the hearers. The result is that the subject matter is not completely apprehended, and as an inevitable consequence is quickly forgotten. Again, the proportion of those who listen to a clever lecture in an appreciative, but otherwise completely inert mental condition, is quite remarkable.

On the other hand, in the Legion system, the member is not allowed to relax. Each one is called upon to render an account of his work. This ensures in his case—on a different grade, it is true, but with equal intensity—the assumption of the effort and the responsibility which in the lecture system falls practically entirely on the lecturer. The member is not merely a listener. His mental state is active, not receptive. He is definitely at work. At the same time his progress is checked and supervised.

The report of each member is delivered sitting. His textbook is before him. Any notes he may have taken are beside him. There is nothing in the surroundings to deprive him of confidence. His report is couched in his own phraseology, and conveys his own thoughts and difficulties in a way which rings simple and familiar to every other ear. There may be comment or questioning from others. Then the next report is taken. It will be seen that the meeting progresses, not as a motor, swiftly carrying its passengers over the ground, but as the plough and harrow painfully tearing it up. By the time the chapter of a book has been dug and re-dug by the succeeding reports of the members of the study group, it will certainly be understood by all, and therefore remembered.

The work of study being one with the general work of the Praesidium, it is certain that it will be animated with the active spirit of the Legion, which will urge the members to put their knowledge to practical use. To that end, Praesidia which have made progress in studies, should consider the taking up of classes, instruction work, Catholic Evidence Guild work, and other means of radiating the special knowledge which the members have acquired. Incidentally, they cannot fail to spread abroad in the Legion a greater desire to be well-informed in matters of the Faith. Knowledge possessed in the Legion must tend to diffuse itself to the general population through the medium of the innumerable avenues of Legionary contact. Thus, a step is made towards "the removing of that deepest disgrace of Catholic peoples, the ignorance of Divine religion."—(Pius XI.: Motu Proprio. June 29, 1923.)

The very first book to be studied should be the Legion Handbook. Indeed it is the essential basis for any other course of study which is in view. For, unless the Legion system is properly understood, it cannot be successfully applied to the work of study or to any type of work. All would regard it as a senseless proceeding to erect a house without looking to its foundations. It would be equally futile to seek to build the edifice of study on the foundation of the Legion system, without giving the latter the solidity which only comes from a complete knowledge of it.

Other branches of study which could most profitably be undertaken would be (in the order suggested):—Dogma and Apologetics, Sacred Scripture, Social Science, Liturgy, Church History, Moral Theology.

A definite portion of the meeting—possibly part of the time following the Allocutio—should be earmarked for the consideration of this work. Special care should be given to this part of the agenda so as to provide a firm framework for this section of the meeting and thereby ensure that it will not develop into a mere desultory discussion.

At each meeting a section of the course will be set for subsequent private study by the members. The members must apply themselves to this work with a high degree of Legionary thoroughness and devotion, for there is a tendency to drift, without realising it, into negligent and unworthy performance. The actual study is free from the effective observation of any but heavenly witnesses. Moreover, the Praesidium is not an ordinary school-class. It is easy to produce a passable report to it, even where the study has been carelessly done.

It is stressed that the work-obligation of each member can only be discharged by the performance of a substantial active weekly task. A smaller amount of active work might be allowed in consideration of the fact that a member is also engaged on study, but it is not permissible to satisfy the work-obligation by study alone. Furthermore, additional ordinary active work should be taken on according as, and to the extent that, the work of study diminishes in quantity or in difficulty.

At each meeting, the members must individually report on their week's work. In their reports they may bring forward any difficulty which has been encountered in the course of the week's reading. Members however, should be discouraged from lightly bringing forward difficulties of a kind which could be solved by a little additional effort on their part.

Self-help and individual effort on the part of the members should be encouraged as much as possible. Care should be exercised that the discussions do not err into unnecessary or undesirable channels, and that points too deep or in any way misleading or irrelevant are not pursued. In all these matters, the chief reliance of the Praesidium will, of course, be the Spiritual Director.

"How closely allied are purity and light! The purest souls are those to whom God gives the most light. That is why our Blessed Lady is of all creatures the most illumined. It has been said of her that she enlightens the angels. But, likewise, she enlightens men, and the Church styles her the Seat of Wisdom. It follows that our studies, our contemplations, our whole life, should gravitate ever more closely around that Woman, of all women the most blessed, the Mother of the Light of light—the Word made flesh. For God has clothed that incomparable creature with the

Sun, and has set her to cast the light of Jesus over the entire world and into every soul which will open to receive it."—(Sauvé: Marie Intime).

9.—RECRUITING MEMBERS FOR PARISH SOCIETIES.

The successful working of the ordinary Church Confraternity or Sodality depends to a greater extent upon the organising of the members than on the qualities or eloquence of the Priest in charge. To keep members, rather than to gain them, is the great problem. The best proof of this is the fact that great numbers join the Parish Societies in response to appeals at Missions or Retreats, yet membership does not grow in proportion or at all. If those who give in their names could only be retained in membership, what a Society! and what an effect upon the Parish!

Now it is certain that many who thus drop out would be retained by looking them up. To do this, and also to canvass for new members, are part of every Prefect's duty. Yet these duties are not usually performed, and probably, indeed, are incapable of being carried out without special organisation directed to that end. Prefects' organisations, meeting regularly, considering membership matters, and supervising the individual Prefect, should be admirable, but do not seem to thrive in practice.

It is suggested, therefore, that the above purpose can be provided for, without the creation of additional machinery, by including the work in the miscellaneous activities of a Praesidium, where it would be attended to, preferably by the very Prefects themselves, become Legionaries.

Such a Praesidium would map out the necessary duties and see that they were faithfully discharged. It would soon have all the better-inclined persons enrolled in Parish Societies and it would seek by various expedients to lift these to still higher levels. Then, through them, it would operate a plan of campaign to reach and influence those who are satisfied with inferior standards of religious living.

Such a Praesidium could be made the heart of a whole town.

"Jesus and Mary are the two primary foundations of the Christian religion. They are the two living sources of each and every blessing which flows to us, the two subjects of our love, the two objects which we must keep in view in all our actions and religious exercises. That person is not a genuine Christian who does not possess devotion to the Mother of Jesus Christ and of all Christians. After God, we must refer to her our whole being and the details of our life. We must place ourselves in dependence on her, and beg her to take charge of all our concerns. We should give ourselves to her and submit ourselves to her as if we were her slaves."—(St. John Eudes, Kingdom of Jesus, 111. Ch. XI).

10.—MISSION TO THE CATHOLIC SERVANT.

This can be carried out as part of the foregoing work or as a special work in itself. Only too often placed in households indifferent or hostile to the faith, viewed as a mere machine, isolated, frequently fresh from the country, thrown upon the city friendless and reduced to forming chance acquaintanceships full of the possibilities of disaster, the Catholic servant is a particularly forlorn class, and the getting into touch with her forms an apostolate of a notable kind.

To her, the weekly visit of Legionaries solicitous for her welfare will come as a ray of light. Generally the object will be to bring the girl into Sodality membership, into suitable friendship, suitable clubs if available, and even in many cases into Legionary membership itself. This work will mean the placing of the feet of many in new and happier ways, leading on to safety and holiness.

"At first sight we might certainly have anticipated that much state and dignity would have been allotted to God's great Mother during some portion, at least, of her life upon earth. How different was the reality, as arranged by the Providence of God. We find Mary in her poor dwelling discharging such homely duties as sweeping the floor, washing the linen, cooking the food, going to and fro to the well with a pitcher on her head, engaged in that kind of work which we, in face of the example set by Jesus, Mary and Joseph, venture to call menial. Mary's hands were doubtless reddened and hardened by toil, she was often weary and overworked; hers were the anxieties of a working man's wife."—(Vassall-Phillips: The Mother of Christ).

11.—WORK FOR SOLDIERS AND SEAMEN.

The circumstances of these men's lives incline them to neglect of religion and expose them to many pitfalls. Therefore an apostolate among them is doubly desirable.

(a) As access to barracks may not always be easy to civilians, effective work for soldiers may require the setting up of Praesidia composed of soldiers. This has already been done in many places with signal success.

(b) Work for seamen will call for the visitation of ships and the provision for various facilities on shore. Praesidia undertaking this work should affiliate with the recognized international society, the Apostolatus Maris, which has branch-headquarters in the majority of maritime countries.

(c) The Legionaries must exhibit meticulous respect for military or marine discipline. Their actions must never run counter to regulations or traditions. In fact, they must aspire to earn for their apostolate the unreserved admission that it uplifts the men in every way, and represents an unmixed asset to those services, and more than an asset—a positive necessity.

"In the second half of the sixteenth century, the Infidels were carrying their bloody scimitars everywhere without resistance and with the design, as they loudly proclaimed, of ravaging Europe and exterminating everything Christian. The holy Pontiff, St. Pius V, seeing the danger addressed himself to God through Mary. Then the Christian fleet sailed to meet the enemy flotilla. The latter awaited them in the Gulf of Lepanto. It had more vessels, superior forces, prestige, pride from conquest, and a reputation of being invincible. The Christians relied on the help of Mary, the Pope, at their departure having commanded them to salute her with one voice before going into action. The Infidel fleet was almost entirely destroyed, and their Empire never recovered from the defeat.

"At the very hour of victory, knowledge of it was revealed to the Pope then at Rome. The people hastened to the churches to Thank God and His Holy Mother. This was the 7th of October and the first Sunday of the month. To perpetuate the memory of this glorious event Pius V ordered that the festival of the Holy Rosary should be celebrated on the first Sunday of October and to the Litanies of the Blessed Virgin he added the words, Auxilium Christianorum, ora pro nobis.

"The naval power of the Infidels no longer inspired terror, but their land forces were still very formidable. It was in the next century, and under the protection of Mary that their power was finally crushed.—(Petitalot: The Virgin Mother).

"In 1683 the Infidels again menaced Europe. Marching on Vienna, they had reduced it to the last stages of despair, when the king of Poland, John Sobieski, came to its aid. He had but twenty-four thousand soldiers, while the Infidels numbered two hundred thousand. But he had fortified himself with the Bread of the Strong and had placed his army under the protection of the Blessed Virgin. His watchword was the invocation of the name of Mary. Scarcely had he appeared on the heights overlooking Vienna, when sudden panic seized the enemy who gave themselves to headlong flight. Soon Sobieski was in possession of the field of battle. Never had victory cost the victors less blood; never was victory more complete. It is in memory of this great event that Pope Innocent XI instituted the feast of the Holy Name of Mary."—(Millot: Toute Grace par Marie.)

12.—THE FORWARDING OF THE PRACTICE OF DAILY MASS AND FREQUENT HOLY COMMUNION.

"I greatly desire that Daily Communion"—and hence Daily Mass—"so salutary and so agreeable to God, may be, by the grace of God, propagated everywhere amongst the Christian people." (Pius X: Decree of June 3rd, 1905.)

Probably this will be carried on less as a work in itself than as one to be kept in mind and assiduously pursued as part and parcel of every Legionary activity. See Section: The Legionary and the Eucharist.

"We see how the Eucharist, sacrifice and sacrament, sums up in the abundance of its richness all that the Cross offered to God and procured for men. It is the Blood of Calvary and the dew of heaven at one and the same time: the Blood that cries for mercy, and the vivifying dew that raises up the drooping plant. It is the price paid for us, and the blessing brought to us. It is life and the price of life. The Cross was not worth more, nor the Supper, nor the two together: and all of it endures, and all of it is fraught with all the hopes of humanity. For these reasons the Mass is well called the Mystery of Faith; not only because the whole Christian dogma—which is the dogma of our ruin in Adam and of our restoration in Jesus Christ—is summed up in it; but also, and chiefly, because the drama, the heroic action by which was accomplished that sublime uplifting of humanity and superabundant compensation for our former losses, continues in our midst by means of it. And it is not a repetition by way of a mere symbol, but actually realises in our midst what was accomplished by Christ Himself."—(De la Taille: The Mystery of Faith).

13.—THE RECRUITING AND AFTER-CARE OF AUXILIARIES.

Every Praesidium which has a sense of appreciation of the power of prayer, will strive to possess a well-filled roll of Auxiliary members. It is the duty of each Legionary to gain Auxiliaries and to try to keep in touch with them.

Consider the generosity of these Auxiliaries who have given up to the Legion part of the precious breathings of their souls. What possibilities of sanctity are in them! The Legion is under infinite debt to them. That debt it can beautifully repay by leading those Auxiliaries on to perfection. Active members and Auxiliaries, both are children of the Legion. The Active members are the elder children; and the Mother of the Legion, as in every family, will look to them to help her with the younger ones. She will not merely supervise that help. She will make it effective, so that in the "after-care" of Auxiliary by Active Legionary lies wonderful things for both of them. In the soul of the Auxiliary rises a great edifice of sanctity; and for the Active Legionary there is the builder's reward.

This work for the Auxiliaries is so full of possibilities that it seems to call for the specialised attention of some highly spiritual members of the Praesidium, who will pursue it in the spirit of the "elder children."

"I think it is evident that in these days of awful sin and hatred of God, Our Blessed Lord wants to gather round Him a legion of chosen souls who will be devoted, heart and soul, to Him and His interests; and upon whom He may always count for help and consolation; souls who will not ask 'How much must I do?' but rather 'How much can I do for His love?': a legion of souls who will give and will not count the cost, whose only pain will be that they cannot do more, and give more, and suffer more for Him who has done so much for them: in a word, souls who are not as the rest of men, and who may be fools, perhaps, in the eyes of the world; for their watchword is sacrifice and not self-comfort."—(Alfred O'Rahilly: Life of Father William Doyle.)

14.—MISCELLANEOUS PAROCHIAL AID.

Important purposes to be served will be:—

(a) The conducting of a religious programme on Sundays and holidays of obligation in places where there is no Priest available to say Mass.

(b) Altar Society work.

(c) The keeping of the Church clean and beautiful.

(d) The care of the blind and the sick, including, where necessary, the preparation of their homes for the visit of the Priest.

(e) Stewarding at Mass. Commonly a lack of attention to order will be followed by unpunctuality and irreverence.

(f) The securing of the recitation of the Rosary at wakes and funerals.

(g) The conducting of instruction classes.

(h) The promotion of all the Catholic Associations and activities, especially those which require the wearing of a badge—so potent (in some places heroic) a method of furthering the interests of the Faith.

(i) And generally the gaining of members for "anything Catholic," with the purpose of bringing every soul in some manner into the protective network of the Church, and thus securing the safety alike of the individual and of the community.

"I desire, like the Mother of Grace, to work for God. I desire to co-operate by my labours and sacrifices towards my own salvation and that of the whole world, as the Holy Scripture says of the Machabees, who in the holy enthusiasm of their courage, 'did not care to save themselves alone, but undertook to save the greatest possible number of their brethren.' "—(Gratry: Month of Mary).

15.—WORK FOR THE FOREIGN MISSIONS.

Even a couple of Legionaries in each Praesidium, assigned to this work, can accomplish much. They might open a branch of the Holy Childhood and surround themselves with a host of children whom they will inspire with love for the Missions ("I would wish every Catholic child to be a member of this admirable Association."—Pius XI.) Or again, they might gather about them a group of those unsuited for full Legion membership and (perhaps organising them on the basis of the Auxiliary degree of Legion membership or of Junior membership) set them to sew, make vestments, etc. Here are three works done in one—(a) the Legionary sanctifies himself; (b) he sets many others to sanctify themselves; (c) the work of the Missions is helped in a practical way.

In connection with this work, it is specially necessary to stress two points, which however apply generally:—

(a) No Praesidium is to be turned into a mere collecting agency for any purpose whatsoever.

(b) The superintendence and regulation of persons engaged on sewing would be a satisfactory employment of the work obligation. But the work of sewing, by itself, is not deemed to represent a substantial active work for a Senior Legionary except in very special circumstances, such as, for instance, actual physical disability.

"When we ponder over the fact that the pagans number even in our day almost a billion, we have no rest in our spirit."—(Pius XI).

16—EACH PLACE HAS ITS OWN SPECIAL NEEDS.

Legionaries will employ any other means of achieving the objects of the Legion which local circumstances may suggest, and which may be approved by the governing authority of the Legion, conformity with Ecclesiastical Authority being always understood. Once again it is insisted that the outlook on possible works should be one of enterprise and courage.

Each deed of heroism done under the Catholic flag has an effect, which may be styled electrifying, upon the modes of thought of that place. All, even the irreligious, are startled into a new seriousness towards religion. Those new standards will modify the way of living of the entire population.

"'Be not afraid,' said Jesus. So let us put away fear. We want no timid ones among us. If ever there is need to repeat those words of Christ: 'Be not afraid,' it is unquestionably in relation to the works of Catholic Action. For fear unfits the mind for action and deprives us of the power to judge truly. So—I say it again—fear must be put far from us—fear of every kind save one alone: that kind I would wish to teach you: It is the fear of God. Possessing it, you will not fear men nor the upsets of this world.

"And as for prudence, it must be such as Holy Scripture defines it and does not tire in recalling: the prudence of the sons of God, the prudence of the spirit. It must not be—it is not—the prudence of the flesh—weak, lazy, stupid, selfish, miserable."—(Discourse of Pius XI: May 17th, 1931).

CARDINAL POINTS OF THE LEGION APOSTOLATE.

1. Active Work must be done.

The Legion without its spirit would be like any other lifeless body. That spirit of the Legion, so transforming of its members, is not floating around in the air, waiting to be breathed in. No! that vital spirit is the product of grace out of effort. It depends on the work which is being done, and on the way in which it is being done by the individual Legionaries. If there is no effort, the spirit flickers low and may die.

Due to (1) a reluctance to embark on work which is considered difficult, or (2) to an inability to discern the work which exists abundantly even in the smallest places, but most of all to (3) a dread of adverse criticism; there may be a tendency to avoid active work, or to allot insignificant tasks to the members. But all are warned that the Legion machinery is designed to supervise substantial active work. **There is no justification for setting up the system at all, unless such work is being undertaken. An army which refuses to engage in battle: what a misnomer! Similarly, members of a Praesidium, which is not engaged in some form of active work, have no right to the name of Legionaries of Mary. It is reiterated that spiritual exercises do not satisfy the Legionary obligation to do active work.**

The inactive Praesidium is not only untrue to the Legion purpose of showing a virile apostolate in action, but it does a further grave injustice to the Legion. It creates the impression that the Legion is not suited to the doing of certain work, whereas the real fact is that the Legion, though perfectly capable, is not even being employed on that work.

2. Material Relief prohibited.

Material relief must not be given—even in the smallest ways; and experience shows that it is necessary to mention that old clothing belongs to this category.

In ruling thus the Legion does not slight the act of relief-giving in itself. It simply declares that for the Legion it is impracticable. To give to the poor is a good work. Done with a supernatural motive, it is a sublime one. The systems of many great Societies rest upon this principle; notably that of the Society of St. Vincent de Paul, to whose example and spirit the Legion rejoices to proclaim itself deeply indebted—so much, in fact, as to make it possible to say that the roots of the Legion lay in that Society. But to the Legion is assigned a different field of duty. Its system is built upon the principle of bringing spiritual good to every individual in the population. This programme and one of relief-giving are not compatible in practice; and this for numerous reasons. Some of these are:—

(a) The visits of an organisation which gives relief will seldom be welcomed by persons who do not need relief. They will fear lest such a visitation would label them in the eyes of their neighbours as benefiting in some material way. So the Praesidium which earns the name of relief-giving will quickly find its field of work narrowed exceedingly. **Material relief may be to other societies a key which opens. It is the key with which the Legion locks itself out.**

(b) Those who expect to receive, and are disappointed, become aggrieved and hence impervious to Legionary influence.

(c) Even among those who are subjects for relief, the Legion will not accomplish spiritual good by giving. Let the Legion leave this to those other agencies whose special work it is, and which have a special grace for it. Certainly, Legionaries will have no grace for it, because thereby they break their rule. The Praesidium, which errs in this way, will find itself involved in grievous complications, and will never bring anything but sorrow to the Legion.

Individual Legionaries may plead the duty of giving charity according to one's means, and may urge that they do not desire to give relief as Legionaries, but in their private capacities. Analysis of this contention will indicate what complications must inevitably arise. Suppose the case—and it is the usual case—of one who did not indulge in such personal relief-giving prior to joining the Legion. In his rounds, he comes across persons whom he deems to be in need in some way or another. He refrains from giving anything on the day of the official Legion visit, but goes some other day "as a private individual," and gives. Surely he is breaking the Legion rule as to the giving of material relief, and surely the double visitation only covers a quibble? He visited in the first instance as a Legionary. The cases came to his knowledge as a Legionary. The recipients know him as a Legionary; and certainly they do not enter into the quibble. To them, the transaction is simply one of Legion relief-giving, and the Legion agrees that they judge rightly.

Be it remembered that the disobedience or the indiscretion of a single member in this direction may compromise the whole Praesidium. The name of relief-giving is easily won. It does not require a hundred instances. A couple suffice.

If a Legionary, for some reason, is set upon helping a particular case, why not save the Legion from all complications by giving anonymously through a friend, or through some appropriate agency? Reluctance to do this, in the circumstances, would seem to indicate that the Legionary is seeking an earthly rather than a heavenly reward for the act of charity.

Legionaries will not, however, be indifferent to the material needs which they will inevitably find in their visitation, and they should bring such cases to the notice of other organisations suited to the type of need which is in question. But should all efforts by the Legion fail to secure the desired help, the Legion is not itself to step into the gap. That is not its work, and it is impossible to conceive that in any modern community no other individuals or agency can be found which will look to the relief of a deserving case.

Much in the same category as relief-giving, and coming under the same ban, would lie the regular utilisation of the Legionary visitation for the purpose of collecting money. Such might secure the money, but never the atmosphere for the accomplishment of spiritual good, and would represent a supreme example of the policy known as "penny wise pound foolish."

"Unquestionably, the pity which we show to the poor by relieving their needs is highly commended by God. But who will deny that a far higher place is held by that zeal and effort which applies itself to the work of instruction and persuasion, and thereby bestows on souls not the passing benefits of earth but the goods that last for ever." (Pius X: Encyclical of April 15th, 1905 on the Teaching of Christian Doctrine.)

3. Home to home visitation desirable.

The Legion visitation should be as far as possible from home to home, irrespective of the type of people reported to be living there. Offence may be taken if persons think they are being singled out for attention.

Even the homes of those discovered to be non-Catholics should not—except strong reasons to the contrary exist—be passed by. These are not to be approached in a spirit of religious aggression, but for the purpose of establishing a footing of friendship. The explanation that all homes are being visited to make the acquaintance of their tenants, will lead to a kindly reception in many non-Catholic homes, a circumstance which Divine Providence may utilise as an instrument of grace to those "other sheep" which He desires to have within the fold. A friendship towards Catholics of the apostolic type will cause many prejudices to die; and a respect for Catholics will unquestionably be followed by a respect for Catholicism. Information may be sought, books asked for, and from all this still greater things may come.

4. The essence of Legion work is its desire to reach every individual, to take into the sphere of its apostolate not merely the neglectful, not alone the Household of the Faith, not only the poor or the degraded, but ALL.

Especially will the presence of heresy or infidelity on a great scale spur on the Legionary to counter-efforts as great; and the most repulsive forms of religious neglect must not intimidate the Legionary. There is no person, however abandoned and hopeless to all appearance, in whom the faith and courage and perseverance of the Legionary will not produce results. On the other hand, it would be an intolerable limitation of the mission of the Legion to confine attention to the graver evils. The special attractiveness of the search for the sheep that is straying or in the hands of the thief, should not blind the Legionary to the fact that a wider field lies to hand in the urging on of that vast multitude who, though called by God to sanctity, are contenting themselves with a life of mere performance of the essential duties. Now, to induce persons, who have been content with merely satisfying their obligations, to take on works of zeal or devotion will only be accomplished by a long-continued visitation, requiring much patience. But if, as Father Faber says, one saint is worth a million ordinary Catholics; and if, as St. Teresa tells us, one soul, not a saint but seeking sanctity, is more precious to God than thousands living common lives, how delightful then the achievement of setting the first steps of many in the path that turns aside from the ordinary rut.

5. No one is too bad to be uplifted; no one too good. Not a single one of those encountered in visitation should be left on the same level as when found. There is no one so good that he may not be brought a great deal nearer to God. Frequently will Legionaries find themselves approaching persons who are holier far than they, but even then it is not for them to doubt their capacity to do great good. They will impart new ideas, new devotions. They may enliven a routine. Certainly, they cannot fail to edify by their cheerful practice of the apostolic life. So, whether the Legionaries are dealing with the saint or the sinner, let them proceed, confident in the knowledge that they are not there in their own spiritual poverty but as the representatives of Mary's Legion, "united with their pastors and their bishops, with the Holy See and with Christ."—(Pius XI: Encyclical of December 23rd, 1922.)

6. A vague apostolate is of little value.

In each case the purpose must be the effecting of considerable and definite good. Great good must be done to a great number, if possible; if not, then great good to a smaller number; never a little good to a great number. The Legionary who is treading the latter path does one evil in that he is labelling as done, work which is, according to Legion ideas, little more than begun, thus preventing others from entering upon it. But another danger lies in the fact that the moment of discouragement will represent the little good done to the many as being in reality no good done to anyone. This feeling of ineffective membership places the latter in peril.

7. The secret of influence is love.

It is to be emphasised that the effecting of real and extensive good can be hoped for only as the result of intensive visitation directed towards the establishing of a footing of intimacy between the visitors and the visited. Good otherwise effected will be only scanty or accidental. This must especially be borne in mind in the case of visitation carried out under the auspices of the Enthronement of the Sacred Heart or of the

Literature Crusade. Though the latter are excellent in themselves and the source of blessings, they are not to be esteemed the principal aim. A visitation that quickly results in the Enthronement, etc., and is then discontinued, would in the eyes of the Legion have reaped but little of the fruits intended. Many and extended visits to each family means slow progress by a pair of Legionaries, and hence the need for many Legionaries and many Praesidia.

8. Visitation in pairs a safeguard of Legionary discipline.

Visitation should be carried out in pairs. In prescribing thus, the Legion has in view the following purposes:—First, the safeguarding of the Legionaries. Ordinarily, it will be less the streets, than the actual homes being visited, which will call for this precaution. Second, the visitation in pairs is a source of mutual encouragement. It is a help against the movements of human respect or common timidity when visiting difficult places or homes where one is exposed to a cold reception. Third, it puts the seal of discipline on the work. It secures punctuality and fidelity in the carrying out of the appointed visitation. If left to oneself, one is easily led to alter the time of, or postpone altogether, one's weekly visitation. Fatigue, bad climatic conditions, natural reluctance to face the unpleasant visit, all operate freely if there is no appointment to be kept with another. The result is that the visitation becomes disorderly and irregular and unsuccessful, and eventually is abandoned altogether.

The usual practice in regard to the situation which arises as a result of a Legionary failing to keep an appointment with his co-visitor is the following. If the work is, say, Hospital visitation, or other work where there is, obviously, no element whatever of risk, the Legionary may proceed to it alone. If, on the other hand, it is work which would throw the Legionary into difficult circumstances, or where disreputable surroundings are in question, the Legionary must forego the visitation. It is to be understood that the above permission to visit alone is exceptional. Repeated failures on the part of the co-visitor to keep appointments should be viewed very seriously by the Praesidium.

This requirement as to visitation in pairs is not to be read as meaning that the two must together address themselves to the same persons. For instance, if a hospital ward is in question, it would be in order, and in fact the proper course, for the two Legionaries to move about separately and devote themselves to different individuals.

9. Control of the work by the Praesidium.

The work is to be appointed by the Praesidium. Members are not free to undertake in the name of the Legion any work they may think fit. This rule, however, should not be interpreted so rigidly as to prevent a member from availing of a chance of doing good which may cross his path. In fact, the Legionary must regard himself as being in a sense always on duty. Work, encountered accidentally, could be brought up and reported upon at the following meeting, and if adopted by the Praesidium would then become ordinary Legionary work. But in all this the Praesidium should be careful. There is a natural tendency in many people of great goodwill to do everything but what they are supposed to do, to wander all over the field instead of standing at the work which has been assigned to them. These persons will do harm rather than good, and if not curbed will do much towards breaking down the Legionary discipline.

Once the sense of responsibility to the Praesidium, the idea that one is its messenger going from it with definite instructions and returning to it to report on the execution of the allotted work is shaken, the work itself will soon cease to be done, or else be a source of danger to the Legion. Should a grave error be the sequel of such independent action, the Legion would be held to blame, although the fault had proceeded from disregard of the Legion system.

When specially enthusiastic Legionaries complain

that their efforts to do good are being fettered by too much discipline, it is well to analyse the matter along the above lines. But it is also necessary to take care that a complaint of this kind is not founded; for the essential purpose of discipline is to drive people on, not to hold them back.

10. In each one worked for, the Legionary sees and serves Christ.

Nowhere and in no case is visitation to be carried out in a spirit of philanthropy or mere human pity for the unfortunate. "So often as you did it unto one of these my least brethren, you did it to Me." With these words written on his heart, the Legionary must see Our Lord in his neighbour (who is all mankind without distinction) and render service accordingly. The evil, the unthankful, the stupid, the afflicted, the despised, the outcast, the greatest objects of natural repulsion, all are to be viewed in this new light. They are surely the least of Christ's brethren and (mindful of Christ's words) to be rendered a princely and reverential service.

Always will the Legionary bear in mind that he is visiting not as a superior to an inferior, not as one equal to another, but as an inferior to his superior, as the servant to the Lord. It is the absence of this spirit that produces the patronising manner. The visitor, possessed of the latter, will accomplish neither supernatural nor natural good. His presence will be tolerated only when he is the bearer of gifts. On the other hand, the gentle, sympathetic visitor, humbly asking admission to the homes at which he knocks, will be joyfully received though his gifts are not material; and he will quickly establish himself on a footing of true friendship. Legionaries should bear in mind that a want of simplicity in dress or accent will raise a barrier between them and those they visit, which no degree of excellence may avail to lower.

11. Every door opens to the humble and respectful Legionary.

Inexperience is apprehensive of the "First Visit," but the Legionary, whether new or tried, who has taken to heart the lesson of the preceding clause, possesses the "open sesame" to every home.

It is insisted that one does not enter by any form of right, but solely by the courtesy of the occupants. Approach must be made cap-in-hand, so to speak, one's whole demeanour showing the respect with which one would enter the palaces of the great. A statement of one's mission, accompanied by a humble request to be permitted to enter, will usually open wide the door and bring an invitation to be seated. Then the Legionaries must remember that they are not there to lecture, or to ask a multitude of questions, but to sow the seeds of that eventual intimacy which will open the floodgates of knowledge and influence.

It has been said that the special glory of charity is to understand others. There is no greater need in this sad world than such a gift. For "the majority of people seem to suffer from a sense of neglect. They are unhappy because nobody takes them in hand, because nobody is ready to accept the confidences they offer." (Duhamel).

Initial difficulties must not be taken too seriously. Even where deliberate rudeness is at work, a meek submission will turn it to shame and produce its harvest at a later stage.

Interest in the children provides opportunity for conversation. Questions as to their religious knowledge and reception of the Sacraments may be asked, which at this early stage might be resented by the elders if asked about themselves; and through the children, efficacious lessons may be addressed to the parents.

Departing, the way must be left open for another call. The simple intimation that one has enjoyed the visit, and hopes to see the family again next week, provides both a natural leavetaking and an effective preparation for the return-visit.

12. The Legionary must not sit in judgment.

Not alone the Legionary manner, but—still more important—the Legionary mind, must be stamped with this delicate respect. It is inconsistent with the mission of the Legionary for him to sit in judgment on his neighbour, or to set up his own standards of thought and conduct as standards which must be conformed to by all. He must not assume that those who differ from him in various ways, who refuse to receive him, or even oppose him, are necessarily unworthy persons.

There are many people whose actions seem open to criticism, but the Legionary is not to be the critic. Too often such persons are like the Saints who were wrongly accused. Again, the lives of many are unsightly with grave abuses. But God alone sees the heart and can judge as to the real position. For, as Gratry says: "many lack the benefit of primitive education. They are born without moral patrimony, and perhaps as food for their journey through this difficult life have received only perverted maxims and examples. But likewise, nothing will be asked of anyone but that which has been given to him."

There are many, too, who parade their riches and whose lives are far from mortified. Of these it is the spirit of the day to speak in bitter words. But here again the Legionary must reflect. There is always the possibility that such persons may resemble Nicodemus, who came to Our Lord secretly by night, and who did much for Him, won Him many friends, loved Him truly, and in the end had the unique privilege of assisting at His burial.

The role of Legionaries is never to be that of judge or critic. They must always consider how Mary's soft eyes would look on all those circumstances and persons. Then let them try to act as she would act.

13. Through the Legionary, Mary loves and tends her Son.

The words of a Legionary explaining the successful outcome of a very unpleasant and difficult visitation:

"We got them to like us," admirably summarise Legionary methods. To awaken this affection, it is first necessary to show it: to love those visited. There is no other way, no other diplomacy, no other key to real influence. St. Augustine puts the same idea in another form when he declares: "Love and do what you will."

But can one love to order in this way? Yes, by seeing in all of those met the Person of Our Blessed Lord. Love is enkindled at the very thought. Again, it is most certain that Mary wills that there be shown to the mystical body of her Beloved Son just such another love as she lavished on His actual body. In this she will help her Legionaries. Where she finds in them the gleam, the readiness to love, she will fan it to a consuming flame.

14. Attitude in an Institution.

Legionaries visiting an institution must remember that they are there simply on tolerance, as much guests as if in a private house. The officials there always look somewhat doubtfully upon the charitable visitor who, coming in to visit the inmates, is apt to forget that deference is also due to the staff and to rules and regulations. The Legionary must never be found wanting in this way. Visiting should never be done at inconvenient hours, nor should medicine or other prohibited articles be brought to the inmates; nor should sides be taken in any of the internal disputes of the place. Inmates will profess to be the victims of ill-treatment by the staff or by other inmates, but it is not the function of the Legionaries to redress these grievances, even if they really exist. They will, of course, listen sympathetically to the woes narrated, and endeavour to instil feelings of resignation, but ordinarily the matter should finish there. Should strong feelings of indignation be aroused in the Legionary, it will serve as a safety-valve to discuss the matter at the Praesidium. The latter will see the circumstances in full perspective and will counsel appropriate action if desirable.

15. The intimate nature of the Legionary work must be safeguarded.

The Legion must guard against the danger of being made use of by too ardent social reformers. The work of the Legion is essentially a hidden one. It commences in the heart of the individual Legionary, developing therein a spirit of zeal and charity. By direct personal and persevering contact with others, the Legionaries endeavour to raise the spiritual level of the whole community. The work is done quietly, unobtrusively, delicately. It aims less at the direct suppressing of gross evils than at the permeation of the community with Catholic principles and Catholic feeling, so that the evils die of themselves through lack of a soil favourable to them. It will consider its real victory to lie in the steady, if sometimes slow, development among the people of an intense Catholic life and outlook.

It is important that the intimate nature of the Legion visitation should be jealously safeguarded. It will not be preserved, if Legionaries gain the reputation of seeking out abuses for public denunciation. The visits of Legionaries to people's homes, as well as their general movements, would tend to be looked on with doubt. Instead of being regarded as friends, in whom complete confidence could be reposed, the suspicion would attach to them that they were engaged on detective work for their organisation. Inevitably their presence would be resented, and this would mark the end of real Legionary usefulness.

Therefore, those in charge of Legion activities will be chary of associating the name of the Legion with ends which, though good in themselves, presuppose methods which have little in common with those of the Legion. Special organisations exist for the purpose of combating the glaring abuses of the day. Let the Legionaries avail of them when the need arises, and lend their support in their private capacities, but let the Legion itself continue to be true to its own tradition and its own methods of work.

16. Outlook on Adverse Criticism.

Frequently in these pages, reference is made to the paralysing effect exercised upon even the best-intentioned by the fear of hostile criticism. Hence, it will be helpful to consider the following principle. A main object of the Legion—that by which it will win its widest results—is the creation of high standards of thought and practice. The members set themselves to live the apostolic life, and thereby hold up a lofty headline of lay life. By virtue of the strange instinct which leads men to imitate, even in spite of themselves, those things which impress them, all will be impelled in varying degrees to approximate to that headline. One sign that an effective headline has been set is that many will openly and with good heart seek to follow it. Another, and more common, sign will be that symptoms of dissent will be evoked. For such a headline is a protest against the lower standards. It is a sting to the popular conscience, and like every other sting, it will provoke the healthy reaction of discomfort and protest, soon to be followed by the upward urge. But if there is no reaction of any kind, it proves that no effective headline has been set.

Therefore, there is no need to be unduly disconcerted should Legionary activities stir up some little criticism; provided always that defective methods are not responsible for that criticism. Bear always in mind another great principle which must govern apostolic effort: "Men are conquered only by love and kindness, by quiet discreet example which does not humiliate them and does not constrain them to give in. They dislike to be attacked by the man who has no other idea but to overcome them." (Giosue Borsi.)

17. There need never be Discouragement.

Sometimes the most devoted labours, heroically prolonged, show little fruit. Legionaries do not set their hearts on visible results, but nevertheless it would not be for their good to work with a sense of frustration. It will console them, and it will nerve them to still more strenuous efforts, if they reflect that even a single sin prevented represents an infinite gain. For that sin would be an immeasurable evil, dragging in its train an endless series of calamitous consequences. "However tiny the mass, it plays its part in the balance of the stars. Thus, in a way that only Thy mind, O Lord, can perceive and measure, the slightest movement of my little pen running across the paper is connected with the motions of the spheres, and contributes to, and is a part thereof. The same takes place in the world of intellect. Ideas live and have their most complex adventures in that world of intellect, a world immeasurably superior to the material world; a world united and compact also in its vast, plenteous, and most varied complexity. As in the material and intellectual worlds, so it is in the infinitely greater moral world." (Giosue Borsi.) Each sin shakes that world. It inflicts hurt on the soul of every man. Sometimes, the first link in this process is visible, when one person leads another to sin. But visible or unseen, sin leads to sin; and likewise one sin prevented wards off another. And similarly does not that second sin prevent a third, and so on unendingly until that chain gathers in the whole world and stretches throughout all time? Is it, therefore, too much to say that each sinner converted to a good life, will eventually represent a goodly host marching behind him into Heaven?

Accordingly, to prevent a grave sin would justify most arduous labours—even the effort of a lifetime—for thereby every soul will feel the glow of extra grace. It may be that the saving of that sin will be a moment of destiny, the inauguration of a process of uplift, which will in time transfer a whole people from a godless life to one of virtue.

18. The Mark of the Cross is a Sign of Hope.

But the chief danger of discouragement does not lie in the resistance—however strong—of the forces against which the Legion finds itself arrayed. It lies in the distress which the Legionary cannot but feel when aids and circumstances, on which he feels entitled to rely, are found wanting. Friends fail, good people fail, one's instruments fail; "and all whereon we lean is traitor to our peace." O what a harvest of good could be reaped—it seems—but for the bluntness of the sickle, but for the deficiencies in one's own camp but for that cross which crushes one!

This impatience at the narrowing down of the possible good to souls may be a danger. It may bring the discouragement which the hostile forces had not been able to create.

It must always be remembered that the work of the Lord will bear the Lord's own mark, the mark of the Cross. Without that imprint, the supernatural character of a work may be doubted: true results will not be forthcoming. Janet Erskine Stuart states this principle in another way. "If you look," she says, "to Sacred History, Church History, and even to your own experience which each year must add to, you will see that God's work is never done in ideal conditions, never as we should have imagined or chosen." That is to say—amazing thought!—that the very circumstance which to the limited human vision seems to prevent those conditions from being ideal, and to spoil the prospects of the work, is not an obstacle to success but the requisite for success; not a flaw but a hall-mark; not a dead-weight on effort but fuel which feeds that effort and aids it to achieve its purpose. For it is ever God's pleasure to show His power by extracting success from unpromising conditions and by accomplishing His greatest projects with inadequate instruments.

But the Legionaries must note this important proviso: If those difficulties are to be salutary, they must not proceed from Legionary neglect. The Legion cannot expect to derive grace from its own faults of omission or commission.

19. Success a Joy. Failure only a Postponed Success.

Viewed aright, the work should be an endless source of joy. Success is a joy. Failure is a penance and an exercise of faith—a higher joy to the thoughtful Legionary, who sees therein merely a postponed and greater success. Again, it is a natural pleasure to be received with the grateful smiles of the many who value intensely the visit. But the doubtful looks of others should bring a deeper consolation, for here is something seriously amiss which has been escaping attention. It is the Legionary experience that true Catholic feeling—even when complicated by some religious neglect—is responsive to the friendly, sympathetic visitor, so that the contrary not infrequently marks a soul in peril.

20. Attitude towards defects of Praesidia and Legionaries.

There must be patience with the defects of Praesidia or individual Legionaries. The fact that zeal is so sluggish, that improvement seems negligible, and that worldly failings are sadly in evidence, should not bring discouragement. The following line of thought will help in such circumstances.

If those Legionaries, with the drive of their system behind them, and unquestionably influenced by its prayer and devotion, are nevertheless found wanting, what would their standards be without the Legion altogether? Again, what are the spiritual levels of the community which cannot produce the few worthy workers required to make a good Praesidium?

Plainly, the logic is that those spiritual levels must be raised at all costs. The best, in fact the only, means of doing this lies in the infusion of an aposolic leaven which will work in the population "until the whole be leavened." (St. Matt. xiii. 33.) Therefore, the apostolic material available must be cultivated with invincible patience and sweetness. Ordinary Catholic spirit itself is a thing of slow growth. Why, therefore, expect the apostolic spirit to be an instantaneous product? If heart be lost, the only remedy is gone. That population is abandoned to its stagnation of soul. Daily the slime will grow thicker, and soon those spiritual swamps will breed nothing but diseases.

21. No Politics in the Legion.

No Legionary body shall allow its influence or its premises to be used for any political purpose or to aid any political party. "Catholic Action," says Pius XI, "is above and outside political party. It does not intend to advance the ideas of a political party."

Neither shall the Legion permit itself to be made an instrument for the personal material benefit of any of its members. But, indeed, no Legionary should have to be admonished against the unworthy exploitation, either inside or outside the Legion, of his membership.

22. No Distinctions in the Legion.

Generally, the Legion is opposed to the formation of Praesidia whose membership is restricted to a particular class or section of the community. Some reasons are:—(a) Too often restrictive will spell exclusive, with consequent injury to fraternity. (b) The best method of recruitment is normally that by the members amongst their friends, and these might not be entitled to join a particular sectional Praesidium. (c) It will almost invariably be the case that Praesidia with a membership representative of various walks of life will prove the most efficient.

Where, however, it is believed that strong reasons exist for setting up a sectional Praesidium, these should be brought before the Curia, which will decide on the matter.

23. To Bridge, not to Separate, must be the Aim.

But there is a consideration more potent than any of the foregoing. Of set purpose the Legion should aim to combat the divisions and the innumerable antagonisms of the world. This process must begin in the Legion's unit of organisation, the Praesidium itself. It would be sheer futility for the Legion to talk of bridging differences, if at the same time it were encouraging the spirit of division by specially catering for it in its own system.

Already ample provision exists in the sphere of general organisation for the needs of this grade or that section. So let the Legion think in terms of the unity and charity of the Mystical Body, and try to organise accordingly. When it has brought together, as fellow-members of the one Praesidium, persons whom the world was keeping apart, it has accomplished something really great. The contact of charity has been made, and out will go the sacred contagion which may seize on and kill the turbulence of the world around.

24. Sooner or Later the Legionaries must Attack the most Difficult Work.

The choice of work may create a doubt. Sinister problems may exist, but perhaps the Priest may fear to entrust them to an infant Praesidium. Motives of timidity should generally not prevail, lest to ourselves be applicable the saying of Pope Pius X. that the greatest obstacle to the Apostolate lies in the timorousness, or rather cowardliness, of the good. Still, if doubts persist, let the beginning be along lines of caution and let the Praesidium feel its way on simpler work. As meeting follows meeting, and experience is gained, certain of the members will emerge as manifestly capable of the most difficult work. Let these be assigned to the work of early doubt: then others as the work requires, and as the members prove themselves. Even if only a couple of Legionaries are engaged on difficult work, it exerts a tonic effect upon the work of the remainder.

25. The Outlook on Danger.

The system will reduce unfavourable possibilities to an absolute minimum, but perhaps an element of risk may attach to some important work. Should calm consideration show (a) that otherwise a work, on which depends the salvation of souls, will in whole or part remain undone, and (b) that everything possible has been done in the interests of safety; then let the attack go on with picked material. It would be an intolerable thing for Legionaries to look on impassively while their neighbours were going to ruin.

26. The Legion must be in the Forefront of the Church's Battle.

If the Legion fails to take in hand the problems and the big evils, be certain that some other organisation will eventually be started to do so. What a reproach to the Legion to be outsoldiered in such fashion!

27. The Legionary must Propagate everything Catholic.

Legionaries will not neglect the use of the Scapulars, Medals, and Badges approved by the Church. In distributing these and spreading devotion to them, channels are set up, along which—as a million instances have shown—it is the will of God that grace will copiously flow.

Likewise, they will promote piety in the homes of the people by encouraging them to hang upon their walls religious prints and pictures, crucifixes and statues, to keep holy water in the house, and beads properly blessed for the Indulgences. The home wherein the sacramentals of the Church are despised runs great risk of gradually forsaking her Sacraments. Children are especially receptive of external aids to devotion, and in a house which lacks a statute or a holy picture they will find it hard to acquire the true and intimate character of the Faith.

Legionaries will also zealously propagate the Sodality of the Children of Mary (so devoted to the interests of their Queen), and the other standard Confraternities and Associations of the Church.

In this connection see the Appendices.

"Jesus Christ associates the Virgin to His plan of forming a precursor by filling the soul of St. John with grace. It is His will that this should be accomplished through her agency. He gives her a share in the spiritual birth of St. John just as she had a share in the mystery of the Incarnation itself. And as St. John represented the Church and all the elect (because it is said of him that he was sent from God that all men might believe through him (St. John i. 7), and because salvation can only be attained by the way of penance which he has pointed out to men), Jesus Christ has thereby taught us that the Blessed Virgin co-operates by her charity in the spiritual birth of all the elect; and that when He, Jesus Christ, visits them by His grace, she, the Virgin, visits them by her charity, for it is her intercession which has won for them His grace.

"Thus she is most really our Mother, and we must ever regard her as united to Jesus Christ in everything that He accomplishes in us, just as was the case in that visit which they made to Elizabeth and St. John."—(Nicole: Essais de Morale).

"GO PREACH THE GOSPEL TO EVERY CREATURE" (St. Mark xvi. 15).—THE PLAN OF ACTION.

1. THE LEGION MUST DIRECT ITSELF TO THE INDIVIDUAL SOUL.

The following general plan of action for the Legion set as it were in array, facing as faithful children of Mary the opposing battle-line of evil, is taken from a document already frequently quoted:—

"We must not allow the crowded altar-rails at the morning's Mass to blind us to the existence of horrible contrasts: entire families where things are wrong, or a whole house, or even whole neighbourhoods, corrupted and abominable, where evil is, as it were enthroned, with its court all around it. Second, we should remember that although sin is in such places congested and doubly repulsive, it is none the less vile where it is more spread out. Third, though we see there the matured fruit—the Dead Sea fruit of evil—the roots lie in the soil of every corner of the country. Wherever neglect is creeping in or venial sin putting up its head, there is a preparation for abominations. Wheresoever the worker may be, there is work at hand to do. Were it nothing else, speak words of consolation to some poor old body in an infirmary, or teach little children to bless themselves and lisp the answer to "Who made the world?" and, little though you realise it, you strike a fierce blow at the whole machinery of evil. Fourth, and this is a message of hope to the Apostolic worker who is over-much inclined to lose heart in the presence of formidable evil, even such a riot of disorder as we have pictured is not incurable. There is a remedy—and there is only the one—and it lies in the intense and patient application of the religious system of the Church.

Under all that crusted depravity, the bare outline of which makes one shudder, there is a faith which in better moments longs for goodness. If, then, there is someone at hand to coax and encourage and speak of better things and hold out hope that all can be repaired, the worst victim of that depravity can be brought to priest and sacraments. With these received, a renovation has taken place which can never be completely undone. Frequently, the great power which goes out from Christ in His sacraments is manifested, and we are left marvelling to find that the miracle of the changed life—an Augustine or Mary of Magdala in a minor key—has been renewed.

For others the cure will be less striking. The draw of the evil habits and the old influences will be irresistible. There will be the falling and rising again. They may never be made into what would be called good citizens, but sufficient of the supernatural will probably find a place in their lives to bring them to port in the end. The great object will have been achieved.

In fact, there will be little failure for the Legionary with simple, courageous faith, no matter where or in what dark and evil places he or she may labour. The rule is short—spread abroad the reign of the Sacraments and the popular devotions, and sin will melt away before you. Do good anywhere, and you raise all; it suffices to break the opposing battle-line at any point. Shape your instruments to the necessity. Six families in a house are standing aloof from Mass and the Sacraments and resist persuasion. Possibly you can induce one of these to do something which requires a smaller degree of co-operation. Get the Sacred Heart enthroned in that home and you have already won the day. They will lift themselves farther and the others with them. In the end people who have dragged each other down by bad example will prove an inspiration to each other."—("Legionary Foundations.")

"This robber stole Paradise! No one before him ever received such a promise; not Abraham, or Isaac, or Jacob, or Moses, or the prophets, or apostles; the thief pressed in before all these! But his faith also surpassed theirs! He saw Jesus tormented, and adored Him as if He were in glory. He saw Him nailed to a cross, and petitioned Him as if He were enthroned. He saw Him condemned, and asked a favour of Him as of a king. O admirable thief! thou didst see a crucified man, and thou didst proclaim a God!"—(St. John Chrysostom).

2. INFINITE PATIENCE AND SWEETNESS MUST BE LAVISHED ON AN INFINITE SOUL.

1. The note of sternness must be banished from the Legionary mission. Qualities essential to success, and above all when dealing with the outcast and the sinner, are those of sympathy and unvarying gentleness. Constantly, in the affairs of life, we persuade ourselves that particular cases are subjects for rebuke or for the cutting word, and we use those words, and later are left regretting. Possibly in every case a mistake has been made. Why cannot we remember in time that it is from rough usage—all no doubt well-deserved—that the hardness and perversity of which we complain have grown up! The flower that would have opened under the influence of the gentle warmth of softness and compassion closes tightly in the colder air. On the other hand, the air of sympathy which the good Legionary carries with him—the willingness to listen, to enter whole-heartedly into the case as put before him—are sweetly irresistible, and the most case-hardened poor wretch, completely taken off his (or her) balance, yields, in five minutes, ground which a year of exhortation and abuse would have failed to gain.

Every Legionary ought to burn into his soul these words applied by the Church to Our Blessed Lady: "My spirit is sweet above honey, and my inheritance above honey and the honeycomb." (Eccl. xxiv, 27.) Others may effect good by stronger methods. But for the Legionary there is only one way of doing God's work—the way of gentleness and sweetness. Let him not depart from that way under any circumstances whatsoever. If he does, he will not achieve good; he will rather work harm. It has been said that Jesus has given to Mary only the Kingdom of Mercy, reserving to Himself that of Justice. Legionaries who stray outside that realm of Mary lose touch with her on whom their work depends. What then can they hope to accomplish?

The very first Praesidium of the Legion was given the title of Our Lady of Mercy. This was done because the first work undertaken was the visitation of a hospital under the care of the Sisters of Mercy. The Legionaries thought **they** were choosing that name, but who can doubt that in reality it was conferred by the sweet Virgin herself, who thereby indicated the quality which must ever distinguish the Legionary soul.

2. Ordinarily, Legionaries are not found remiss in their pursuit of the sinner. Frequently years pile up in the tireless following of some determined defaulter. But sometimes persons are encountered who put one's faith and hope and charity to trial. They appear to be outside the category of the ordinary sinner; persons of superlative badness, incarnate selfishness, or bottomless treachery; or full of hatred of God or of a revolting attitude towards religion. They seem not to have a soft spot in them, a spark of grace, or a trace of the spiritual. So utterly detestable are they that it is difficult to believe that they are not equally repellent to God Himself. What can He possibly see in the midst of disfigurements so frightful, to make Him desire closest intimacy with them in Holy Communion, or their company in Heaven?

The natural temptation to leave such a one to himself is almost irresistible. Nevertheless, the Legionary must not let go. Those human reasonings all are false. God does indeed want that vile disfigured soul, so much, so ardently, that He has sent His Son, our most dear Lord, to that soul, and He is with it now!

Here is the motive for Legionary perseverance, exquisitely put by Monsignor R. H. Benson: "If a sinner merely drove Christ away by his sin, we could let such a soul go. It is because—in St. Paul's terrifying phrase—the sinful soul holds Christ, still crucifying Him and making Him a mockery (Hebr. vi. 6), that we cannot bear to leave it to itself."

What an electrifying thought! Christ our King, in the possession, so to speak, of the enemy! What a watchword for a lifelong campaign, for the grimmest battle ever waged, for an unrelenting pursuit of the soul that must be converted in order that Christ's agony be ended! Everything that is natural must be burnt up in the white-hot act of faith that sees and loves and stands by Christ Crucified in that sinner. Even the toughest steel turns to liquid at the touch of the blow-lamp. Can any hardened heart of man withstand the steady flame of such a charity!

A Legionary of wide experience of the most depraved sinners of a great city was asked if he had met any that were absolutely hopeless. Reluctant, as a Legionary, to acknowledge the existence of that category, he replied that many were terrible but few were hopeless. Being pressed, he eventually admitted that he knew of one who seemed to be capable of being so described.

That very evening he received his overwhelming rebuke. Quite accidentally he met in the street the person he had named. Three minutes' conversation, and the miracle of a complete and lasting conversion took place!

"One episode stands out in the life of Saint Madeleine Sophie, in which the faithful pursuit of a soul is seen in all its pathos. For twenty-three years she clung with persistent love to one whom God's providence had brought across her path: a lost sheep, who but for the Saint could never have found the fold. Where Julia came from, no one ever knew—she never told her own story twice in the same way. But she was alone and poor, and of a difficult and wayward disposition; like nothing in ordinary life, it was said; deceitful, treacherous, mean, passionate to the verge of frenzy. But the Saint saw only a soul, found in dangerous places by the Good Shepherd, and put into her care by Him. She adopted her as her own child, wrote more than two hundred letters to her, and suffered much on her account. Repaid by calumny and ingratitude, the Saint still held on, forgave her again and again, and ever hoped. . . . Julia died seven years after the Saint and in peace with God."—(Monahan: Saint Madeleine Sophie Barat.)

3. THE SEEKING OF CONVERSIONS TO THE CHURCH.

"The Church," Pius XI has solemnly declared, "has no other reason for its existence than to extend over the earth the Kingdom of Christ and so to render all men sharers of His saving Redemption." It is sad, therefore, that Catholics should live in the midst of multitudes who are not of the Church, and make little or no effort to win them to it! Sometimes this arises from the fact that the problem of shepherding those who are in the fold is thought so grievous that those outside it are lost sight of as part of the problem. Need one be surprised if, in the end, neither those inside are preserved nor those outside brought in?

Make no mistake about it: The Faith must be brought to the notice of every person outside the Church. Timidity and human respect and difficulties of one kind and another must all be swallowed up in the supreme desire to share that gift of Faith with those who have it not. The Gospel must be preached to every creature. (St. Mark xvi. 15.) The exertions to that end must be like those of men beside themselves, thought Francis Xavier. But others will counsel prudence. Yes, much depends on it in its true sphere, which is that of safeguarding necessary action, not of crippling it. The rightful place of prudence in a system is that of brake, whereas the error is almost invariably made of supposing that it is to be the engine. And then there is surprise at the inaction. Oh! there is need for those men beside themselves, who do not think in terms of caution, who live above fear. For souls are being swept along in the rapid-flowing river of time. Delayed effort will gather in other souls; but not **those** souls—the abyss of eternity will have enfolded **them**!

Persons outside the Church toss on a sea of doubt from which their hearts crave rest, but they need to be persuaded that in the Church there is really faith and calm. The first step towards convincing them must necessarily be the approaching of them. How can they understand the truth unless some man show them? (Act. viii, 30, 31.) How can fantastic misunderstandings be dispelled if Catholics ever preserve a stately silence on the subject? How can the opponents of the Church guess from the outward chill of Catholics the warmth of faith that lies beneath? And are they not to be excused for thinking that Catholic belief, which seldom shows any enthusiasm, is little or not at all removed from their own admitted unbelief?

There is a tendency to think that sufficient has been done when the Catholic claims have been set abroad by the radio, by the wide circulation of the printed word, or by the addressing of public meetings. But in fact, the approach becomes the less effective according as it loses the personal touch. If conversions depended on the reaching of people in bulk by means such as the above, the present age of scientific publicity should also be one of conversions on a grand scale. But, instead, it is found difficult to keep even the Catholic fold intact.

No! The approach to be really effective must be an individual and intimate one. The radio, the Press, etc., can all be made to play an awakening or supporting part in a scheme to bring those "other sheep" to the Good Shepherd, but the centre of that scheme must be the appeal of one person to another person. According to the laws that rule the spiritual world, as Frederick Ozanam puts it, the attraction of one soul is needed to elevate another. In other words, the law of charity must operate; and the gift without the giver is bare. But only too often does the individual Catholic assume an attitude of helplessness. He believes that those outside the Church are too firmly rooted in prejudice and in ignorance to be moved. Admittedly, the prejudices are many, traditional, almost inborn, and hardened by education. What resources has the simple Catholic to oppose to this array of unbelief? He need not fear. He possesses in the doctrine of the Church, however simply explained, a shining sword whose efficacy is best described in Newman's noble words: "I have an intense feeling in me as to the power and victoriousness of truth. It has a blessing from God upon it. Satan himself can but retard its ascendancy; he cannot prevent it."

As has been repeatedly urged in these pages, the approach to those whom it is desired to win must be like to that which the Divine Shepherd would make in such a search. There must be nothing of the controversial, nothing overbearing. Every word must breathe humility, affection, sincerity. And actions as well as words must show forth one essential thing, that they are backed by a genuine belief. Then, they will seldom be seriously resented and will never fail to leave a deep impression, which will ripen in a high proportion of cases to conversion.

If personal contact is necessary, not many cases can be dealt with by the individual worker. Therefore for many conversions many workers will be required. Legionaries must be multiplied.

As part of any scheme the following should receive attention:—

(a) The work of study should be undertaken, not for the purpose of mere controversy, but to fit oneself to assist the sincere enquirer.

(b) Existing converts should be looked up in order to ensure that they have the support of Catholic friendships, or to bring them, if suitable, into Legion membership. None will be more qualified than they to meet the difficulties of their former brethren.

(c) The following up (from lists supplied by those who specialise in instruction) of those who had embarked on a course of instruction in which they did not persevere. Experience indicates that the default is usually due, not to a loss of the desire to become a Catholic, but to accidental circumstances which cause a break in the attendance; shyness or procrastination then prevents resumption.

"Take away Our Blessed Lady's contribution to the Gospel testimony, efface her testimony to Christianity, and you find not simply a link broken, but the very fastening of the whole chain wanting; not merely a gap, or a break, made in the structure, but the foundation gone. The belief in the wonders wrought in the Incarnation, of ages, and of the world, rests upon one point of testimony, a unit, a single voice—that of the Blessed Virgin Mary." —(Cardinal Wiseman: The Actions of the New Testament).

4. THE HOLY EUCHARIST AS AN INSTRUMENT OF CONVERSION.

Too much time is often spent on arguments which —even if they are proved—do not attract to the Church. The aim in all discussions should be to make those outside the Church catch a glimpse of the treasures which are within. There is no more effective way of doing this than by the presentation of the doctrine of the Eucharist, which summarises in a sentence the vastest boon imaginable.

Even those who know Jesus dimly and uncomprehendingly, are lost in admiration of Him. On the strength of human evidence they acknowledge that He exercised an unexampled power over nature, so that the elements obeyed Him; the dead returned to life; and infirmities fled at His command with such completeness that their former victims are said to have lived unusual spans of life. He did all these things directly of His own power, because, though man, He was likewise the Eternal God Himself, Who made all things, Whose word is might.

The Scriptures tell how once that God-Man—among innumerable other wonders—accomplished the sweet miracle of the Eucharist. "He took bread, and blessed and broke: and gave to His disciples, and said: Take ye and eat: This is My Body." (St. Matthew xxvi. 26.) This is a mighty scripture, but for how many has it not been a sealed one? "This saying is hard, and who can hear it!" (St. John vi. 61.) The objection of some even of His own disciples has echoed down through the centuries to the infinite loss of souls: "How can this man give us His flesh to eat?" (St. John vi. 53.) Those disciples could almost be pardoned for their unbelief, for they had not grasped the real nature of Him who stood in their midst. But what is it that clouds the minds of those persons who acknowledge the Divinity and hence the omnipotence of Christ? Surely these should see how deceptive—how unthinkable therefore—it would be for that same Divine Person—

when solemnly addressing simple folk—to say "My Body," while meaning "not My Body." Let them absorb the ruthless logic of Pascal: "How I detest this folly of not believing in the Eucharist. If the Gospel is true; if Jesus Christ is God; where is the difficulty in the matter?"

The challenge of so overwhelming an idea as the Eucharist cannot be heard unheeding. To hold up persistently to the notice of the separated ones this crowning glory of the Church must force their minds to contemplate its possibility; so that many of the worthier sort will reason to themselves: "If this is true, how dreadful is my present loss!" In the pang of that thought will come the first big impulse towards their true home.

Many earnest persons outside the Church read the Scriptures, and in meditation and sincere prayer seek to draw Jesus out from the dim past of history, rejoicing if their imagination creates a vivid picture of their Lord engaged in His works of love. O! if these souls could only understand that in the Church there is the wonder of the Eucharist, which could bring Jesus as He is, whole and entire, in all His physical reality, with all His Divinity, into the sphere of their present lives! If they could realise that by this means they could touch Him, talk to Him, contemplate Him, or busy themselves about Him more closely, more intimately by far than did His dear friends at Bethany. Nay more! by Holy Communion in union with Mary they could render to that Divine Body all the loving cares of a Mother, and thus, in some sense, thank Him adequately for all that He has done for them. Surely the unsurpassable good of the Eucharist has only to be explained to multitudes outside the Church to cause them to yearn for light. Then Jesus will give them understanding of the things that are concerning Him. Like the disciples journeying to Emmaus, their hearts will burn within them as He speaks on the way and opens to them the sense of that "hard saying" of His: "Take ye and eat: this is My Body." And their eyes will be opened, and they will know Him in the breaking of the Bread Divine. (St. Luke xxiv. 13-35).

In this recognition of the Eucharist, the misconceptions and prejudices which chilled the understanding and darkened the view of heaven, melt away like snowflakes in a burning sun, so that he who had walked unseeing, will exclaim with overflowing heart: "One thing I know, that whereas I was blind, now I see." (St. John ix. 25.)

"Our Lady of the Blessed Sacrament is Mary receiving, in her capacity as universal dispenser of grace, the full and absolute disposal of the Eucharist and of the graces which it comprises. For this Sacrament is the most efficacious means of salvation, the most excellent fruit of the redemption brought by Jesus Christ. Consequently it is for her to make Jesus known and loved in this Sacrament. It is for her to spread the Eucharist all over the world, to multiply churches and to plant them among infidel peoples, to defend the belief in the Eucharist against heretics and the impious. It is her work to prepare souls for Communion, to move them to visit frequently the Blessed Sacrament, and watch constantly before it. Mary is the treasury of all the graces which the Eucharist contains, of all which lead to it, of all which flow from it."—(Tesniére: Notre Dame du T. S. Sacrement.)

5. SOULS ARE NOT APPROACHED EXCEPT WITH MARY.

Sometimes Mary is kept in the background so as to meet the prejudices of those who make small account of her. This method of making Catholic doctrine more acceptable may accord with human reasonings. It does not reflect the Divine Idea. Those who act in this way do not realise that they might as well preach Christianity without Christ as ignore Mary's part in Redemption. For God Himself has thought fit to arrange that no coming or giving or manifestation of Jesus should be without Mary. The Redemption was the ardent desire of God. But in this, as in all matters minor to it, He would not force the will of man. He would offer the priceless boon, but it was for man to accept it, and man was at liberty to refuse it.

Consider the awe-inspiring working out of the merciful design of God. Attend in spirit the greatest Peace Conference ever held. It is a Peace Conference between God and mankind, and it is called the Annunciation. In that Conference God was represented by one of His high Angels, and mankind was represented by her whose name the Legion is privileged to bear. She was but a gentle maiden, yet the fate of all mankind hung upon her in that day. The Angel came with overwhelming tidings. He proposed to her the Incarnation. He did not merely notify it. Her liberty of choice was not violated; so that for a while the fate of mankind trembled in the balance. The moment had arrived to which generations had looked forward, just as ever since all generations have looked back to it. It was the crisis of all time. There was a pause. That maiden did not accept at once; she asked a question, and the answer was given. There was another pause, and then she spoke the words: "Be it done to me according to Thy word," those words that brought God down to earth and signed the great Peace Pact of humanity.

The Father made Redemption depend on her.—How few realise all that follows from that consent of hers. Even Catholics in the main do not realise the importance of the part that Mary played. The Doctors of the Church say these things: Supposing that maiden had refused the offer of motherhood that was made to her, the Second Divine Person would not have taken flesh in her. What a solemn thing that is! "What a terrible thought to think that God has made the entrance of the Redeemer dependent upon the 'Be it done to me' of the handmaid of Nazareth; that this saying should be the termination of the old world, the beginning of the new, the fulfilment of all prophecies, the turning-point of all time, the first blaze of the morning star which is to announce the rising of the sun of justice, which as far as human will was able to accomplish, knit the bond that brought heaven down upon earth and lifted humanity up to God!" (Hettinger). What a solemn thing indeed! It means that she was the only hope of mankind. But the fate of men was safe in her hands. She pronounced that consent which, though we cannot fully understand, commonsense nevertheless tells us must have been inconceivably the most heroic act ever performed in the world—such that in all ages no other creature but she could have performed it. Then to her came the Redeemer; not to herself alone, but through her to poor helpless humanity, on behalf of whom she spoke. With Him, she brought everything that the Faith means, and the Faith is the real life of men. Nothing else matters. Everything must be abandoned for it. Any sacrifices must be made to get it. It is the only thing in the world of any worth. Consider, therefore, that the Faith of all generations: those that have passed away up to the present, and the uncountable millions yet to come: the Faith of all has depended on the words of that maiden.

No True Christianity without Mary.—In return for this infinite gift, all generations must henceforth call that maiden blessed. She who brought Christianity on earth cannot be denied a place in Christian worship. But what of the many people in this world who hold her cheaply, the many who slight her, the many who do worse? Does it ever occur to those people to think that every grace they have they owe to her? Do they ever reason that if they were excluded from her words of acceptance that night, then Redemption has never come on earth for them? They stand outside its scope. In other words, they are not Christians at all, even though they may cry: "Lord! Lord!" all the day and every day. (St. Matt. vii. 21). And on the other hand, if they are indeed Christians, and if the gift of life has come to them, then it has only come because she gained it for them, because they were included in her acceptance. In a word, the Baptism that makes a person a child of God makes one simultaneously a child of Mary; and this, though he ignore her, or even (in the words of Shakespeare) "turn all her mother's pains and benefits to laughter and contempt; that she may feel how sharper than a serpent's tooth it is to have a thankless child."

Gratitude, therefore—a practical gratitude—to Mary must be the mark of every Christian. Redemption is the joint gift of the Father and of Mary. Therefore, with the words of thanks to the Father must go up the word of thanks to Mary. If there is default in this, behold that worst of all types of people: the ungrateful child—more hideous, as Shakespeare says, than the sea-monster!

The Son is always found with His Mother.—It was God's Will that the reign of Grace should not be inaugurated without Mary. It was His pleasure that things should continue in the self-same way. What had been done in secret at Nazareth has to be confirmed openly in the Temple. He will make offering of Himself to the Father, but it is between the arms and by the hands of His Mother, for that Babe belongs to its Mother; without her, the Presentation cannot be made. When He desired to prepare St. John the Baptist for his mission of going before Himself, He sanctified him by the charitable visit of His Blessed Mother in the Visitation. On the first Christmas night, those who turned her from their doors turned Him away. They did not realise that with her they refused Him whom they awaited. When the shepherd-representatives of the chosen people found the Promised of All Nations, they found Him with her. If they had turned away from her, they would not have found Him. At the Epiphany, the Gentile races of the world were received by Our Lord in the persons of the three Kings, but they only found Him because they found her. If they had refused to approach her, they would not have reached Him.

Proceed, and it is learned from the Fathers that Our Lord did not enter upon His public life without her consent; likewise her request at Cana of Galilee was the beginning of the signs and wonders and mighty deeds by which He proved His mission. When the last scene came on Calvary which finished the whole awful drama of Redemption, she stood at the foot of the Cross, not merely because she was a fond Mother, not in any accidental way, but precisely in the same capacity as she was present at the Incarnation. She was there as the representative of all mankind. Our Lord did not offer Himself to the Father without her assent and offering made on behalf of all her children; the Cross was to be their Sacrifice and His Sacrifice.

The Holy Ghost Operates always with Her.—Come a little further to the feast of Pentecost—that important occasion when the Church was formed by the descent of the Holy Ghost. Mary was there; it was by the Holy Ghost operating with her that the Church was formed. How natural this is: What is the Church but the Mystical Body of Our Lord? What was Pentecost but a sort of new Incarnation? The same law applies: again was Mary an essential part. And so of all divine things to the end: If Mary is left out, God's Plan is not conformed to, no matter what one's prayers and works and strivings may be. If Mary is not there, the grace is not given. This is an overpowering thought. It may provoke the question: "Do those who ignore or insult Mary receive no graces?" They do indeed receive graces, for failure to acknowledge Mary may be excused on grounds of utter ignorance. But what a sorry title to Heaven! and what a way of treating her who helps one thither! Moreover, the graces which come in such circumstances are but a fraction of what should flow, so that one's life's work is largely failing.

What Place must we Assign Her?—Some, too, may take alarm and say it is a slight to God to credit such a universal power to a creature. But if it has pleased God to make it so, how does it slight His Dignity? How foolish it would sound were anyone to say that the Force of Gravity derogated from God's Power! That law of Gravity is from God, and accomplishes His purposes throughout all nature. Why should one think it disrespectful to allow as much to Mary in the universe of Grace? If the laws which God has made for nature show forth His might, why should the law which He has made for Mary do otherwise than manifest His Goodness and Omnipotence?

But even if it is conceded that acknowledgment is due to Mary, there still remains the question of its manner and amount. "How"—some will say—"am I to apportion prayer to Mary and prayer to the Divine Persons or to the Saints? What is the exact amount—neither too much nor too little—which I am to offer to Her?" Others will go further and their objection will present itself as follows: "Would I not turn away from God were I to direct my prayers to Her?"

All these grades of doubt proceed from applying earthly ideas to heavenly things. Such persons are thinking of the Father and the Son and the Holy Ghost, and of Mary and the Saints, as if they were so many statues, so that to turn to one they must necessarily turn away from others. Various examples might be utilised to help towards a better understanding of the true position. But, strange to say, the simplest and at the same time the holiest solution of such difficulties lies in the recommendation: "You must indeed give all to God, but give it all through Mary." It will be found that this apparently extreme devotion to her is free from the perplexities which measuring and moderation bring.

Every Action should Endorse Her Fiat.—The justification of this method is to be found in the Annunciation itself. In that moment all mankind were joined with Mary, their representative. Her words included their words, and in a sense she included them. God viewed them through her. Now, the daily life of a Christian is nothing else than the formation of Our Lord in that member of His Mystical Body. This formation does not take place without Mary. It is an outpouring and a part of the original Incarnation, so that Mary is really the Mother of the Christian just as she is of Christ. Her consent and her maternal care are just as necessary to the daily growth of Christ in the individual soul as they were to His original taking of flesh. What does all this involve for the Christian? It involves many important things of which this is one: he must deliberately and whole-heartedly acknowledge Mary's position as his representative in the sacrificial offering, begun at the Annunciation and completed on the Cross, which earned Redemption. He must ratify the things she then did on his behalf, so that he can enjoy, without shame and in their fulness, the infinite benefits thereby brought him. And that ratification: of what nature is it to be? Would a once-repeated act suffice? Work out the answer to this question in the light of the fact that it was through Mary that every act of one's life has become the act of a Christian. Is it not reasonable and proper that likewise every act should bear some impress of acknowledgment and gratitude to her? So the answer is the same as that already given: "You are to give her everything."

Magnify the Lord with Mary.—Have her before the mind, at least in some slight way, at all times. Unite the intention and the will to hers in such fashion that every act done during the day, every prayer you utter, is done with her. She is left out of nothing. Whether you pray to the Father, or to the Son, or to the Holy Ghost, or to a saint, it is always to be prayer in union with Mary. She repeats the words with you. Her lips and your lips form the words together, and in everything she has a part. Thus she is far more than at your side. She is, as it were, in you; your life is you and she together giving to God all you jointly have.

This all-embracing form of devotion to Mary acknowledges handsomely the part she played and daily continues to play in the workings out of salvation. Likewise it is the easiest devotion to her. It solves the doubts of those who say "how much?" and of those who fear lest giving to her is taking from God. But even some Catholics may say "It is extreme." Yet where does it offend against sweet reason? And wherein does it deny His due to the Almighty? The latter fault is better laid to those who say that they are zealous of the Dignity of God, but will not work the

Plan which He has made; who say they hold the Scriptures as the sacred word of God, yet will not hear the verses which sing that He hath done great things to Mary, and that all generations shall call her blessed. (St. Luke i. 48-49.)

To all these doubting ones it is best to speak in terms of this rich and full devotion. But how indeed can Legionaries talk in any other terms of her? Minimising and reduction only leave her a mystery. If Mary is a shadow or a sentimental notion, then surely not the Catholics, but those who treat her lightly are justified! And, on the other hand, the statement of the fulness of her claims and of her essential place in Christian life contains a challenge, which cannot be ignored by any heart in which grace has some dominion. Then calm examination of the role of Mary will leave such people at her feet.

The purpose of the Legion is to mirror Mary. If true to this ideal, the Legion will share her crowning gift to cast the light into the hearts of those who are in darkness of unbelief.

"The great master of Thomas Aquinas, Albertus Magnus has a delightful phrase in a commentary on the Annunciation portion of the Gospel, which rendered freely says that Mary's Son gives infinitude to His Mother's excellency, there being also in the tree which produces the fruit some of that infinite perfection which belongs properly to the fruit.

"In practice the Catholic Church looks upon the Mother of God as being an unbounded power in the realm of grace. She is considered as the Mother of the redeemed on account of the universality of her grace. In virtue of her divine motherhood, Mary is simply the vastest, the most efficient, the most universal supernatural power in heaven and on earth, outside the Three Divine Persons."—(Vonier: The Divine Motherhood.)

6. THE PROBLEM OF THE IRRELIGIOUS POPULATIONS.

Then there is the awful problem of irreligion on a great scale. In very many of the world's centres of population entire districts, which are nominally Catholic, are leading lives in which Mass or the Sacraments or even prayer play no part whatsoever. In one such case, a survey discovered only 75 practising Catholics out of a total population of 20,000. In another case, 400 attend Mass out of 30,000, and in another 40,000 out of 900,000. Only too frequently the irreligion of such areas is left to fester and to grow in peace. No effort worthy of the name is made to deal with it. It is argued that direct approach would be fruitless or would be resented, and perhaps prove dangerous. And, strange to say, such arguments are accepted even by those who think it natural that missionaries should go to the ends of the earth to face danger and even death.

The saddest thing about such places is that the clergy are practically debarred from that direct approach. One of the dire complications of the frenzy of irreligion is that its victims turn against their fathers in God and drive them from them. Here is the unique value of the Legion. It represents the Priest and carries through his plans; yet it is of the people, so that it cannot be kept at arm's length. It lives the life of the people, so that the irreligious cannot destroy its work and even prevent its approach by the smoke-screen of lies, which can so easily be raised against a separated order like the clergy and the vow-bound classes.

"What shall a man give in exchange for his soul?" (St. Mark viii. 37.) What effort shall a man make for the soul of his neighbour? Assuredly, it must be a supreme effort—even to the peril of death, were such necessary. Those great irreligious areas must be evangelised with no less determination than are the far-distant mission fields. It is not suggested that those who cry "hopeless," or those who allege "danger," should be entirely ignored. Possibly something they say will conduce to the success and to the safety of the Legion campaign. But in no circumstances should any word of theirs be allowed to paralyse that attack. Great faith must be shown if mountains of evil are to be removed: faith akin to that referred to by St. Ignatius, when he said that so great was his trust in

God that he was prepared to commit himself to the deep in an oarless, sail-less skiff.

It will be found that martyrdom does not await the Legionaries, but that a remarkable degree of success does await them. A fair number of souls are actually waiting for the first direct appeal to them.

A method of approach.—In conditions such as those supposed, where the most elemental obligations of religion are being ignored, the first efforts of the Legionaries might be applied to the emphasising of that great cental requirement—attendance at Mass. Let a leaflet be secured which sets out in simple but effective language the beauty and power of the Mass. If the leaflet bears a coloured picture illustrative of its subject, its effect will be enhanced. Armed with a supply of these, the Legionaries will proceed to a home to home visitation. To each person, who will accept one, a copy of the leaflet is given, accompanied, if possible, by a gentle exhortation on devotion to the Mass. Legionaries need not be reminded that their attitude in all circumstances must be one of infinite sweetness and patience; never one of mere interrogation; never one of rebuking neglect.

Rebuffs at first may be many, but these will be compensated for by many immediate successes. The ordinary methods of Legion visitation will be followed, the underlying idea being the effort to establish relations of true friendship with the persons visited. That gained, almost everything is gained.

Each individual case of resumption of the practice of religion must be regarded as soldiers would view the capture of a point of vantage in war, for each one will bring others. As the captures grow in number, public opinion will begin to suffer modification. All in the area are observing the Legionaries. All are talking, criticising, thinking; and hearts that were chill begin to burn. Year will follow year, each with its substantial list of captures. For many years the general attitude of the populace towards religion will seem to be unchanged. Then, just as a touch causes an ant-eaten fabric, which looked sound, to fall suddenly into dust, some event reveals that the hearts of the people have returned to God.

The result of effort.—Of a certain town, with a population of 50,000, it could be said that hardly any were practising their religion. This condition of neglect was complicated by abnormalities of every kind. A Priest could not pass through many districts without insult. A Praesidium was started in a spirit of faith, and the apparently hopeless task of visitation was embarked upon. All were surprised by an immediate flow of results, increasing in number and in importance as the Legionaries gained numbers and experience. After three years of unexpected success, the Church authorities were emboldened to call for a General Communion of men, and ventured to hope for an attendance of 200. The actual number that participated was 1,100, showing that the entire population had been stirred to its depths by the three years' apostolate. Plainly, the end is already in sight, so that the next generation in that town will be born into a changed order of things. Holiness will reign where once the Mass had been universally scorned and its ministers were derided. Other places, similarly circumstanced, should seek a remedy in the same way.

"And Jesus answering saith to them: Have the faith of God. Amen I say to you, that whosoever shall say to this mountain, Be thou removed and be cast into the sea, and shall not stagger in his heart, but believe that whatsoever he saith shall be done; it shall be done unto him. Therefore I say unto you, all things whatsoever you ask when ye pray, believe that you shall receive; and they shall come unto you."—(St. Mark xi. 22-24.)

7. THE LEGION AS THE HANDMAID OF THE FOREIGN MISSIONARY.

Many form the erroneous impression from the reading of the Handbook that only persons of advanced spiritual development and fair education could be attuned to the high ideals and the very detailed system proposed by the Legion. They tell themselves that they have no such material available, and therefore that it is not practicable to have the Legion. Thereby they reject what might be their greatest asset. For universal experience has shown the adaptability of the Legion to every grade and type of mind and education and race. In fact, if the Legion has a special joy, it is that persons and races, whom the world would call depressed or primitive, come into the Legion in great numbers, accommodate themselves to it with amazing facility, and prove themselves second to none in its service and in their conquests.

Is suitable material available?—There is no population without its cream, and the latter is always good enough for Legion membership. Standards of quality, which result in declarations that no suitable material exists, are incorrect standards. They mean that no one is deemed worthy of trust or responsibility. This outlook will produce a Catholicism which may indeed believe, but will not raise a hand to spread the Faith. Therefore, the opposite policy must prevail. Interest and responsibility must be widely spread, and many must be enlisted in the apostolate. Only in the mobilisation of vast numbers of the native Christians themselves does any prospect lie of the complete conversion of the pagan peoples amongst whom they live. Such is the conviction of Pius XI himself. In his "Message from the Holy Father to China," on August 1st, 1928, he impresses on the Ordinaries that Catholic Action forms an essential element in the work of evangelisation.

Hence, Missionary Bishops and Vicars Apostolic are urged most earnestly to utilise determinedly the ready-to-work system which the Legion unquestionably affords of developing and directing apostolic energy even among the simplest folk.

Knocking the material into shape.—The first step would be the establishment of a Praesidium under the direction of each Priest and each Religious in the Vicariate. These Directors will regard the development and successful running of these radiating-points of Faith as a test of the real success of their mission. Thus, they are not to be disconcerted by early disappointments. At the least, there should be given to the all-important work of raising up key-Catholics a degree of patience and thoroughness equivalent to that which military officers would give to the work of making reliable soldiers out of crude material. For —let it be repeated once again—it is only in proportion as apostolic mechanism is set up and worked by the Missionary that he will possess the power to reach the teeming pagan multitudes around him. The most strenuous efforts on the part of the Missionary to do everything himself by direct action will never achieve anything but a comparative success. A goodly number of converts may be gained. But the Gospel preached to every creature! Never! still less every creature won to the Faith! Not though that Missionary's life were to be prolonged to cover twenty lifetimes!

"Go preach the Gospel to every creature."—As the membership and the quality of the Praesidia grow, it may be possible to increase the number of Praesidia. Perhaps the Directors may be able to assume the control of more than one Praesidium each. Perhaps, too, it may be possible to utilise Catechists and other experienced persons in the capacity of Presidents or Tribunes for the training and inspiring of Praesidia. Each new Praesidium means ten to twenty additional soldiers of the Faith in action. Each one of these Legionaries is of the people, living their lives, attuned to their minds, and hence able to influence them towards the Faith in a way to which the foreign Missionary would seldom attain.

Success in this policy of multiplying Praesidia would mean that in the course of time each Priest would be organising the efforts of a great number of apostolic workers, so that he would veritably play, in all but the supreme functions, a part analogous to that of a Bishop. As to the Bishop, he would find himself in possession of an innumerable and irresistible hierarchy of workers for the Faith, through whom he would be in the position for the first time of being able to preach the Gospel to every creature in his territory.

A definite duty for each Legionary.—A well-defined sphere of action would be assigned to each Legionary. Each area of work would be surveyed and reduced to terms of individual duties for assignment to the Legionaries, each one of whom would be held strictly responsible for the proper performance thereof. The Legionaries must be made to realise that in the discharge of their duties they are the hands and feet and ears and eyes and mouth of their Spiritual Director. One of the main objects of the Legion system will be the bringing home of this responsibility to each Legionary, and the fitting of each one to bear it creditably.

Elemental items of duty which will fall to be performed would be (a) the effort to bring Baptism to the dying—not only to the infant, but to all; (b) the ensuring of the Sacraments to the sick; (c) the stimulation of the neglectful; and (d) ultimately the addressing to each individual person outside the Church of an appeal to enter.

Must the Legionaries be advanced in knowledge?—It may be objected that a fair degree of knowledge of the doctrines of the Faith is required to render such an appeal effective. Respectfully, a contrary opinion is advanced. Consider that the conversions of the early days of Christianity were wrought by the common people—the workman, the slave, the little, feeble and oppressed members of that powerful, rich, enlightened society in which they lived. Here is not question of formal instruction (which would constitute another problem), but of the effort of one heart to pour its supreme possession into another heart. This is accomplished most effectively when like deals with like. Each convinced Catholic, however imperfect his knowledge, has a certain mental picture of his faith, and possesses the capacity to convey this impression to the mind of another whom he seeks to influence. But he will not exercise that capacity unless moved thereto by force of organisation or other strong impulse.

The Legion means Mary at work.—The introduction of the Legion means the application to the work of the Missions of two great forces:—(a) the principle of methodical organisation, which is always attended by increase in interest and power; and (b) that most potent element, the mother-influence of Mary, which is attracted in fulness by the Marian system of the Legion and is lavished on souls through the medium of its intensive apostolate. In very fact, the spreading of the light of faith cannot be accomplished other than in concert with her. Efforts over which she does not preside are like the illuminant without the lamp. Perhaps it is an insufficient appreciation of this fact that accounts for the rarity of magnificent conquests for the faith to-day. In earlier ages whole peoples were rapidly converted, and St. Cyril did not hesitate to declare at the Council of Ephesus that it was by Mary they all were won to Christ. Moreover, the great patron of the Missions, St. Francis Xavier, gave it as his own experience that wherever he omitted to place at the foot of the Saviour's cross the figure of the Divine Mother, those countries revolted against the Gospel which he had brought to them.

If, through the Legionary apostolate, this most fruitful action of Mary can be enabled to exert itself in the Mission fields, why should not those days, referred to by St. Cyril, come once again on earth, so that whole territories and nations will put aside their errors and joyfully embrace the Christian Faith?

"How foolish the presumption, or how sublime and heavenly the inspiration, which has now taken possession of those fishermen! Consider for a moment their enterprise. Never has prince, or empire, or republic conceived so lofty a plan. Without any apparent chance of human aid, these Galileans, partitioned out the whole world for future conquest. They formed a determined plan to change the religion established all over the world, whether false or in part true—whether Jewish or Gentile. They desired to establish a new worship, a new sacrifice, a new law, because, said they, a certain Man whom men crucified at Jerusalem so ordained it."—(Bossuet.)

"THE GREATER OF THESE IS CHARITY."—
(1 Cor. xiii. 13.)

Mary was so utterly full of charity that she was found worthy to conceive and bring into the world Him who is Charity itself. The Legion of Mary, depending for its very life on devotedness to her and imitation of her, must necessarily be distinguished by this self-same quality of intense charity. It must be full of charity: then only it will bring charity into the world.

Legionary Charity requires:—

1. For entry to the ranks of the Legion, there shall be no social or political or national or colour discrimination. Fitness for membership is to be the only test. Did Christian Charity not demand this, Legionary policy would. The Legionary Apostolate will accomplish even more by indirect action (i.e., as the leaven in the community) than directly by the actual works in hand. If the entire community is to be brought fully under the influence of Legionary action, it follows that the Legion's ranks must contain representatives of every grade and section. But the words of Pius XI, which follow, sufficiently establish this principle.

"In order to bring back to Christ these whole classes of men who have denied Him, we must gather and train from among their very ranks auxiliary soldiers of the Church, men who know their mentality and their aspirations, and who with kindly, fraternal charity will be able to win their hearts. Undoubtedly the first and immediate apostles of the workingmen must themselves be workingmen, while the apostles of the industrial and commercial world should themselves be employers and merchants."—(Pius XI.: Encyclical on the Social Order.)

2. Within its own ranks an unaffected simplicity and sincere mutual charity amongst the members, all distinctions being non-existent except those which may arise from proficiency in the spirit and work of the

Legion. If love is due to those least ones whom one sets out to serve, it is due in higher degree to one's brethren in organisation. The spirit of distinction is evidence, not merely of an imperfect carrying out of membership, but of the absence of the first qualification for membership, which is the spirit of love. The whole idea and spirit of the Legion is one of intense charity and sympathy, which before radiating its warmth outside, must first of all burn brightly and strongly on the domestic hearth of the Legion itself. "By this shall all men know that you are my disciples, if you have love one for another." (St. John xiii. 35.)

Charity practised in its ranks will soon be practised at large. Chasms bridged by membership are on the way to being bridged amongst men outside.

"That unity which Paul, Ignatius, Cyprian and Augustine celebrate over and over again with enthusiasm as the blessed gift of our salvation, that *vinculum pacis, spiritus unitatis, unitas caritatis*, is no longer, or at least in no sufficient measure a regular constituent of Christian sentiment. . . . Here is the widest gulf between our piety and that of the early Church. How vividly did the Christians of the early centuries realise the truth —and how deeply they were penetrated by it—that they in Christ their Head were united and formed into a new supernatural unity, a spiritual temple, a chosen generation, a royal priesthood, a holy nation. (1 Peter ii. 5-9)"—(Karl Adam: Christ Our Brother.)

3. Towards other organisations a spirit of readiness to give unstinted co-operation and assistance, desirous only that good may be done, by whomsoever it may be accomplished.

The Legion will jealously guard itself against meriting even in the slightest degree the reproof of the Apostle:—"All seek the things that are their own; not the things that are Jesus Christ's." (Ep. to the Philippians, ii. 21.)

But the Legion's attitude towards those other organisations must not merely be passively virtuous. It must be actively helpful. As a main principle of its work, the Legion must seek to aid in the building up of each and every Society which is worthy of the name Catholic. Through its own zealous Active membership, through the great numbers whom it touches in connection with its works, and especially through its numerous Auxiliary members, the Legion is in a favourable position for recruiting for and strengthening the Catholic associations around about it. Not all can be brought into the Legion's own ranks, for its requirements are far from easy. But almost everybody—indeed let one boldly say everybody—should be brought into membership of a Catholic Society or Association of some kind, and by this means be caught firmly in the arms of Mother Church and pressed closely to her life-giving bosom. In this manner would Catholic Action be made a vital force, a glorious thing, the safeguard of the individual and the mainstay of the Church.

"One of the qualities most needed at the present day is concerted action. 'Has fate decreed,' it has been asked, 'that the wicked will always be as one in their brutal hatred, while good people never learn to be united?' It is necessary to be united. An association without concerted action is like a flock of sheep. Members must agree as to the end to be obtained, accept the same authority, and obey in everything that the success of the common enterprise demands. Otherwise you have anarchy. Catholic associations are opposed by associations which are both united and powerful. If they are to win, they must above all strive for unity: unity among the members of the same association; unity with other associations."—(Raoul Plus: Facing Life.)

4. Towards the Pastors of the Church unreserved loyalty and loving obedience—qualities which must spring naturally and abundantly from the very status of the Legion as the supplement of the Priestly Ministry.

Imitating her who is the "Handmaid of the Lord," the Legion of Mary, under her patronage and guidance, aspires to the honour of being the handmaid of the Ministers of the Lord. It regards as its function to aim at rendering all the ground into which the seed of the word of God is cast good ground, bearing fruit a hundredfold: here removing the thorns and briers by exerting its influence on worldly minds; there deepening the soil by strengthening religious convictions and encouraging the weak and despairing;

and lastly, softening the hard ground by its Christlike charity and the dew of prayer and self-sacrifice. The Legion, while being a part of the flock itself, aspires also to be the link between the shepherds and the flock, facilitating the work of the pastors and enabling them to be in constant personal touch with all the sheep of the flock; and on the other hand, keeping the sheep always under the warm benign influence of their pastors. Thus multiplying the priest; casting abroad his zeal, his personality and his very word; representing him everywhere and to everyone; the Legion makes it possible to have renewed the literal fulfilment of Our Divine Lord's words: "I am the good shepherd, I know my sheep, and my sheep know Me"; and those other words: "Other sheep I have that are not of this fold: them also I must bring, and they shall hear my voice, and there shall be one fold and one shepherd." (St. John x. 14-16.)

"If I speak with the tongues of men, and of angels, and have not charity, I am become as sounding brass, or a tinkling cymbal. And if I should have prophecy and should know all mysteries, and all knowledge, and if I should have all faith, so that I could remove mountains, and have not charity, I am nothing. And if I should distribute all my goods to feed the poor, and if I should deliver my body to be burned, and have not charity, it profiteth me nothing. Charity is patient, is kind; charity envieth not, dealeth not perversely; is not puffed up; is not ambitious, seeketh not her own, is not provoked to anger, thinketh no evil; Rejoiceth not in iniquity, but rejoiceth with the truth; Beareth all things, believeth all things, hopeth all things, endureth all things. Charity never falleth away: whether prophecies shall be made void or tongues shall cease, or knowledge shall be destroyed."—(1 Cor. xiii. 1-8.)

APPENDIX I.

The Roman Legion.

The Roman Legion was probably the most magnificent fighting unit the world has ever seen. The secret of its invincibleness lay in the marvellous spirit of its members. The soldier had to merge his personality in that of the Legion to which he belonged. An unquestioning obedience to his commanding officer was demanded, such that he was expected to obey "ad nutum," that is at "the nod," irrespective of the merits of the officer or of the soldier's personal likes or dislikes. There might be no grumbling if promotion did not come, and if resentment happened to be felt, it might not be allowed to appear either in word or deed. Hence all moved together as one man, because directed by a common purpose, each bound to the leader and to one another. Shoulder to shoulder and flank to flank, their hosts patrolled the world and upheld Roman prestige and Roman law wherever they appeared. Their devotedness made them resistless in the face of the enemy, their undaunted courage and dogged perseverance wearing him out and compelling him either to surrender or to fly. They were the outposts of the Empire: on them fell the brunt of maintaining it in its integrity. Such examples as that of the Roman Centurion found standing at his post when Pompeii was excavated, or the famous Theban Legion—massacred in the persecution of Maximian—illustrate their unflinching heroism.

The spirit of the Roman Legion may be summed up as one inspired by submission to authority, an unflagging sense of duty, perseverance in the face of obstacles, endurance in hardship, and loyalty to the cause in the tiniest details of duty.

Such was the Pagan ideal of reliable service. The Legionary of Mary must also have this virility, but supernaturalised and tempered and sweetened by contact with her who can best teach the secret of loving, gracious service.

"Standing before the Cross, the Centurion watched the Saviour die. Struck by the cry He had uttered before rendering up His soul, he glorified God, saying: 'Truly this man was the Son of God.' (St. Mark xv. 39.) And the Legionaries that were with him watching Jesus, having seen the earthquakes and the things that were done, were sore afraid, saying: 'Indeed this was the Son of God.' (St. Matt. xxvii. 54).

"The soldiers of the Roman army thus became the first converts.

"The Church of the future which must, to the great shame of the Jews, be called the Roman Church, began in a mysterious manner around Calvary the function which she was destined to fulfil in the world. The Romans it was who offered up the victim and elevated it in the sight of the multitude. These future guardians of the unity of the Church would refuse to tear the tunic of Jesus. These depositaries of the faith would be the first to write and to uphold the principal dogma of the new faith—the royalty of the Nazarene. They would smite their breasts at the moment when the sacrifice should be consummated, saying: 'Truly this was the Son of God.' Lastly, with the same spear which would open up to the Gospel all the highways of the universe, they would open the Sacred Heart of the Master, from whence flow streams of benediction and of supernatural life. Since all humanity is guilty of the death of the Redeemer, since all have steeped their hands in His blood, and since therefore the future Church could not be represented but by culprits, does it not seem as though the Romans, as early as the time of Calvary, were, though unconsciously, inaugurating, substantiating, their immortal destiny.

"The cross had been fixed in such a position that the back of Jesus was turned upon Jerusalem, while His face was to the West, towards the Eternal City."—(Bolo: Tragedy of Calvary).

APPENDIX II.

The Archconfraternity of Mary, Queen of Our Hearts.

1. Blessed Grignion de Montfort, in his treatise on the True Devotion to the Blessed Virgin, expresses the desire that all those who practise this devotion should be grouped together into a Confraternity. This wish was realised in the year 1899, when the Confraternity of Mary, Queen of our Hearts, was established at Ottawa, Canada. On April 28th, 1913, it was canonically erected as an Archconfraternity in Rome. Divisional Centres now exist in many countries.

2. The object of the Archconfraternity is the establishment of the reign of Mary in our souls so that Jesus Christ may reign in them more perfectly. The method is the practice of the form of devotion to Mary taught by the Blessed Grignion de Montfort, and defined as follows by him:—

"This devotion consists in giving ourselves entirely and altogether to Our Lady, in order to belong entirely and altogether to Jesus by her. We must give her (1) our body, with all its senses and its members; (2) our soul, with all its powers; (3) the exterior goods of fortune, whether present or to come; (4) our interior and spiritual goods, which are our merits and our virtues, and our good works, past, present, and future. In a word, we must give her all we have in the order of nature and in the order of grace, and all that may become ours in future in the orders of nature, grace, and glory; and this we must do without any reserve of so much as one farthing, one hair, or one least good action; and we must do it also for all eternity, and we must do it further without pretending to, or hoping for, any other recompense for our offering and service, except the honour of belonging to Jesus Christ by Mary and in Mary, even though that sweet Mistress were not, as she always is, the most generous and the most grateful of creatures."

3. The Conditions are:—(a) The inscription of one's name at any Centre. The Head-centre is at 44 Via Romagna, Rome. The principal one for U. S. A. is at: Montfort Preparatory College, Bay Shore, Long Island, New York, and for Canada: De Montfort Fathers, Eastview Center, Ontario, Canada.

(b) The Consecration of oneself, body and soul, to Mary. Some notable day, especially one of her Feasts, should be chosen for this, and a deliberate preparation should be made. The form of Consecration composed by the Blessed Grignion should be used, if at all possible. This Consecration should be renewed: the more often the better: certainly not less frequently than once a year. An ejaculation embodying the idea of this

Consecration should begin the day and be frequently on one's lips: "I am all thine, my most loving Jesus, and all that I have I offer to Thee through Mary, Thy holy Mother" (300 days' Indulgence). This form would also satisfy the Morning Offering of the Apostleship of Prayer. Another form would be that so dear to the Legion: "I am all thine, my Queen, my Mother, and all that I have is thine."

(c) To live habitually and always (this is the essence of the devotion) in a state of complete dependence on Mary's will, after the example given by the Son of God at Nazareth; doing all our actions through her, with her, in her, and for her; in such manner that we consider her as acting always in union with us, directing all our efforts and administering all their fruits. See Article on Duties of Legionaries.

4. Advantages and Privileges: Plenary Indulgences on the usual conditions, on the day of admission, on the Feasts of the Annunciation, the Purification, Christmas Day, the two Feasts of Our Lady of Dolours, the Visitation, the Assumption, and at the moment of death; and also on the Feasts of the Immaculate Conception and of the Blessed Grignion de Montfort, subject to the additional condition that one's Consecration be renewed. A Partial Indulgence of 100 days may be gained each time that one does any good work in union with Mary. This alone will prove a treasury of Indulgences for the faithful Legionary.

Priests who become members of the Archconfraternity are by the fact itself Priests of Mary, and by Papal Decree of December 18th, 1913, the favour of the Privileged Altar, three times a week *in perpetuum,* was accorded to them.

All the members have a share in the merits, prayers, and good works of the two Congregations founded by the Blessed de Montfort, i.e., the Fathers of the Company of Mary and the Daughters of Wisdom.

5. The principal Feast of the Archconfraternity is the Annunciation, and the Secondary Feast is that of Blessed Grignion de Montfort (April 28th).

6. For the proper understanding and practice of this devotion it is essential that one read not once but frequently Blessed Grignion de Montfort's "True Devotion to the Blessed Virgin," and his smaller work, "The Secret of Mary."

"Pius X, especially, has set out vividly the doctrine of the universal mediation of Mary and of her spiritual Maternity in his beautiful Encyclical 'Ad diem illum,' which is substantially but a transposition of the Blessed de Montfort's book of the 'True Devotion.' The Holy Pontiff was a fervent admirer of this celebrated little treatise. He particularly recommended all to read it, and he conferred his Apostolic Benediction on those who would do so. Moreover, in that Encyclical of his on Mary are to be found not only the most familiar thoughts of the great servant of Mary, but often his very expressions." (Mura: Le Corps Mystique du Christ.)

"Those who undertake this holy slavery should have a very special devotion to the great mystery of the Incarnation of the Word on March 25th. Indeed the Incarnation is the proper mystery of this practice, inasmuch as it was a devotion inspired by the Holy Ghost, first, to honour and imitate the ineffable dependence which God the Son had been pleased to have on Mary for His Father's glory and our salvation; which dependence particularly appears in this mystery, where Jesus is a captive and a slave in the bosom of Mary, and depends on her for all things; secondly, to thank God for the incomparable graces He has given Mary, and particularly for having chosen her to be His most holy Mother, which choice was made in this mystery. These are the two principal ends of the slavery of Jesus in Mary." —(Blessed Grignion de Montfort.)

APPENDIX III.

The Medal of the Immaculate Conception called the Miraculous Medal.

"Then the Blessed Virgin said to me: 'Get a medal struck after this model; those who wear it when it is blessed will receive great graces, especially if they wear it round their neck. Graces will be abundant for those who have confidence.'" (B. Catherine Labouré.)

Legionaries should greatly esteem this Medal, which

has been prominently associated with the history of their organisation. It was not the result of deliberation that a statue of the 1830 model graced the table at the first meeting, yet it effectively summarised the devotional outlook of the organisation which came into life around it.

The use of the Medal in the work was then recommended. The invocation which appears on the Medal commenced to be said at that first meeting and now, as part of the Catena, is recited daily by every member. The design of the Medal is incorporated in the Legion Vexillum.

It is provocative of thought that the Medal should in this manifold way insert itself into the Legion devotional system. Whether accidental circumstances were at work, or yet another of the delicate and wonderful fashionings of Providence, may be judged from the following additional considerations:—

(a) The aim of the Medal is the furthering of devotion to the Immaculate Conception. But the Medal likewise exhibits Mary in her role as Mediatrix of Grace, thus comprehensively showing her in the various aspects under which she is regarded by the Legion, viz., Mary Immaculate, Mother and Mediatrix.

The representation of the Immaculate Conception is complemented by that of the Immaculate Heart on the reverse of the Medal. The former portrays Mary stainless in her conception; the latter shows her sinless ever after.

(b) The reverse of the Medal bears the images of the Sacred Heart of Jesus and of the Immaculate Heart of Mary, both of which have been invoked in the opening prayers of the Legion from the very first meeting. This representation of the two Hearts, the one pierced with a circlet of thorns, the other by a sword, the two surmounted by the Cross and the letter M, recalls the Passion and the Compassion, which earned those graces which Legionaries pray to be privileged to bear to others in company with Mary.

(c) An astonishing circumstance is that it was at the precise moment of the Centenary of the Apparition to Catherine Labouré (which had special reference to France) that the Cardinal Archbishop of Paris opened the audience in which he gave his approbation and blessing to the Legion.

Thus, one can almost say that the Medal has been assimilated by the Legion, so that the mission of the Legionary includes that of the Medal. The Legionary is, as it were, a living Miraculous Medal, a humble instrument of Our Lady's graces to the world.

As Legionaries are encouraged to regard themselves as soldiers, likewise should they look upon the Medal as their especial ammunition. To a certainty, Mary will impart to it a double power in the hands of her Legionaries.

Pius X. furnished a new motive for spreading devotion to the Virgin of the Miraculous Medal by erecting the Association of the Miraculous Medal, the members of which participate in the Indulgences and privileges granted to the Scapular of the Immaculate Conception (the Blue Scapular).

Legionaries should join this Association, which is in the charge of the Priests of the Congregation of the Mission, from whose houses information as to enrolment may be obtained.

A special Feast in honour of the Manifestation of the Miraculous Medal is celebrated on the anniversary day of the apparition of the Blessed Virgin, Nov. 27th.

"Mary brought into the world apostolicity itself—Him who came to cast fire on earth and willed that it be enkindled. Her role would now have been incomplete if she had not been in the very centre of the tongues of fire which the Spirit of her Son sent upon the Apostles to make them burn with His message even to the consummation of the world. Pentecost was Mary's spiritual Bethlehem, her new Epiphany, in which, as Mother standing by the crib of the Mystic Christ, she makes Him known once again to other shepherds and other Kings."—(Sheen: The Mystical Body of Christ.)

APPENDIX IV.

The Apostleship of Prayer.

1. The Apostleship of Prayer is a League of prayer and zeal in union with the Sacred Heart of Jesus. It was established in 1844 and has since spread over the world. It now embraces 25,000,000 members, ever increasing, grouped in 100,000 aggregated Centres.

2. Chief among the practices of the Apostleship are "The Three Degrees":—(a) The First Degree includes those members who make the "Morning Offering," that is who offer in the morning the prayers, works, and sufferings of the day for the Intentions of the Sacred Heart. And of course, all will make this offering through Mary, thus adding greatly to its value. (b) The Second Degree comprises those who, in addition to the Morning Offering, offer daily to the Blessed Virgin one Pater and ten Aves for the Pope's intentions. Every month His Holiness declares his Intention, which is to be thus prayed for by the Apostleship. (c) The Third Degree comprises those members who go to Holy Communion once a week, or even once a month, in Reparation to the Sacred Heart. (d) Members may pass from one Degree to another at their own wish without any formality.

3. The advantages are: (a) The members espouse the cause of the Sacred Heart and become His apostles. By their prayers, works, and sufferings in union with His, they make His labours, sufferings, and death fruitful for the saving of the souls of men. (b) Thus they attract to themselves the fruits of the Promises made to St. Margaret Mary. (c) They increase the merit of each of their prayers and actions. (d) They share in the prayers and works of their countless fellow-members, including an immense number of Religious. (e) They participate in the merits of almost all of the Religious Orders. (f) They can gain Indulgences—Plenary and Partial—so numerous that to set them out would occupy about two pages of this Handbook.

4. For admission, one must be enrolled on the Register of any Centre, and receive a Certificate of membership. The Society of Jesus is in charge of the Apostleship, and all information may be obtained from any one of its Priests or Houses.

5. The organ of the Apostleship is the Messenger of the Sacred Heart. There are now 65 Messengers published in 40 different languages. A sovereign way to spread devotion to the Sacred Heart is the spreading of the sale of this beautiful little magazine.

6. The obligations are so light, the benefits to the member are so great, the joy given to Mary so exquisite, the profit to the Kingdom of Christ so immense, that every human being should be a member of the Apostleship, and Legionaries in their works should labour to bring this desirable thing to pass.

"Mary is the inseparable companion of Jesus. Everywhere and always the Mother is beside her Son. Therefore, what binds us to God, what places us in possession of the things of Heaven is—not Christ alone, but that Blessed pair—the Woman and her Seed. Hence, to separate Mary from Jesus in religious worship is to destroy the order established by God Himself."—(Terrien: La Mere des Hommes.)

APPENDIX V.

The Confraternity of the Most Holy Rosary.

1. This is an Association of the Faithful who undertake to recite the fifteen Decades of the Rosary at least once in the week. There is no more richly indulgenced Confraternity in the Church, and membership in it is necessary for all who wish to gain the full advantages of the Rosary.

2. The fact that the Blessed Grignion de Montfort was not only a member of the Confraternity, but devoted himself ardently to is propagation, should be a headline for Legionaries. The following interesting document is still in existence: "We, the Provincial of the Order of Preachers, do certify and declare that Louis-Marie Grignion de Montfort, Brother of our Third Order, preaches everywhere and with much zeal, edification, and fruit, the Confraternity of the

Rosary in all the Missions which he gives continually in the towns and country places."

3. In order to join, one's full name must be enrolled on the Register in a Church where the Confraternity has been established, and one's beads must be blessed by a Dominican Priest or a Priest having the faculties to do so. The fifteen Decades of the Rosary must be said at least once each week, meditating on the mysteries while doing so. This obligation does not bind under sin. The ordinary daily Rosary more than fulfils it. The entire Rosary need not be said together; the Decades may be recited one or more at a time according to convenience. There is no meeting, no subscription.

4. Some of the advantages of the Confraternity are as follows:—(a) The special protection of Our Lady, Queen of the Rosary; (b) a share in all the good works and spiritual benefits of the members of the Dominican Order, and of the Rosary Confraternity, the world over; (c) a share, after death, in the prayers and suffrages offered by the same for the dead; (d) very great indulgences, partial and plenary, daily, monthly and annually, all of which are applicable to the dead; (e) a special indulgence for every work of charity or piety performed; (f) an indulgence of 2,025 days for each Hail Mary in the Rosary, by saying the Holy Name reverently; (g) a plenary indulgence every day (applicable to the dead) for those members who go to Confession and Communion, visit a Church, and recite the complete Rosary (Fifteen Mysteries) within the natural day, for the triumph of the Catholic Church; (h) a plenary indulgence at the hour of death.

Enquiries may be directed to Rosary Headquarters, 141 East 65th Street, New York City; or to 5375 Notre Dame de Grace Avenue, Montreal, P. Q. Canada.

"The Holy Rosary is the fairest flower of our Order. Should it come to pass that this flower withers, simultaneously the beauty and lustre of our Institute is seen to fade and disappear. And on the other hand, when that flower revives, forthwith it draws down on us the heavenly dew, imparts to our stem an aroma of grace, and causes it to bring forth, as from a root of piety, fruits of virtue and of honour."—(Master-General de Monroy, O.P.)

APPENDIX VI.

The Confraternity of Christian Doctrine.

OBJECT.— 1. To instruct and train children, and even adults, in the knowledge and practice of Christian Doctrine. This is done mainly by teaching and explaining the words of the catechism; and particularly by instruction in the use and value of prayer and the Sacraments. But more advanced instruction may be undertaken.

2. To retain a religious and moral hold upon the young after they have left school. It is the business of the Director to determine what means for this purpose may be useful and practicable.

3. Visitation of the homes of children to recruit for classes, or in the event of absenteeism, or for the purposes of the after-care contemplated in the preceding paragraph.

4. The carrying on of religious correspondence courses for children or adults, as has been found necessary in many places.

5. Care of religious libraries.

ERECTION.—1. In his Encyclical of April 15th, 1905, Pius X ordered that the Confraternity should be erected in every Catholic parish.

2. The only essential for the erection of the Confraternity of Christian Doctrine is the decree of erection by the Ordinary.

No special formality is prescribed for the actual erection. Since, however, it is a public act which concerns all the faithful, the Decree of the Bishop should be published in some way, that is, publicly notified in the church where the Confraternity is being erected.

The Confraternity of Christian Doctrine can only be erected in a church or public oratory or at least a semi-public oratory.

3. Once it has been canonically erected, the Confraternity is *ipso jure* affiliated to the Archconfraternity of Christian Doctrine in Rome, and at once participates

in the blessings, the indulgences, and the privileges of this Archconfraternity.

ORGANISATION.—1. Membership is open to all Catholics who are able to render to the Confraternity some real service, either by teaching, reading, superintending, and keeping order, or by visiting, gathering others for the meetings from their homes or from the streets or otherwise by promoting the work of the Confraternity.

2. Each branch shall be under the control of a Director, who shall be the Parish Priest or some Priest appointed by the Ordinary.

3. The details of the actual organisation, i.e., as regards officering, government, meetings, scope of work, and method, may be determined by each Ordinary.

INDULGENCES.—1. Plenary (on the usual conditions) on the day of admission on the Feast of SS. Peter and Paul, at the hour of death, and twice in each month if Christian Doctrine be taught or learned on not less than two occasions in that month.

2. Partial Indulgences are attached to the performance of the duties of the Confraternity.

NOTE.—In the event of a Bishop's appointing a Praesidium to discharge the purposes of the Confraternity, it is suggested for consideration by His Excellency that, in view of the considerable quantity of prayer already required from the members of that Praesidium, he might dispense them from any special prayers of the Confraternity where such are prescribed to be said.

"This work of teaching catechism is nothing else than the everyday putting into effect of the command given by Jesus: 'Go preach the Gospel to every creature.' For the catechism is the teaching of the Christian truths, and the explanation, in greater or lesser detail, of the Gospel. Hence it is that the Directors in charge of this work are actually engaged in the forming of those whom St. Paul refers to as the men and women who have laboured with him in the Gospel."—(Discourse of Pius XI: March 12th, 1926).

APPENDIX VII.

A Portrait of Mary.

"My Lady is beautiful, beautiful beyond compare; so beautiful that when one has seen her once, one would wish to die so as to see her again; so beautiful that when one has seen her, one can on longer love anything earthly."—(St. Bernadette.)

"St. Epiphanius, quoted by Nicephorus, has left us a charming portrait of the Virgin. This portrait, sketched in the fourth century, from traditions now effaced, and from manuscripts which we no longer possess, is the only one which has come down to us.

"The Virgin, according to this bishop, was not tall of stature, though her height was a little above the middle size; her colour, slightly bronzed, like that of Sulamite, by the sun of her country, had the rich tint of ripe ears of corn; her hair was light, her eyes lively, the pupil being rather of an olive colour, her eyebrows perfectly arched and black; her nose, remarkably perfect; was aquiline; her lips rosy; the shape of her face a fine oval; her hands and fingers long. She was utterly full of divine grace and loveliness; all the fathers eagerly attest, with one accord, this admirable beauty of the Virgin.

"But it was to this assemblage of natural perfections that Mary owed the power of her beauty; it emanated from a higher source. St. Ambrose understood it well, when he said that this attractive covering was but a transparent veil which let all the virtues be seen through it, and that her soul, the most noble, the most pure that ever was, next to the soul of Jesus Christ, was entirely revealed in her look. The natural beauty of Mary was but the remote reflection of her intellectual and imperishable beauties. She was the most beautiful of women, because she was the most chaste and most holy of the daughters of Eve.

"The greatest propriety reigned in all the actions of the Virgin; she was good, affable, compassionate, and never tired of hearing the long complaints of the afflicted. She spoke little, always to the purpose, and never did an untruth defile her lips. Her voice was sweet and penetrating; and her words had something gracious and consoling which shed calm over the soul. She was the first in watchings, the most exact in fulfilling the divine law, the most profound in humility, the most perfect in every virtue. She was never seen in anger; she never offended, afflicted, or railed at any one. She was an enemy to pomp, simple in her attire, simple in her manners. Never had she a thought of displaying her beauty, her ancient nobility, or the rich treasures of her mind and heart. Her presence seemed to sanctify all around it, and the sight of her banished the thought of the things of earth. Her politeness was no vain formality, made up of words of falsehood: it was an expansion of universal benevolence which came from the soul. In fine, her look already revealed the Mother of Mercy."—(Orsini: History of the Blessed Virgin.)

"Identity of blood implies between Jesus Christ and Mary a similarity of formation, of features, of inclinations, of tastes, of virtues; not only because identity of blood very frequently creates such a similarity, but because in Mary's case (her maternity being altogether a supernatural fact—the effect of overwhelming grace), this grace took hold of this more or less general principle of nature and developed it in her in such a manner as to make her the living image and portrait in every thing of her divine Son; so that whosoever could see her, could admire the most exquisitely formed image of Jesus Christ. This same relation of motherhood established between Mary and her Son an intimacy not only as to intercourse and communion of life, but as regards an interchange of hearts and of secrets; so that she was the mirror reflecting all the thoughts, feelings, aspirations, desires and purposes of Jesus, as He in turn reflected in a more eminent manner, as in an unspotted mirror, the miracle of purity, of love, of devotedness, of immense charity which was the soul of Mary. Mary could, therefore, say with greater reason than the Apostle of the Gentiles: I live, now not I; it is Jesus who lives in me."—(De Concilio: The Knowledge of Mary.)

INDEX

IMPORTANT NOTE—HOW TO USE THE INDEX:—

Items, not independently indexed, should be sought under appropriate general headings which are set out in heavy type, as follows:—**Apostolate, Mary, Membership, Outlook, Spirit, System, Visitation, Work.**

"Per te, O Maria, resurrectionis nostrae tesseram certissimam tenemus."—(St. Ephraem).

The address

of the CONCILIUM LEGIONIS is:—

DE MONTFORT HOUSE,

NORTH BRUNSWICK STREET,

DUBLIN, IRELAND.

Following her, thou strayest not;
invoking her, thou despairest not;
thinking of her, thou wanderest not;
upheld by her, thou fallest not;
shielded by her, thou fearest not;
guided by her, thou growest not weary;
favoured by her, thou reachest the goal;

—St. Bernard.